Acclaim for Neal Pollack's **ALTERNADAD**

"*Alternadad* is a very straightforward and honest account of Gen-X parenting, and in particular the strange and irresistible yearning of many thirtysomethings to become not merely good parents, but 'cool parents.' . . . Rings true for any parent, cool or square."
—*The Capital Times*

"Revelatory and funny. . . . More traditional dads surely love their kids just as much, but rarely has the bond felt more moving than it does here." —*Los Angeles Times Book Review*

"What happens when a party animal becomes a dad? It's his own story that Neal Pollack tells in his funny, poignant memoir *Alternadad.* . . . Pollack's tale is as offbeat as is his lifestyle but the fundamental dilemma he describes in this memoir will be familiar to parents of all kinds." —*The Christian Science Monitor*

"Highly enjoyable." —*The Boston Globe*

"Frequently amusing and disarmingly touching. . . . It's heartening to find a different Pollack—whose great, previous work was well-armored with its opinionated cynicism—who has put a vulnerable side on full display here." —*Houston Chronicle*

"With his new memoir, the recovered satirist follows in the grand tradition of books like Bill Cosby's *Fatherhood.* For Pollack, it's a drastic reversal . . . but we're lucky that he acquiesced." —*Details*

"Hard to resist. . . . Proves [parenting] is partly poignant, partly funny—and mostly hard." — *Austin American-Statesman*

"A witty, postmodern paean to parenthood." —*New York* magazine

"Very funny. . . . Pollack shouldn't simply be lumped in with a spurious hipster parenting movement. His book reveals that the core aim of fatherhood has barely budged: provide food, clothing, shelter."
—*Slate*

"Surprisingly heartwarming, considerably jarring and funny."
—*Philadelphia City Paper*

"With his signature wit and candor, Pollack describes his unique approach to parenting. . . . *Alternadad* offers a peek into the world of the modern family, where anything-but-typical parents are raising kids differently than their own parents, but with all the love and responsibility (and sense of humor) that the job requires."
—*UrbanBaby*

"An honest and true story, just beyond the ordinary, of two people with a child trying to make their way in the world."
—*Poets & Writers*

"Very funny. . . . Neal Pollack chronicles his version of rock'n'roll fatherhood." —*Child* magazine

"*Alternadad* works because it's got a lot of heart. Neal tells his story without the shrill judgment and holier-than-thou attitude that's prevalent in so many parenting books and blogs. It's an honest, funny, and ultimately moving story, one that dads (and moms) will love." —*DadCentric*

"Pollack treats the subject of fatherhood with humor and honesty. . . . He succeeds in writing about parenting and reveals himself as an ever-evolving writer who's not afraid to call life as he sees it."
—*Playboy*

Neal Pollack

ALTERNADAD

Neal Pollack is the author of the satirical cult classic *The Neal Pollack Anthology of American Literature* and the rock'n' roll novel *Never Mind the Pollacks*. He's the creator of www.offsprung.com, an Internet humor magazine and parenting community, and he keeps a semidaily blog at www.nealpollack.com. He lives in Los Angeles with the painter Regina Allen, who is also his wife, their five-year-old son, Elijah, their dogs Hercules and Shaq, and a goldfish named Hingy Dingy Bingy Bangy Bongy Pee Wee Herman. Elijah named the fish.

ALTERNADAD

ALTERNADAD

Neal Pollack

ANCHOR BOOKS

A DIVISION OF RANDOM HOUSE, INC.

NEW YORK

FIRST ANCHOR BOOKS EDITION, FEBRUARY 2008

Copyright © 2007 by Neal Pollack

All rights reserved. Published in the United States by Anchor Books, a division of Random House, Inc., New York, and in Canada by Random House of Canada Limited, Toronto. Originally published in hardcover in the United States by Pantheon Books, a division of Random House, Inc., New York, in 2007.

Anchor Books and colophon are registered trademarks of Random House, Inc.

Portions of this book have been previously published, in slightly different form, in the following publications: *Child* magazine, *The New York Times Magazine*, *Ready-Made*, Salon.com, *Tango*, and the anthologies *Maybe Baby*, *Proud to Be a Liberal*, and *The Worst Noel*.

The Library of Congress has cataloged the Pantheon edition as follows:
Pollack, Neal, [date]
Alternadad / Neal Pollack.
p. cm.
1. Pollack, Neal, 1970—Family. 2. Fathers—United States—Biography.
3. Husbands—United States—Biography.
4. Child rearing—United States—Case studies.
5. Family—United States—Case studies.
6. Fathers and sons—United States—Case studies.
I. Title.
HQ756.p645 2007
306.874'2092—dc22
2006043795

Anchor ISBN: 978-1-4000-9558-2

Author photograph © Andrew Southam
Book design by Wesley Gott

www.anchorbooks.com

Printed in the United States of America
10 9 8 7 6 5 4 3 2 1

This book is dedicated with love and gratitude
to my parents, Bernard and Susan Pollack.
Mom, Dad: Please don't read chapter seven.

Everybody works but father
And he sits around all day,
Feet in front of the fire—
Smoking his pipe of clay,
Mother takes in washing
So does sister Ann,
Everybody works at our house
But my old man.

—JEAN HAVEZ, 1905

CONTENTS

Contents

ACKNOWLEDGMENTS

ETERNAL FLAME OF MY HEART: Regina Allen.

BELOVED SPAWN: Elijah Pollack.

BELOVED PET: Hercules.

INTERMITTENTLY BELOVED PET: Gabby.

NOT-SO-BELOVED PET: Teacake.

EDITOR: Andrew Miller.

AGENT: Daniel Greenberg.

LOS ANGELES BUREAU: Shawn Hopkins, Justin Manask, Steve Golin, Rene Reyes, Marcy Morris, Joe Cohen, Greg Lessans, Alix Madigan, Kim Randall, Kevin McCormick, and Ryan Kallberg.

TRUSTED FRIENDS AND COLLEAGUES WHO READ THE BOOK ALONG THE WAY OR PROVIDED COUCHES AND/OR BEDS DURING VARIOUS EDITORIAL MISSIONS: John Hodgman, Todd Pruzan, Joy Bergmann, Jane Lerner, John Senseney, Jack Peasley, Liam Ford and Ann Weiler, Jim Arndorfer and Paula Wheeler, Shoshana Berger.

AUSTIN BUREAU: Ben Brown, Katie Spence, Scott Richardson and Kathleen Scanlan, Zach Horton and Debbie Smith, Michael and Kristina Barnett, Shannon McCormick and Lacey Eckl plus Emmett, Micki Gibson and Jennings Crawford plus Eamon, Jenna and Shelby plus Mia, Jennifer and David plus Sam, the ladies of the Book Club/Hedonist Society, Owen and Jodi Egerton, Milton, Mary

Acknowledgments

Jane, Tessa and Emma Matus, Mike Donohoo, Denise Daley, Heather Crist, Alex Brown, and whoever cleaned up the messes Elijah made at Central Market.

THE NEAL POLLACK INVASION: Dakota Smith, Jim Roll, Jon Williams, and Neil Cleary (version 1.0). John Grey, Rob Timbrook, Todd Dwyer, and Nigel Smith (version 2.0).

BELOVED FAMILY BESIDES MY PARENTS, TO WHOM THIS BOOK IS DEDICATED: Margot, Lloyd, and Ali Hummel; Rebecca, Alex, and Jane Smith; Mary Allen; Brett, Donna, Westlund, and Mackenzie Allen; Larry and Estelle Dougherty, Captain Rick, Gigi, Michael, Simona, and Alana King; Liz, Drew, Luke, and Nicholas Porter; Michael, Catherine, and Enzo Dougherty; Jon King; Chris Dougherty; Sarah Dougherty.

BLOGMASTER: Kenan Hebert.

PANTHEON BUREAU: Farah Miller, Liz Calamari, Dixon Gaines, and Jenna Bagnini.

THE HERCU-FRIENDS: Bruno and Charlie.

SPECIAL THANKS: To Henri Mazza, for giving me a hot, dusty room to write in when I needed it most.

ALTERNADAD

PROLOGUE

I was napping pleasantly on a futon one Saturday afternoon when my wife flung open the door. She held a filthy sponge in her left hand. A look of terrified desperation clouded her eyes.

"Catastrophe!" she said.

"What?" I said.

"*Your son* took off his diaper. He's throwing shit all over his bedroom! And he's enjoying himself!"

"That's bad."

"It's disgusting, that's what it is! Now get out of bed and help me clean!"

I'd woken up with the kid, who had just turned two, at 6:20 a.m., and I was tired. Plus, allergies had mashed my brains into lentil soup. They call it Cedar Fever here, which is an insult to cedars, and even to fever. It's horrible. My head was encased in a stack of hay. My eyes had been scraped dry. I needed a nap. No. I deserved a nap. But this situation required a dad.

"Dammit all to hell!" I said, and I got up.

Elijah stood in the middle of the living room. He was naked, flapping his arms, and hopping around like a Packers fan on Wild Card Sunday.

"Ah-ha-ha!" he said. "Elijah bad!"

Regina was in Elijah's room with a roll of paper towels and a bottle of industrial cleaner. She scrubbed the wall next to his bed with unrestrained fury. Elijah had thrown his blankies on the floor. Little chunks of poo corrupted all three of them. I cursed the fact that I was alive.

"He smeared it all over the slats of his crib," Regina said. "It's on his stuffed animals. It's everywhere. I really think I'm gonna puke. I see carrots. Oh no! There are peas! And *corn!*"

She wasn't looking at me as she said that. I think she was speaking to some kind of abstract God of Parenting. Then she turned to me with a command.

"Entertain him! Now!"

I looked at Elijah, who was cackling and turning in a circle. He didn't need to be entertained; he needed to be pacified. I turned on the TV. It was that *Little Bear* program where the Maurice Sendak–created animated bears are such a happy family and they always solve life's little problems, like getting lost in the woods or attacked by a puma, because their lives are based on sincere friendship and good judgment.

Oh, how I loathe *Little Bear.*

Regina emerged from the bedroom and pointed the sponge at me. Threat brewed in her gaze.

"You need to run him a bath!"

"Right."

She returned to the bedroom. I went into the bathroom and turned on the faucet. Elijah made a beeline down the hall. I grabbed him around the waist and twisted him upward. He howled with glee.

"Don't you dare," I said.

"Daddy-doo!" he said.

He looked so cute. I just had to tickle him right then. Regina continued her attempts to contain the situation. She ordered me to put bubbles in his bath, even though I always put bubbles in his bath and wouldn't consider doing anything else. But I understood. Sometimes, when matters spiral, you just need to control what you already know.

By the time the bathtub was filled, the trauma of the afternoon had already waned. Regina had picked up all the larger poo-chunks. She looked like a field surgeon three days after Antietam. All that remained was two loads of laundry.

"Do you want help?" I asked.

"No." She sighed.

"Are you sure?"

"Elijah take a baf!" Elijah said. "In da water! With Cookie Monster and ducks in da bubble baf!"

Regina was the motor of my ambition, the bulwark of my soul, the apple of my eye, and the pearl of my heart. She handed me an afternoon's worth of our baby son's shit.

"Just get rid of this," she said.

I took it, because I loved her.

I walked outside. The wind nipped. I was wearing a white T-shirt, gray boxer briefs, and black socks pulled up to my knees. Also, I was holding a plastic Walgreens bag full of human excrement. A chill gust stopped me for a moment, and I had a premonition.

Someday, I realized, I'll look like this *all* the time.

1

BEFORE

ONE

Positively Chase Avenue

1993–1997

I n the early 1990s, years before I became a father, I lived in a neighborhood called Rogers Park, on the far North Side of Chicago. The neighborhood held a dozen blocks north to south that were lined with wide, shady trees. Thick-grained Lake Michigan beaches made up its eastern border. But despite its natural advantages, Rogers Park wasn't one of the fancier parts of Chicago at the time. We didn't get the upscale retro diners, loft condos, or bars that catered to Indiana University graduates who seemed to spread throughout the city as if hatched from pods. Instead, the streets of Rogers Park dripped of mild neglect. This made them interesting but not particularly dangerous.

The apartment buildings in my neighborhood looked a little ragged, but you often heard guitars playing from inside them as you walked. No major trend had touched the neighborhood in decades; the people who lived there deliberately defied trendiness. The nightlife tried but failed. Hip-hop DJs, start-up rock bands, and small independent film societies ran up against the same frustrations. No one in the neighborhood could afford to go out, unless they could, and then they went out in other neighborhoods. My cohabitants were poets and drunks, low-end shop owners and itinerant musicians, union organizers and shifty-eyed permanent graduate students who slept on the floor. At the time, I described the people of Rogers Park as the sediment left over after you put the city of Chicago through a sifter. It was a neighborhood for people who didn't belong in any other neighborhood.

I lived on Chase Avenue, at the far northern end of the city, in a quasi-communal apartment with a female construction worker from rural North Carolina named Rachel. We shared the apartment with a thin-fingered graduate student who possessed a bad temper and a cat whose name, Trakl, will be obscure except to those familiar with Norwegian philosophy. I had the room off the living room, which was separated from the rest of the apartment by a plyboard wall painted with a mural depicting lush greenery that somehow also managed to be ugly. Previous residents of the apartment had constructed it during a drunken party, and it looked like something that amateurs slapped up during a weekend fund-raiser at an elementary school. They'd included one nice feature, a window from which I could peek out into the rest of the apartment, like a guest star dropping in on Pee-wee's Playhouse. I got an actual window view as well, of a parking lot and beyond that a concrete pier and a gray swirl of Lake Michigan surf.

Rachel was a hippie, albeit one who spent her nights reading Russian novels. She hung out with a loose coalition of assorted weirdos. Some of her friends even had children, or were in the process of making children, which I couldn't believe.

Her best friend had a little daughter, about four or five. The girl seemed perfectly happy. She ran around barefoot and dressed like a princess, as a little girl must. But she also colored and read books in a dingy café while her mom smoked cigarettes and did her *own* homework. Sure, my mom had gone to graduate school when I was a kid, and sure, she'd smoked a lot of cigarettes back when that was socially acceptable in the suburbs, but hanging out in a café? That was crazy. My parents only took us to Chinese restaurants. The little girl's parents attributed her conception to a bottle of wine, a lack of birth control, and a Hawkwind album. They lived in an apartment and were marginally employed! How, I wondered, could people like this possibly have kids?

In Rogers Park, it seemed impossible to be any kind of parent other than an eccentric one. One couple I got to know owned the No Exit Café, a place that had existed in several shades of brown since 1958 and practically screamed Leo Kottke Slept Here. They raised three kids in a world of folk music, bad poetry, and men with food in their beards who played backgammon and Go for money. I hung out with them from time to time because I liked them, but also because I had trouble believing they were real. I wanted to say, You're parents? But you make your own jewelry and attend Native American coming-of-age ceremonies in South Dakota! It's not possible. My father is president of the Phoenix Rotary Club and eats hot dogs at Costco. *That's* what dads are supposed to do.

I became friends with a guy named Lou, a Vietnam veteran and computer animation specialist in his early fifties who liked to drink, and had therefore met all the women in the neighborhood under thirty who went to bars. He threw Sunday potluck dinners at his condo, which he shared with a rotating roster of young roommates, a pit bull, and an utterly horrifying hairless twenty-one-year-old cat. The dinners were like a halfway house version of Brigadoon. Every poet, freeloader, harmonica player, and semi-insane drug fiend in the neighborhood showed up, sometimes as many as a hundred a week, only to disappear until the next dinner. This went on for years and eventually led to the cancellation of the dinners because Lou had a taste for the finer meats and couldn't afford the filchers anymore. I went nearly every week and filched as well, though I was one of the few people who at least brought a bottle of wine or a six-pack.

Lou had two children, late-teenage variety, that hung out at the potlucks. His daughter sang folk songs, played the guitar, and sometimes kissed girls. His son dropped in and out of college and seemed to like to hang around his dad all the time. Then there was another son, a little red-haired kid who was ten when I met him. Lou would drive to South Carolina every summer to fetch the kid from the kid's mother. He and the kid did a lot of normal things, like go to the beach and roller-skate and play basketball, but the kid also spent a lot of time at restaurants with bars, where Lou drank beer.

Lou didn't seem like a worse parent, or a better one, than any other I'd known. It had never occurred to me that kids would choose to hang out with their parents. I would no sooner go out drinking with my dad than I would go skydiving with him. And while my folks had always been very generous about throwing parties, I really couldn't imagine them, or want them to consider, smoking pot with my friends.

I grew up in high-upper-middle-class suburban Phoenix. When we moved there, in 1977, my father was a marketing executive for a large corporate hotel chain. His employment situation, and our material circumstances, went up and down throughout my child-hood. But we were never forced to abandon our house, which had an unobstructed view of Camelback Mountain and its adjacent two acres of uncultivated desert brush. We had orange, lemon, grape-fruit, and fig trees, a kidney-shaped swimming pool, and a cool, inviting back porch. I got my own shag-carpeted bedroom with built-in bookshelves, a desk, and corkboard; it was the size of an average Manhattan studio apartment, with a connecting bathroom that had a glass-stalled shower and Saltillo tile floors. My parents planted us in a pretty exclusive neighborhood. My first Arizona play-mate, a neighbor from down the road, was the heir to the Camp-bell's Soup fortune.

This was a land where parents were named Diane and Ted. They coached baseball, ran bake sales to raise money for the eighth-grade cheerleading squad, and had closets bigger than most people's garages. Several friends of mine practiced on personal tennis courts.

On the other hand, the father of the kid whom I'd carpooled with to Hebrew school went to jail for some naughty legal work he did for Charles Keating. The dad of one of my co-editors on the high school paper suffered a similar fate for running a corrupt S&L. Those kinds of things never happened to parents in Rogers Park.

I knew a young Rogers Park woman who'd worked in every café in the neighborhood. When I learned that she had a little daughter, it just seemed impossible.

"But she sleeps with guys!" I said to Rachel.

"So?" Rachel said.

"She has a kid!"

"And what's your point?"

I really was that naïve. But suddenly, parenthood no longer seemed like something exclusive to stable adults in boring suburbs. It seemed like everyone I knew suddenly had kids. Maybe, I thought, a guy like me could become a dad after all.

About a year and two roommates after I moved in with Rachel, her friend Ned came to live with us. Ned had a lot of problems. He got really depressed. Once he told me that vampires were hovering outside the apartment and that they wanted to eat his brain while he slept, neither of which he could objectively prove. He wasn't capable of working a normal job, or of waking up before noon, but he was quite sweet and funny, played bass reasonably well, and could draw brilliantly, though to no end other than filling sketchbook upon sketchbook.

Ned was kind, almost guileless. He was also a dad. Years before, he'd gotten his high school girlfriend pregnant. She'd kept the baby, and he'd left town. He knew his daughter, a little. Sometimes he'd visit his hometown for a week or two and come back with pictures of his smiling girl. He became the star exhibit in a Museum of Weird Parenthood that existed only in my mind. When my parents came to visit, I liked to show him off, as if to say, "See, not everyone lives in bourgeois comfort like you do." My mom, who'd spent much of her teenage life hanging out with actors in Greenwich Village, and my dad, who'd grown up in the Bronx with Jewish parents who'd left Germany, not by choice, in the mid-1930s, weren't impressed with the bohemian authenticity of my circumstances. I, on the other hand, looked at Ned as a piece of living, breathing outsider art, and couldn't believe that my life had moved in such a fascinating direction, or that it contained such original people.

Somewhere along this important voyage of personal discovery, I got my own place. Rachel moved back to North Carolina with a boyfriend. Ned became the senior resident of the apartment on Chase Avenue, which was by now so far removed from the original lessees that it had become a de facto squat. I started hearing stories. Hanging out at the No Exit Café, Ned met Jill, a sophomore journalism student from Northwestern, my alma mater. They drove around in her car all night, talking. For days they talked and talked and then they were in love. I went over to the apartment for dinner one night, and it was a lot cleaner than it'd been the last time. Jill had moved in.

They got a little careless with the birth control. Jill wasn't feeling so good one evening. The next day, she and Ned took a bus to the doctor on Western Avenue, who told them the news. They went to a diner and gazed at each other over their favorite sandwich, which they shared because they could only afford one. The next time I saw Ned, he said, "Jill and I are having a baby."

"Oh," I said. "That's great."

"I'm gonna get a job."

"Good for you."

"I want to be a real dad this time."

"I think you'll be a wonderful dad."

In reality, I had no idea, because I didn't know what it meant to be a wonderful dad, or any kind of dad at all. Here were a college student and an unemployed, mentally ill musician, and they were about to bring a child into the world. My head nearly exploded at the thought. I had to understand. One night, I went over to the apartment and sat them down.

"I want to do a story about you guys," I said.

Soon after moving to Rogers Park, I'd been hired as a reporter at a weekly "alternative" newspaper. It wasn't a typical job. I never had to go into the office unless I wanted to, and I usually didn't want to. My editors gave me few deadlines and even fewer assignments. I was completely free. On days when I didn't have anything else to do, which were frequent, I'd hop the El and ride it to a stop I'd never visited before. I covered whole wards with my notebook and tape recorder, hanging out in taverns and junkyards, on piss-stained Lake Michigan piers and in strangers' basements. Every experience seemed important and precious. I conducted four-hour interviews with coffeehouse owners and popcorn-stand proprietors and played beach volleyball with drag queens. Among my friends I counted a Colombian cab driver, a Korean liquor-store owner, a flamboyantly gay black barbecue entrepreneur, and an eighty-year-old former exotic dancer who illegally sold used furniture from her front yard in the shadow of Wrigley Field.

But I wanted to write a story that, to me, exemplified the neighborhood I called home. Ned and Jill were it. I approached my editor with the story idea.

"It's about hippies having kids," I said.

My editor wasn't impressed. She had two children herself.

"No, really," I said. "It's a good story. It's *emblematic of the culture of the neighborhood.*"

Every editor has his or her weak spots, and writers who don't want to work very hard need to discover those weak spots if they want to survive. I'd hit on one of her tics. My paper, like many urban weeklies, specialized in amateur urban anthropology, and I was a leading practitioner.

"All right," she said. "But keep me updated."

That meant "call me in three months."

"No problem," I said.

I went to the doctor with Ned and Jill. We got a sonogram. Jill and I went shopping for vitamins. Once a week, I attended birthing classes, which were conducted on soft pillows in the den of a late-nineteenth-century house in Evanston owned by a young, good-looking couple to whom the Clinton years had obviously been kind. We sat for hours in Ned and Jill's apartment talking about their dreams and possible baby names. Jill would go to school part-time, and also work part-time. Ned would work part-time, too, and take care of the baby when Jill was busy. He really wanted to be a hands-on dad. Theirs, they thought, was the perfect setup. It was hard for me to keep a reportorial distance, so I got excited along with them. I felt a little bit like a member of the third gender in *Stranger in a Strange Land,* though I hate it when people use the verb "to grok."

Around the eighth month, I declared myself on call at all times. If Jill had even a twinge of labor, she and Ned needed to call me. They'd agreed to allow me into the birthing suite, and I wasn't about to miss that show. Twice I roared out of the house, interrupting sleep and even *Jeopardy!,* and I would have been at the hospital within five minutes if I'd had a car. Instead, it was thirty minutes on the El, including a transfer at Belmont to the Brown Line. Both times, the labor didn't take, and it was back to long walks by the lake for Ned and Jill to jar that little sucker loose.

One night, I came home drunk to find the message on the answering machine. Jill's water had broken. They were hanging out at a friend's house until labor progressed to the point where they needed to go to the hospital; someone would call me at the appropriate hour. Though I didn't witness this myself, intrepid background reporting later revealed that Ned lay on his side next to Jill, rubbing her back and whispering supportive things to her. Finally, around dawn, it was time. Their friend drove them to the hospital down Lake Shore Drive, in a car without shock absorbers. Jill didn't enjoy this drive much.

At six a.m., the phone rang.

"Whuhhhh?" I said.

It was Jill's friend. They needed a reporter posthaste to witness the birth. This time, I avoided risk. Ten dollars and I part hard, but I took a cab and got there in time.

The lights were dim and the room felt calm, as homey as things get in a hospital. It was quiet and sanctified, almost like they'd piped in the silence. I smelled disinfectant. Jill lay on a queen-size bed that looked warm and relaxing. Ned lay behind her, forever rubbing her back. I was tired and still pretty drunk. I turned on my tape recorder, because it's important to capture the audio squish of the birth canal for a newspaper article.

"Hi, Neal," Jill said.

"Shh," I said, as I sat in a chair that would place me in the same relative proximity to the birth as an umpire has to a cleanup hitter. "Pretend like I'm not here."

Jill had determined that she'd do the birth without any painkillers unless it was really necessary, with the meaning of "necessary" very much up to her discretion. Impressively, she endured. The midwife came in at crunch time. Jill pushed. Her vagina opened like a flower in a stop-motion nature video, she let out a throaty moan, and a boy emerged from her womb.

I got out of there quickly. Any tears shed between Ned and Jill in the next hours weren't my business until they told me about them later. I found myself shaking, and profoundly moved. It was like I'd seen a Faces of Death video, but in reverse. Reproduction was magic and the birth had been flawless. Someday, I thought, when I have a child, it will go exactly like that.

A couple weeks later, I turned in my story, with the happy ending I'd witnessed. My editor rejected it.

"Something about this feels false to me," she said.

I murmured something like "You're such a bitch, bitch, bitch" in my mind. Three months of work! *Three months!* I was an artist! Didn't she understand?

But she was right. Birth is just the opening scene of a more complicated, more difficult, and far more interesting story.

Time passed without me seeing much of Ned and Jill. Neighborhood bars were shutting down all over Chicago, and I'd made it my professional duty to attend the closing nights of as many of them as I could. But things rarely shut down in Rogers Park, or if they did, not too many people cared, so I spent a lot of time away from the neighborhood.

About six months after the birth, I ran into Jill at the No Exit. She'd returned to school, with much success, but was having a lot of trouble finding someone to take care of the kid. Ned certainly didn't help. He'd decided that he needed to spend a lot of time at band practice in the suburbs. On a good day, Ned was home from noon to five. Sometimes he'd stroll the baby down the street to a coffeehouse and flirt with the girls who admired his sensitive fathering manner.

Jill had an important three-hour class one evening, and she couldn't find anyone to take the kid. By 4:30, Ned still hadn't shown up, and she was getting worried. Five passed, then six. The class started at seven. Ned came home after eight, and she was done with him.

At the end of the semester, after she'd graduated from the best journalism school in the country with honors while caring for an infant full-time, Jill took the baby to visit her father in Montana. She didn't come back. A few months later, Ned went out to visit them. He really wanted to see the kid, so he did, staying there for a little while. Then he returned to Chicago, but not for long, because he couldn't pay rent on the apartment anymore. He was going back to his hometown to live with his mother.

"I want to see my daughter," he said to me, the last time I saw him.

I'd realized that, regardless of a family's financial circumstances, there are good parents and bad parents, and a whole bunch of possibilities in between. Aesthetics mattered a little bit, but they weren't all that mattered. Eccentricity is not a virtue unto itself. I resolved to apply this knowledge on the off chance that I ever became a dad. Unfortunately, I've never been good at remembering what I've learned.

For a while, I stayed in touch with Jill. She got a job at a newspaper and found a good school for her son. There were wide-open spaces and goats and she had family nearby. She moved in with a grown-up man. Once in a while, she sent along pictures of the boy, who was handsome and healthy. But I felt an odd disconnect between that child and the one I'd seen born. I changed my e-mail address and forgot to CC Jill on the announcement.

I still lived in Rogers Park, but the neighborhood's mystique had begun to recede from my life. It had helped foster a self-perception that I was a lonely poet of the city, destined to forever walk on Chicago's icy winter streets under flickering yellow streetlamps. But a guy's self-perception can change, particularly when he meets a girl.

TWO

Love, Exciting and New

1997–2000

I n those years, my love life was extremely annoying, both to me and to everyone I knew. An affair with a beautiful and mysterious young woman collapsed when the ghost of her dead policeman father told the family that he didn't approve of me. That was admittedly the most extreme case, but my other entanglements didn't trail by much: I picked up the owner of a used-bookstore coffee bar, who took me to a party where she alternated between kissing me and a guy in drag. I had a lot of sex with a very nice schoolteacher, but only during the halftimes of televised Bulls games. I ended a tête-à-tête with a contraceptive educator because I hated her poetry. A brief Instant-Message and phone affair with a Boston-area woman provided some solace until she dumped her husband and moved in with a female nurse. I fell very much in love with a young sculptor who had a chronic back problem, but I had a girlfriend at the time. When I emerged single, the sculptor had latched onto a roadie for Poi Dog Pondering. It was a typical, or maybe hyper-typical, catalog of moronic romantic missteps for a twenty-seven-year-old man. My friends endured a lot of "But I just want to find someone who loves me for who I am, not for who they want me to be," though I had no idea what that meant.

One Thursday afternoon, I checked out the personals section of my newspaper. This was before the era of Friendster and Nerve Personals and craigslist. Hooking up with other sexually frustrated neurotics took more than a few e-mails and a quick subway ride. Surprise was still possible.

"Wayward Southern Belle," went the Ad of the Week, "seeks single gentleman with penchant for scatological humor."

Not only did I want to respond to the ad, but I also got phone calls from several female friends, telling me that I had to get in touch with this woman immediately. She sounded like I'd made her to order. Many of my favorite women are Southern and a little naughty; in addition to being the sexiest things on the planet, they have manners. They also like to boss people around, and I needed bossing. So I called the personals number, which cost me ninety-nine cents a minute despite my years of service to the company, and punched up her mailbox.

A few days later, I stood on the top step of the Film Center of the Art Institute of Chicago, which has since moved downtown and been renamed after Gene Siskel. I'd made the obvious first-date choice of a six p.m. screening of *The Tarnished Angels,* a 1958 Douglas Sirk movie about stunt fliers starring Rock Hudson and Robert Stack. Mainstream movies at corporate movie theaters, unless Quentin Tarantino directed them, were simply out of the question for me in those years, but I never missed a showing of *Funny Face* at the Music Box.

Regina had said she might be late because she was working for a mural-painting company, and they had a job out in the suburbs. She showed up with her hair drawn back, and she was wearing a nice skirt-and-blouse number and knee-high black boots. Cute, I thought. Not just cute for someone I met through a personal ad. But objectively cute.

"Hi," I said.

"Hi," she said.

"You're late."

"I told you."

"Well, you're really late," I said. "You made me miss the first five minutes."

We were married already.

After the movie, we went to an Italian restaurant in Wicker Park that isn't there anymore. She drove because I didn't have a car. I ate a lot of pasta way too fast. Midway through the meal, I excused myself. I'd spent the day on a rooftop in the hot sun, interviewing an eccentric Chicano art collector. He'd poured me a few liberal helpings of vodka, with not much cranberry juice to cut it. That night, the heat and the vodka took their revenge.

I returned to the table.

"Are you OK?" she said.

"Oh, I'm fine."

"You were gone a long time."

"Do you have any gum?" She did, fortunately.

We talked of art and books and music and food and life, all of which we said we loved. The conversation flowed without pause or disagreement. Soon, it turned to childhood. She'd grown up in Nashville, under economic circumstances more or less similar to mine; she'd attended the same private girls' school as Reese Witherspoon, and her manners were just as good. We also had a Phoenix connection: Her aunt and uncle had lived within walking distance of my grade school. While I really don't like Phoenix, because no sane person does, it still gave us an extra thing in common. There were also important differences.

"I'm adopted," she said.

"Oh."

"I was in a foster home for a year, and then my parents came and got me."

"Do you know anything about your birth parents?"

"I was born in Knoxville. My mom says my birth mom was a

cheerleader at the University of Tennessee. I don't have any more information."

"That must be hard."

"It's like there's this gap in my identity. I don't know who my people are. That's why I'd really like to have children. Because I need something to biologically call my own. Some sort of physical connection to the world."

A short but meaningful pause later, she asked, "So what do you think about kids?"

"Oh, I love kids," I said. "I always have. I'm really good with them."

The question hadn't bothered me or put me off, and I didn't really think about why she looked excessively pleased at my response. I was just excited to be having dinner with a woman who didn't seem to care that I was nerdy. In fact, she snorted rather easily at my jokes, and had a Jean-Luc Picard figurine on her dashboard, so she didn't have any nerdiness leverage on me. She was exactly the woman I'd been searching for: a smart, confident, talented, patient, bossy, good-looking Southern nerd.

It was getting late, but I proposed that we become even drunker. On the way back to my place, we stopped at a bar called the Great Beer Palace, which also isn't there anymore. My stomach gave out on me anew.

"Could you please excuse me again?" I said.

After I was done regurgitating the rest of my dinner, I *really* needed some gum. I asked her to stop at a White Hen Pantry on the way home. All the while, I talked to her about how I didn't believe in monogamy. At the time, I was under the influence of left-wing friends who spent a lot of time decrying the bourgeois constrictions of contemporary heterosexual relationships.

"Why should we be restricted to just one partner?" I said to my future wife on our first date.

"We just should."

"That's very conventional of you to think so."

I chomped on my gum. She pulled up to my apartment building. I leaned toward her, tongue a-blazin'. A few minutes later, we unclenched. That had been some pretty great smooching. I desperately wanted to see her again.

A week later, we met at a bar. I was there first. In fact, I'd been there all day, or at least since 3:30, when *Jeopardy!* aired in Chicago. Again, she arrived about five minutes late.

"Sorry if I stink," she said. "I went for a run and didn't take a shower."

"That's OK."

I tried to kiss her.

"I don't think it's going to work out," she said.

To recap: On the night I met Regina, I nagged her because she was late to a movie, vomited twice without telling her, and then made out with her for a while, and went on a long, ill-considered rant about how I didn't believe in monogamy.

"Why?" I said.

After a drink, she agreed to drive me home. I pressed my case because I'd decided I was in love with her, though I didn't admit that out loud because it's generally not a good idea to tell a woman you're in love with her while she's breaking up with you.

"But you don't believe in monogamy," she said.

"Oh, come on. Do you really think I meant that?"

"Why wouldn't I?"

My belief felt genuine, at least abstractly. But here I found myself confronted with someone whom I already knew I wanted to marry. She was sweet, kind, warm, practical, and fun. From our conversations, if not actual experience, she had no sexual neuroses and seemed to enjoy sex a lot. I'd never met a sexually confident woman who seemed able to deal with my irrational mood swings. While those two qualities don't necessarily have anything to do with each other, it was still a new combination for me. I got excited.

My favorite movie is *Airplane!*, I know all the lyrics to the original Broadway soundtrack of *Annie*, and my first rock concert was the Huey Lewis and the News *Sports* tour in 1983. And she didn't care. She owned a dozen Kate Bush records and even more Lyle Lovett albums, and I didn't care either. I couldn't imagine losing Regina, even after just one date.

I've always tended to fall in love quickly and dramatically, so it was time for me to get drastic. I'd recently seen the Baz Luhrmann–directed *Romeo + Juliet* and had found it quite moving. Just like Leonardo DiCaprio, I raised my hands above my head.

"I am fortune's fool!" I shouted.

Regina looked genuinely worried, possibly because she didn't get the reference right away.

"No you're not," she said.

"I am! I am! I am fortune's fool!"

Three weeks passed, and I thought about her often. In fact, I called her twenty times a day. I did this out of enthusiasm rather than obsession, though I guess the line between the two depends on whether or not you're making or receiving the calls. In retrospect, our son owes his existence to the fact that Regina didn't have caller ID, voice mail, or an answering machine.

It also helped that her other current boyfriend was an accountant whose dominant trait seemed to be his desire to hide his frequent marijuana use from her. Over the Fourth of July weekend, while visiting friends in St. Louis, she realized that I was, in fact, the better option. Perhaps I was even the best option in the whole world; I'd already promised that I'd *never* hide my frequent marijuana use from her.

We arranged to meet at a club called Schuba's, where a band called the Handsome Family was playing on a Friday night. The Handsome Family are a married couple who for many years have taken various mental problems and dark obsessions and spun them into lyrical, haunting songs reminiscent of Nick Cave, Vic Chesnutt, and the Louvin Brothers. They're based elsewhere now, but at the time, they lived in Chicago. They liked to vacation in the Wisconsin Dells and sang incessantly about suicide, making them a popular model for every Chicago couple with a vaguely alternative bent. Regina and I more closely resemble the family on *Seventh Heaven* than the Handsome Family, but we liked the band regardless.

I don't remember the name of the opening band, but I do remember that they hung piñatas above them on the stage. One piñata in particular, a roundish pink ghost with puckered lips, caught Regina's attention.

"That's Pinky," she said. "I love Pinky."

"He's pretty cute."

She put her head in my lap and gave me a goofy smile.

"Hiiiiiiiiiii!" she said.

"Well, hello there," I said.

All night, possibly to the Handsome Family's annoyance, Regina and I crooked our pinky fingers at each other and squealed, "Pinky! Oooooh! Pinkeeeee!" I went up to the lead singer of the opening band after the show and asked him how much money he wanted for Pinky. He said that Pinky wasn't for sale. We were disappointed, but I suddenly wanted to do something very nice for Regina.

The next time she and I got together, she saw my apartment for the first time, just for a few minutes. As we were getting ready to leave, I said, "Do you hear that noise? It's really strange."

"What noise?" she said.

"Just a noise," I said. "It sounds like someone trying to get out of somewhere. Why, where could it be coming from?"

She began to look nervous.

"Wait!" I said. "I think it's coming from this closet over here."

I opened the door to my coat closet. A yellow papier-mâché giraffe hung from the ceiling. I'd bought it earlier that day at a Mexican grocery store.

"Look at that!" I said. "I think he's saying he wants to go home with you."

"You got me a piñata!" she said.

"It chose me."

Soon thereafter, we began to spend the night at each other's places. I preferred mine; it was large and relatively quiet. Furthermore, I had a brand-new queen-size bed of medium quality, while Regina slept on an uncomfortable futon with a dreamcatcher hanging overhead. She had a roommate who was going through some depression and had begun to exhibit jealous symptoms toward me. Also, an elderly German brother and sister lived below them, and at any manifestation of noise after ten p.m., the brother, Gunther, would come up the stairs, pound on the door, and moan, "Please! I am desperate for sleep!" Who needed that crap? Also, Regina and her roommate got into some weird psychological battle about garbage. They'd leave bags festering for weeks on their back porch until finally, with a heaving sigh of frustration, I'd lug them away, saying something endearing like "You guys are such fucking slobs."

And then there was Growltigger.

Regina owned two male gray tabby cats, both of which weighed more than twenty pounds. One of them, which she'd pretentiously named Teacake after the male lead in Zora Neale Hurston's *Their Eyes Were Watching God,* was harmless enough if you kept him fed and allowed him to drink out of the bathtub faucet at all times. The other, Growltigger, was one of those special-needs pets that can turn the hardiest female soul into a crazy cat lady. Teacake was a big cat, but he wore his weight well, almost like a puma would. Growltigger, on the other hand, was just fat. A great sac of blubbered fur hung from his belly, spreading like pond ripples wherever he lay.

He slept with Regina, and I don't just mean "on the bed." Every night around eleven p.m., Growltigger would curl himself around Regina's head, place his paw on her cheek, and begin purring lustily. More than once, I woke to see the two of them nuzzling like lovers.

Finally, I called her on it.

"Are you making out with Growltigger?"

"Nooooo." But she blushed.

"Look, he's a sweet cat. But would you please stop kissing him? It's freaking me out!"

Growltigger made an unreliable bedmate. Occasionally, at dawn, he'd stand up and secrete a foul-smelling viscous white liquid from his anal glands. Because Growltigger slept so close to Regina, sometimes her hair bore the burden of his leakage. She called this process "getting assed." It smelled exactly like you think it might, but much worse. I know this because she occasionally put her hair under my nostrils after it happened, so I could share in the experience. Once, after one of the rare nights we spent apart, I got a call long before my usual wake-up time of ten a.m.

"Oh no!" Regina said.

"What?"

"You're not going to believe it."

"Just tell me."

"Growltigger assed in my nose!"

"Come on."

"I woke up and he was standing on my chest. I saw it coming out of his butt but I couldn't stop him!"

She sounded genuinely miserable, but I suspected she'd enjoyed it, albeit so subconsciously that even her subconscious wasn't aware.

"I'm sorry," I said.

"I've washed inside my nose three times," she said. "And it still smells like ass!"

After six months or so, we moved in together despite Growltigger's ass problem. Our new home was a really nice three-bedroom, two-bathroom one block away from Hollywood Beach. It had a two-person tub with massage jets, front and back porches, and rent low enough to make everyone jealous. The cats joined us.

In addition to Teacake and Growltigger, I had two female cats, Gabby and Zimmy, who themselves weren't exactly hot-fudge sundaes. Gabby is skeletal, whiny, and affectionate to the point of obsession. She'll live for a long time because she can lithely jump to a high place very quickly, from a standing start. But poor little Zimmy was a fluffy, unathletic, long-haired gray-and-white fragile princess cat. Growltigger, the kind of cat that intentionally knocks over a vase if you're not paying attention to him, swatted her on the head every time he saw her. Zimmy spent most of the rest of her time with us under the bed.

With such troublesome animals in our lives, Regina and I needed to escape relatively often. We took a short vacation to the Wisconsin-Iowa border, where no cat would ass us. Regina brought her banjo. She'd recently expressed interest in learning how to play, so I'd bought her a used one for her thirtieth birthday. The banjo didn't come out of its case the entire trip, but she took it everywhere nonetheless. The fact that she'd even considered playing the banjo on a hike in Wisconsin merely confirmed that I'd chosen my partner well.

On our way back home, we spent the night in Galena, Illinois, a Midwestern town that reflects our nation's deep nostalgia for the glory days of the Rutherford B. Hayes presidency. Regina and I went to see a Mark Twain impersonator, who was always in residence, and dined on poorly sauced food under faux-gaslit chandeliers. For some reason, this cheap 1880s theme-park setting inspired one of the most important conversations of our lives. We walked along the Mississippi, oblivious to the camera-snapping tourists around us.

"I really hope I can make a living as a fiction writer someday," I said. "I've never wanted to do anything else."

"I wish my painting could support me," she said. "But there's no way."

"That's the most important thing," I said. "To support yourself doing what you love. I'm going to live by that principle no matter what."

"Yeah," she said.

There are innumerable reasons, good and bad, why people choose to get married. Some marriages are bound together by sexual passion, while others more closely resemble platonic friendship or a business deal: Ours contained elements of all three. Regina and I looked at each other and held hands. At that moment, though we didn't say anything, we knew that we had sealed the eternal bond, forever declaring that, unto death, our mutual love was to be the agent of our fondest individual artistic dreams. We would never allow the other to fail.

The night we returned home to Chicago, we got naked and lay in bed.

"I think we should get married."

"Is this it?" Regina said.

"Yep."

"Oh, baby."

And then we kissed.

This stands as the third-happiest moment of my life, behind only the birth of my son, which was still more than three years away, and Kirk Gibson's game-winning home run in Game One of the 1988 World Series. I would have placed my engagement second, but as soon as we were done kissing, Regina called her mother. That knocked it down one place on the list, but it was still definitely above Game Five of the 1993 NBA Finals.

The next night, as Regina and I relaxed in the dining room, I took a sip of Scotch and said, casually, "Our life is pretty great right now. I don't know if I want to have kids."

A thick rain began to fall outside. Our windows slicked with the torrent. Agonized lightning flashes mixed with organ peals of thunder. The wind called the lost ships of Lake Michigan home from the deep.

"What do you mean?" she said.

"Um . . . I don't want to have kids, maybe?"

There's no way for me to write Regina's response without it

sounding like dialogue from *The Young and the Restless,* so instead, indulge me while I invoke the spirit of Shakespeare, one of the few writers capable of registering the intensity of her response.

"Show your false self no more before my wet-veiled eyes!" she said. "Thine fickle promises are cast upon the rocky shores of hope! O, castle of barren desire! I plead mercy on this forsaken womb!"

"Maybe I do want to have kids."

She sniffled.

"Are you sure?"

"Oh, yes," I said. "Very sure."

THREE

The Nest Tightens

June 2000–December 2001

About a month after we returned from our honeymoon, Regina took a trip to visit some friends of ours who'd just moved to Narberth, a hilly, verdant, close-in suburb of Philadelphia, a place with a neighborhood bar on Main Street and a hundred-year-old independently owned general store. From that cozy launching pad, our friends took Regina on forays into the city, showing her Philly's rich, weird outdoor market culture and outstanding art museum. In the evenings, they supped with interesting people of substance and a certain income level. Regina called me.

"You need to take a serious look at this place," she said.

Two months later, I did. Our friends showed me the same things they'd shown Regina: The old neighborhoods with small streets, the food carts, and the Reading Terminal Market, where I ate a roast turkey sandwich with gravy at an Amish diner. On my own, I discovered bars full of smoke and original wood, places with surly bartenders, bad jukeboxes, and unappealing clientele. One morning, we went to the Italian Market in South Philly and saw vegetable vendors warming their hands over trash-can fires in the middle of the street. Then, on a drive through the neighborhood just north of the

Art Museum, I spotted a kid in a Phillies cap bouncing a ball repeatedly against his stoop, like he was one of the Ducky Boys in *The Wanderers,* just waiting for his chick to call him on a Saturday night. That kid with the ball made something bloom in my heart.

I'd been growing disenchanted with Chicago. All the things that I'd loved about the city—the diversity, the weirdness, the old buildings—seemed to be disappearing. The incessant gentrification, and the incessant bitterness of the people (like me) who tried to prevent or at least limit it, had begun to wear on me. For many years, I'd romanticized what I thought was the "old Chicago," a weird, dirty, corrupt machine town where downtown was sleazy and junkies owned the nightlife district. Of course, I'd spent my best years of the '70s watching television in suburban Phoenix, and therefore I had a limited perspective. Indeed, an old neighborhood pol I knew once told me, "You know, things weren't so great here in the nineteen seventies." But I wasn't listening. Perhaps I'd written too many stories about people and businesses getting displaced by real-estate development, or perhaps I was an idiot. Regardless, I was in the middle of a city that felt more generic to me every day. I needed a break.

Regina and I sat up late nights trying to gather the courage to relocate. I loved my newspaper job, but the work had begun to feel repetitive to me. I really wanted to write fiction. A few years close to New York, I figured, would help me find an agent, and maybe get a book deal. Regina wanted to paint, but her space in our apartment was a badly lit, skinny room that overlooked a busy street. In Chicago, it was too expensive for her to rent a space outside the house, but in relatively ungentrified Philly, there were lots of abandoned industrial buildings that were renting out raw spaces to artists before the loft developers descended.

Our decision got a lot easier when Regina received a small inheritance from the estate of her father, who'd died the year before she and I had met. We wanted to buy property with the money. It wouldn't have landed us a small studio in the least desirable neighborhood in New York, but it was just enough to get a little house in Philly, one of the few affordable East Coast cities. We had very little to lose by moving there.

But the main reason I wanted to live in Philly was that it still felt old, and was still really strange. It was what I imagined Chicago had been like in the 1970s. That may be the least reasonable motivation ever for moving to a place, but it's genuinely what I believed at the time.

"Philly?" people said. "Why are you moving *there*?" Or, if they were already living in Philly, they said, "Why are you moving *here*?"

If we didn't feel like getting weird looks, Regina would say something like, "Well, Neal really needs to be closer to New York for his work. And plus, it's cheap, so I might be able to afford a studio." But the real reason, at least the one in my mind, came out sometimes anyway. I'd say, *"Because we saw a fishmonger warming himself over a garbage-can fire in the middle of the street!"*

We house-hunted in mid-August, during the Republican National Convention. I thought, for some reason, that I was covering the convention and its associated protests for *Rolling Stone,* so I spent many useless hours witnessing the usual melodramatic scene of the police doing battle with radical left-wing puppeteers. As the tear-gas canisters exploded, Regina was calling me with real-estate updates. I kept telling her to call me back after the people's struggle was over. Didn't she understand that democracy was at stake here? Then I got chased down an alley by some motorcycle cops, and I decided that house-hunting might not be such a bad alternative.

To help us find our Philadelphia dream home, we engaged a kind and sophisticated Realtor named Ingrid, who charmed us with a client newsletter that described all the fine books she'd read recently. Ingrid immediately deduced that Regina and I could afford a house in a neighborhood in the middle stage of its urban pioneer period. She showed us several places out of our league, just to whet our appetites, and a couple of really nice buildings in the middle of blocks that otherwise looked like London after the Blitz. Then she took us down Poplar Avenue, a minor thoroughfare at the northern edge of central Philly.

We beheld a dumpy little townhouse on a block of dumpy little townhouses. The house Ingrid showed us had cracked, bulging sidewalks, wainscoting with peeling dark-green paint, and brick that, because of deteriorating mortar, looked as though it had been pared down with sandpaper. Not very promising, we all agreed.

Inside was a different matter. The paint colors were a little off, but the house had some charming original cabinets, a cool decorative fireplace, and a nice seat in the bay window, which would be perfect for pillows on which our cats could then pee. Upstairs were a nice big bedroom with a skylight and large built-in closet, an extra bedroom with a built-in cedar wardrobe that had once been utilitarian but was now nearly an object of art, and a small bathroom with low-quality Mexican-style tile. The big winner, however, was the kitchen, large, with a cork floor, an island, and funky red cabinets that wrapped around the room. Regina and I began to act impressed.

"This is a nice house," Ingrid said, matter-of-factly, almost surprised.

A middle-aged Jewish couple occupied it. She was a sculptor who taught pottery classes. He was a record producer who'd been instrumental in developing the Philly soul sound of the '60s and currently did work with the Roots. They'd raised one daughter and a couple of golden retrievers in that little place. We felt as though we'd be buying the house from an older version of ourselves.

Our housing philosophy, which has remained consistent over the years, was: Move into a house only if the people living there before you had the same income level or above. This often lands us in a pretty nice house in a pretty sketchy neighborhood. It had been relatively easy to avoid real-estate hypocrisy when I was a single guy renting an apartment. But homeownership, especially homeownership with a $712 monthly mortgage, muddied the political waters. For someone who didn't like gentrification, I was certainly spending a lot of time gentrifying. The possibility of profit had joined the equation, but my old priorities lingered.

We went out back to the tiny patio, which was occupied mostly by plant boxes, raccoon turds, and shards of broken pottery. I saw that one plant, off in a corner, had a familiar if illegal-looking leaf. Leaning in, I took a sniff. My nose never fails me in such matters.

"We'll take it," I said.

Growltigger wasn't well. He developed a heart murmur. As we prepared for our move in the fall of 2000, he began to have breathing problems. Regina took him to the vet, who told her that the cat's heart had enlarged. Medication kept him comfortable for a while, but gradually, he turned listless and surly. He lay in the middle of the living room, heaving. Regina fell to the floor, sobbing.

"I love him so much!" she wailed.

We went to the vet, who examined the cat and nodded somberly. We had a choice, he said. We could increase the dose of medicine and try to keep Growltigger going for a few months. But he would inevitably suffer. Or we could put him down right now.

"Can we have a few minutes with him?" Regina said.

"Of course," said the vet.

Growltigger lay on a metal table. Regina touched his head. He looked at her, purred, and rubbed his head against her hand. Then he did the same thing to me.

"Good-bye, buddy," I said.

The vet came in with a long needle.

"Are you ready?"

"Yes," said Regina.

He caressed Growltigger's head.

"It won't hurt at all."

The needle went into Growltigger's thigh. Instantly, the cat began to shudder.

"I think he's going," I said.

"He's already gone," said Regina.

She was weeping when I led her out of the office. I wasn't much better. Our dear Growltigger would ass no more.

Growltigger's death magnified my wife's need to nurture; those cats had been child substitutes for years. Maybe it was because she felt like a child substitute herself. She had a loving family, but what she'd told me on our first date still held true. She didn't have true blood relations.

Under Tennessee law, at the time we met, Regina had no legal right to know anything about her birth mother. On the last day of our honeymoon, which we'd spent driving around the Smoky Mountains until we ran out of money, we took a detour to Knoxville.

You know you're married when you find yourself searching through yearbooks at the University of Tennessee library for a thirty-five-year-old photograph of someone who might sort of resemble your spouse. We went up into the stacks and Regina handed me a couple of yearbooks. I looked at two on the early side, while she checked the back end. Nineteen sixty-six yielded no fruit for me, nor did 1967. Regina crapped out on '69 and '70. Nineteen sixty-eight was the key year, in Regina's mind. We pored over separate copies of that yearbook like CSI investigators, but with no skills and no clues.

"This one!" Regina said.

Her eyes welled.

"It's my mother! She looks like me!"

"Are you sure?"

"She does! She looks like me! And . . . and . . . her name is Gina! That's my mother. I know it."

A few months later, Tennessee adoptees won a big lawsuit. Soon afterward, Regina received a packet that told her everything. Her mother was alive and in Atlanta. Regina had her name, her address, and a copy of her driver's-license photo. Of course it wasn't the woman from the yearbook. Her birth mother was divorced and had no other children. She'd been a student at the University of Georgia when she'd gotten pregnant, but had given birth to Regina in Knoxville. Even Regina's birth grandparents were still alive.

Unfortunately, none of them wanted to meet Regina. The agency informed Regina that if she or anyone she knows ever attempts to contact her birth mother they'll get thrown in prison. This news set off the snooze alarm on Regina's biological clock.

"I need something that I can call my own," she said.

"I understand," I said.

She put her head on my shoulder and started nuzzling my neck. She gave a sweet smile that said "I love you" on the surface but contained a more specific message beneath.

"What do you want?" I said.

"Nothing. I just think you're so handsome, that's all."

"Uh-huh. Now what do you want?"

"Puppy."

"No."

"Awww. Puh-peeeeeeeeeeeee!"

I didn't want a dog, because the arrival of a dog always means that children are next. In theory, I liked children. In theory, I didn't mind having my own. But theory and practice are different. Plus, dogs create their own special set of problems, particularly when combined with cats.

"Pleeeeeeeeeease? Please can we get a puppy? Oh, pretty please?"

Her begging increased in intensity once we moved to Philly, a town that tends toward cruelty and lonely-making even if you know a lot of people.

"We really need a puppy."

"There are three cats in this very small house. We can't have a dog."

"*Puppy!* Come on. They're so cute."

She started doing research on the type of dog that would fit us perfectly. We needed something small, amusing, and affectionate, but that wouldn't shed. That narrowed the search to a few breeds. Apparently, shelter dogs have all kinds of health problems. Regina didn't just want baby practice. She wanted purebred baby practice. Specifically, she settled on purebred Boston terrier baby practice, and she found websites for me to examine.

"Look at their scrunchy little faces!" she said.

"What are you, eight years old? They're not Cabbage Patch Kids. You have to clean up their poop and stuff."

She pointed to a picture.

"That one, in particular, wants to come live with you."

"No!"

Now deep inside the puppy matrix, Regina found a breeder outside of Pittsburgh, then made sure that the American Kennel Club had certified the breeder because, according to her research, ill-bred Bostons develop all kinds of crazy breathing problems. This amateur medical analysis was another sign that she was in mommy mode. It was her version of puppy prenatal care.

She told me she'd reserved us one of the next litter, which was scheduled to pop in July.

"You did *what*?"

"I put a deposit on a dog. It's my birthday present!"

I couldn't argue with a birthday present. I was defeated.

"Oh, all right," I said. "I guess I like dogs."

In mid-August, the breeder sent us a JPEG of "Tubs."

"Everyone loves our little Tubs," she wrote.

"Awwwww, he looks like a mole," Regina said.

"He is pretty cute," I said. "But I'm not calling him Tubs."

She ceded me at least that ground. And thus on a Wednesday morning, Regina and I drove five hours across Pennsylvania. We pulled up at a ranch-style house about fifteen miles west of Pittsburgh and beheld an assortment of purebred Boston terriers jumping inside a series of wire-mesh pens. The roundest one in the new-puppy chamber belonged to us.

"There he is," Regina said.

"Yep," I said.

"What we should call him?"

"Hercules!"

"I was kind of thinking Iggy."

"Iggy isn't a bad name, but Hercules! Come on."

She regarded our puppy. He pawed at the pen, tongue out, eyes bulging hilariously.

"OK," she said. "Hercules."

Hercules slept curled in my lap all the way home. He didn't move for hours.

"I think there's something wrong with him," Regina said.

"There's nothing wrong with him."

I stroked his tiny head.

"Isn't that right, wittle boy?"

I had already become mushy, even cheesy, but it didn't matter, because I had a pup. The next two months were a self-guided high school health class, except instead of being forced to take care of a mannequin baby, we raised ourselves a fine young dog. We got up near dawn every morning for Hercules' outdoor pee, the first time in a dozen years that I'd woken up early for anything except to wait in line for concert tickets. At night, Regina prepared a hot-water bottle wrapped in a towel for Hercules to sleep with in his crate. The breeder said it would remind him of his mother.

Every evening, I'd take Hercules for a walk around our neighborhood in Philly. He charmed all who approached him, the old and the young, the lame and the able, by licking with ardor. It didn't occur to him to discriminate. He was such a sweet boy, and he never pooped inside. On the other hand, he humped all our pillows until they popped their stuffing. Every time anyone raised his or her voice over conversation level, even implying that something was wrong, Hercules would huddle in the corner. His ears would droop and he'd shiver as though we'd put him in the freezer. While playing with our cats, he'd bite their tails. They'd retaliate by pissing on our sofa. I'd blame the cats. My animal sympathies had been transferred.

One day it began to sleet fiercely during our afternoon walk. I picked up Hercules and tucked him inside my pea coat. He shivered with fear and confusion and cold. I felt like a true man. The well-being of this absurd creature was my responsibility, and it pleased me to feel that way.

"Don't worry, Hercu-baby," I said. "Daddy's gonna save you."

I was perfectly happy with the family as it stood, but soon enough Regina put her head on my shoulder and began nuzzling my neck again. She gave a sweet smile that said "I love you" on the surface but contained a more specific message beneath.

"What do you want?"

"Baby, baby, baby. Bay-beeeeeee!"

It was time.

FOUR

Wave of Incubation

December 2001–August 2002

A book called *Taking Charge of Your Fertility* appeared on our coffee table. Regina's friend Angela, who'd already taken charge by producing a human baby named Graham, had sent it along. Regina attacked *Taking Charge of Your Fertility* with more enthusiasm and attention than she'd attacked any book since *Optimum Wellness.* She more or less had to. She was thirty-two, beyond the stage where a man could get her pregnant by looking at her cockeyed. I ignored the book, half-assuming that it would end up in the rack by the toilet or on the upstairs bookshelf where Regina kept all the Native American novels she'd read in college. Still, I was secretly impressed by Regina's efficiency. She treated baby-conception like it was a science experiment, which, in many ways, it was.

But I still made fun of her when she began to take her temperature every morning with a digital basal thermometer. Where the thermometer came from, I don't know, but I do know it was the first of many products to mysteriously appear. From here on, though I didn't realize it at the time, my life would be a gradual accumulation of things that weren't for me.

A woman trying to discover her ovulation date, I've learned, needs to take her temperature before she gets out of bed in the morning. She should move as little as possible while executing the maneuver. Regina followed these instructions as though they were military writ. In the mornings, I felt the barest shuffle in the bed next to me. Thirty seconds later, I heard three short beeps in a row. Regina extended two fingers and stuck them under the covers, where they headed toward her crotch.

"That makes me hot," I said.

"I'm checking the viscosity of my cervical fluid," she corrected.

"Oh."

"If it's clear and stringy, that means I'm ovulating."

"I see," I said, though I actually didn't. "Don't you ovulate the same time every month?"

She looked at me like I hadn't finished my math homework.

One day, while at the painting studio she shared with a friend downtown, she felt a little cramp on the left side of her crotch. She rushed to the bathroom. The results were substantial. She called me.

"I'm coming home for lunch!"

She rarely came home for lunch.

"Why?"

"My cervical fluid is clear and stringy!"

"My God! That's terrible!"

"Don't you remember? That means I'm ovulating."

"Oh. Great!"

About a half hour later, Regina dragged her bike into the entry-way. She gave me a long, deep kiss.

"I'm getting into bed," she said.

"Already?"

"This is the optimal moment."

"We can't do it tonight?"

"If we don't do it now, I'll never get pregnant."

Normally, it didn't take much to get Regina and me to sleep

together. But there had been a very distinct lack of foreplay this time; I don't necessarily need much, but a little drama in bed is always nice. Only one thing could get me ready for this encounter in the requisite amount of time. Fortunately, the Internet is full of pictures of Lynda Carter in her Wonder Woman costume. And I know where to find them all.

Regina lay in bed, looking beatific. She opened her arms to me. We were about to perform a ritual dance of pure trust and devotion. It would be lovemaking in every sense of the word, a holy, if secular, bow toward the perpetuation of the species.

"Come here, sweetie," she said. "I'm ready."

Nearly twenty seconds passed before I finished. Wonder Woman had gotten me quite worked up.

"That wasn't much fun," I said.

"We'll do it again. This usually takes a few months."

For some of our friends, making a baby has been a nail-biting melodrama of sleazy fear-mongering fertility doctors, sperm washing, false alarms, and miscarriages. Regina has spent many tearful nights on the phone with them. But for us, that one nooner under a skylight in an old townhouse in a transitional neighborhood just north of downtown Philadelphia was enough. A few days on, Regina was driving us home from the grocery store. She parked across the street from our house and put her head on the steering wheel.

"Whoo. I'm dizzy."

"You'll be all right."

"Seriously, Neal. I feel really strange."

The reality of permanent adulthood loomed before me, an endless plain of responsibility and difficult decisions. It was frightening, and I come from melodramatic, slightly manic-depressive stock that tends toward needless panic. I banged on the dashboard, clawed at my eyes, and tugged at my hair.

"You're pregnant!" I said. "Damn your damn cervical fluid chart! I knew it! I knew it! You tricked me!"

"Calm down."

"Shit, shit! Fuck! Fuck! Fuck!"

Regina started spending nights, and some afternoons, on the couch in her bathrobe, watching television while she ate nothing but cheese, crackers, and grapefruit. I found myself getting drunk fairly often, and I wasn't usually much of a drinker. Many nights, I paced upstairs in my undershirt and boxers, cursing the rumbles of the city buses that passed under our window every fifteen minutes, imagining our future child running into the street and getting run over by one of them. The weather was lousy. Money was tight. We were far away from family and friends, and we were scared. As soon as Regina had gotten pregnant, it seemed, life had become difficult and unhappy.

We tried to make Philadelphia work. I developed a taste for Yuengling beer and a justified prejudice for Pat's cheese steaks. During Allen Iverson's Finals year, I wore my Sixers ski cap with pride. We put a Philly Phanatic bobblehead doll on top of the TV and got a subscription to the *Philadelphia Daily News,* choosing it over the *Inquirer,* because the *Daily News* was the paper that city-dwellers read. I began going to weekly pub quizzes at a downtown Irish bar. Regina got some teaching gigs at local colleges, and I helped organize a reading series at the public library. But our world was still crusted with gloom.

The clerk at my neighborhood convenience store sat behind bulletproof glass. Police helicopters would sweep searchlights through our windows at two a.m. The park where we walked Hercules was littered with broken glass, used needles, and discarded mattresses. One night, the cop who lived across the street from us got mugged on our block. I got off the bus from downtown to find him, blood pooling in the snow, surrounded by emergency personnel. Apparently, he had lain there for an hour before anyone called the cops. I asked a guy in uniform what had happened. He grunted, "Robbery," turned away, and walked back to his car.

Anyone but me could have seen the irony coming from a thousand miles away. I'd wanted an ungentrified city, but the reality of one made me uncomfortable. We hadn't expected fancy, but the town was even harsher than we'd thought.

We lived next door to a mailman who claimed to have once been a major player in Philly's poetry-slam scene. He had a lot of kids, or at least, through the thin wall that our houses shared, they sounded like a lot of kids. I never could quite figure out how many, exactly. A twelve-year-old daughter was always around; she was a sweet kid and he was definitely her dad. But her brothers and sisters seemed variable in number. It didn't help that the mailman himself wouldn't tell us which kids were his and which weren't.

At night, the mailman and I sat on our respective stoops. I drank beer, and he didn't. A churchgoing woman had recently captured his heart, and he wanted to appear worthy.

"I'm thinking about leaving," he said. "Get an RV and we'll drive out to Nevada or something. Someplace warm. It'll be hard to leave all this luxury, but I'll manage."

"So you and your . . . how many kids do you have again?" I said, trying a sneak attack.

"Maybe we'll go to Arizona," he said.

Our block captain was a retired music-industry bodyguard named Butter. He drove a white Cadillac DeVille. Butter kept the block relatively safe, because he was thick, fast, and he carried a baseball bat. If you needed some work done on your house and were too lazy or incompetent to do it yourself, you could ask Butter, because he'd lived in the neighborhood a long time. He'd walk north a few blocks, and fifteen minutes later, you'd have your guys. Because he had a taste for rare tropical plants, Butter's house was about 95 degrees and stupefyingly humid at all times. He hung outside.

One night, he pulled his Cadillac onto the sidewalk in front of my stoop. I sat on the trunk with him and the mailman and we looked down the street at the bridge, which had a guardrail bent up at a 90-

degree angle from an accident that had happened there two years before. Beyond that was Fairmount Park.

"It used to be something else here, in the sixties," Butter said.

"I bet," I said.

"You know who used to sit up there on that hill in the park?"

"No."

"John Coltrane."

"*NO!*"

"Damn right! Coltrane used to sit up there and play his saxophone all day long. It was his favorite practice spot."

"That must have been something."

"It was really nice to come home from work every day to a free John Coltrane concert. It made a fine soundtrack for getting with your woman, too."

"With my luck," the mailman said, "my woman would have left me for John Coltrane."

Butter then did something corny but also beautiful. He put a Coltrane cassette in his car deck. We watched the sun set over the trees with a sweet saxophone melody in the background.

An ambulance roared by, full siren blaring. Pregnant Regina came out of the house in her bathrobe.

"What the hell was that?" she said.

Two police cars followed, equally loud. They hung a right up 30th Street and headed north. A chopper appeared over the buildings in front of us, spotlight searching even though it was barely dusk. *Ride of the Valkyries* would have been a more appropriate soundtrack than John Coltrane.

"Arizona," the mailman said. "I'm definitely going to Arizona."

We knew one other family in Philly besides the mailman's. They were a slightly more traditional model of modern parenting, bohemian division. The dad co-owned a used-book store and watched their daughter during the day. So they could pay their tiny mortgage, the mom worked a boring but easy office job, tinkering with her novel at the frequent moments when she had nothing else to do. They took their three-year-old girl to parties and plays, keeping her up past eleven with a steady supply of sugared foods. It wouldn't have been my choice, but it worked for them. Maddy was hard-wired to enjoy dressing like a fairy princess. In that sense, she was like many little girls. In other ways, she was a shining example of cute hipster urban precociousness. I adored her. When her parents had parties, she was usually my main conversation partner.

"We're going to have dim sum tomorrow," she said to me one Saturday night.

"Really?"

"Uh-huh. Dim sum is yummy."

"That's true."

"It has MSG in it, which makes your head hurt sometimes."

"That's also true."

"My daddy works in a used-book store."

"No, Maddy," I said. "Your daddy *owns* a used-book store. There's a difference."

Some vaguely incomprehensible avant-garde jazz from the late 1960s was playing on the stereo.

"That's my daddy's music," she said.

"Do you like it?"

"No," she said. "But he plays it anyway."

Though they weren't rich, and they also weren't Jewish, they still sent Maddy to an expensive Jewish preschool. Maddy liked this because the school let her dress as Queen Esther, the Jewish version of a fairy princess, whenever she wanted, even when it wasn't Purim.

"What about public school?" I asked her parents.

"Yeah, right," her mom said.

A good public education, to me, is a birthright, not a privilege. But I'd attended public school in Scottsdale, Arizona, and now I lived in North Philadelphia. I'd read about lousy urban schooling in Jonathan Kozol's books, but I never thought that would apply to *my* kid. While we lived there, Philadelphia mayor John Street showily barricaded himself inside school-board headquarters because, he said, he didn't even want to consider letting a private corporation take over partial control of the city's school system. This was a noble sentiment in theory. But in reality, he was trying to protect the teacher's union because it was a major funding source for his political machine. On the day the story broke, I said to Regina, "Maybe we shouldn't live in the city."

"I was thinking the same thing," she said. "But I don't *not* want to live in the city. We should at least live in some city, somewhere."

"I feel guilty."

"Why? You don't owe anything to Philadelphia."

"Yeah, but I made a commitment . . ."

"Do you want to honor your abstract commitment that no one cares about but you?" she said. "Or do you want your child stepping on a needle in the park?"

"So where should we raise our child?"

"I don't know."

Perhaps, we realized, we should have thought this detail through a bit more carefully. Life's learning curve, once you get pregnant, is steep and immediate. It wasn't long before we got our health-care lesson.

Despite the fact that we had many friends in Philly who received good medical care, including one whose father was a respected local pediatrician, we picked a prenatal doctor out of the phone book. Our doctor in Chicago had been a dashing young figure who wore a fedora and a camel's-hair coat when he wasn't in the office. He spent his weekends at *Iron John* male-encounter workshops in the Wisconsin woods, and he sometimes prescribed Chinese herbs and acupuncture. For some reason, we didn't realize that he'd been an unusual fellow. Predictably, our random choice in Philly led us to a medical center downtown where the elevator was broken and the stairwell smelled like urine. I was the only father in the waiting room.

Into the examining chamber walked a sour-smelling doofus with a voice like Eeyore's. He had a mustache that curled at the ends, which turned out to be his most redeeming quality. We planned to use a midwife for the birth. We should have used one right away.

"First of all," he said. "Congratulations."

"Thanks," I said.

"Are you taking prenatal vitamins?" he asked Regina.

"Yes," she said. "Good ones. Rainbow Light. They have added nutrients that are supposed to be good for mom *and* baby."

"Never heard of them," he said.

I wondered if Regina knew more than he did. She'd done an almost impossible amount of research on pregnancy: Her body had become a holy shrine of well-informed childbearing. About four months before she got pregnant, Regina switched to decaf. After a while, she decided that the smell of decaf was too tempting for her, and besides, it still contained a little caffeine. For two weeks, she frequently had her head on the dining-room table, her palms over her temples. Then the withdrawal ended.

After that, she started drinking red-raspberry-leaf tea. This, she told me, was supposed to be beneficial to the female reproductive system. It toned the uterus and regulated hormones. Also, she gave up alcohol, reduced her sugar intake to ice cream, and increased the amount of protein she was eating. She kept this approach up throughout her pregnancy, and also through eighteen months of breast-feeding, though she occasionally had a glass of something alcoholic after the baby was born.

Meanwhile, she did regular kegels, which is more or less an exercise where you contract your sphincter area, or, as the pregnancy books call them, "the pelvic floor muscles"; she stopped inhaling when she was around household cleaners, perfumed lotions, paint, solvents, hair dye, and the like; during her third trimester, she started eating wild salmon and walnuts, which contain omega fatty acids vital for brain development, and she avoided shellfish, raw eggs, sushi, and anything else that contained a risk of food poisoning or heavy-metal consumption. Speaking of heavy-metal consumption, she stopped going to rock shows with me because she didn't want to inhale smoke and thought the amplified noise would hurt the baby's ears. I, on the other hand, had increased my consumption of beer, marijuana, and red meat, and I also spent a lot of time biting my nails.

"I'm having trouble finding a heartbeat," our "doctor" said.

"What?" I said.

"It's probably nothing to be worried about," he said. "I'm ordering an ultrasound anyway."

Of course the ultrasound showed a heartbeat. In fact, the fetus was holding up a sign in the womb that read SWITCH DOCTORS NOW. But because of this, when it came time for Regina's five-month ultrasound, which actually *was* necessary, our insurance refused to pay. We'd already had an ultrasound, the letter said.

I called the insurance company.

"You'd better fucking pony up for the fucking ultrasound," I recall myself saying.

And thus we tasted the first bitter fruit of our choice to become "self-employed." The freedom to work where and when you want becomes entrapment when you consider health coverage. When I'd had a job, my insurance covered everything, including dental and psychiatry. Now, on the verge of becoming a father, I faced enormous bills just to get my pregnant wife's temperature taken. I'd joined the National Writers Union because it offered its members good, affordable insurance. But I quickly learned that before you join an independent health-care group, you should make sure you know who else belongs. We were already well on our way to parenthood before I realized that most of my collective bargaining partners were unpublished and over sixty. At this time, the insurance industry was beginning to completely divest itself of people it would actually have to insure, like the elderly and the sick. Pregnancy wasn't afforded any special privileges, either.

Six months into Regina's pregnancy, we received a letter from the union.

"Our health insurance carrier is dropping our policy," it said. "We're currently in negotiations to find a new . . ."

I was on the phone before the end of the sentence.

"My wife is six months pregnant! What do you mean we don't have any insurance?"

"Sir, we're working on it," said the person with the worst job in America.

At our next visit, the doctor informed us that he was leaving. Pennsylvania's malpractice-insurance costs were skyrocketing for OBs. I could see why.

"Who's going to take care of her?" I said.

"Oh, we'll find someone around here," he said.

That week, the union informed us that they'd contracted with a company with the homey name of Unicare for a policy that would cost us $700 a month, which would rise to $1,200 a month once we had the baby. Good lord, that was a lot of money. And thus we were faced with an all-too-typical American choice. Either we could have health care, or we could eat. While Regina was pregnant, we had no choice but to pay the premium. We didn't qualify for Medicaid, and $700 a month, though almost exactly the amount of our mortgage, was a lot less than the $20,000 we would have had to pay without health insurance. But after that, we'd have to find our own coverage.

Thus temporarily if uncomfortably insured, we drove around the Philly metropolitan area, looking at houses for sale in suburbs populated by people who'd given up around the time that *All in the Family* premiered. They were places full of sadness, drawn shutters, and carpets that smelled like forty years of bad stew. I imagined life as lonely and unpleasant; I'd only see my neighbors on garbage night, when we'd exchange nervous nods at the curb. On Sunday, Regina and I would drive to Costco for pantry supplies, then hurry home so I could watch the Eagles game in my easy chair. Occasionally, I'd take the train to Penn Station so I could fool myself into thinking that I had access to Manhattan. I saw myself bilious and bitter, Regina drunk on cheap wine, our kid a glue-sniffing, hate-crime-committing skate punk.

We had to find something else. Soon, I would head off on a three-week book tour. The secondary purpose of the trip, we decided, was to scout out a new home for us. We were as surprised as anyone else when it turned out to be in Texas.

Regina lay on our cat-shredded couch that stank of cat pee, moaning and nearly unable to move, as a living creature began to churn inside her, displacing her gastrointestinal tract. It was her first trimester, she was hundreds of miles from any relative, and she lived in a city where she had few friends. Her life, once so expansive, seemed to shrink as the baby grew. The house was dark and damp and full of street noise. She was as sad and lonely as she'd ever felt.

One night, I called home.

"I'm in San Francisco," I said. "It's so beautiful here."

"I took some butter out of the refrigerator today and it smelled so disgusting that I threw up."

"I'm sorry."

"I threw up crackers."

"That's terrible."

"Please come home now."

"I'll be home soon."

"Not soon enough."

Only a year and a half earlier, a few months after our wedding, she and I had gone on a cross-country twenty-city book tour. It was my first one, fueled only by my ambition, Regina's willingness to drive for twelve-hour stretches, and our credit cards. It takes a good, trusting person to go to Las Vegas with her husband, not on vacation, but so he can do a reading at 11:30 on a Sunday night in their hotel room in front of four people. It takes a heroine to drive on a fool's errand from Seattle to Los Angeles without stopping. We lived on Corn Nuts, beef jerky, truck-stop Subway sandwiches, and twenty-ounce bottles of caffeinated diet soda. Every time we got into the car we sang "On the Road Again," no matter how tired we were, before we started bickering over the map. It was hard for me to imagine taking a trip like that without her, though I hardly protested when one manifested itself. Still, I was thinking about the family's future.

I'd persuaded my publisher that it would be great for my book if they sent me to Austin, Texas, for the South by Southwest music festival; I'd become adept at creating free vacations for myself and passing them off as work. There were more than 700 bands playing around the city all day and night, sometimes for free. That's where people were turning their entertainment attention, so it was easy to get a gig at the large independent bookstore downtown.

"Hey, man," said my bookstore liaison when I arrived. "Welcome to Austin."

It was the second time I'd visited Austin. The first time, I'd been there with Regina. We'd found it really laid-back and fun. There seemed to be a lot of parks, and a lot of families with small children. But it was in Texas. That was very far away from anything we needed to do.

"Nice to be here," I said.

"Right on," he said.

He seemed like a bit of a conspirator.

"You know anyplace around here I can get high?" I said.

"A bunch of us were about to head up to the top floor of the parking garage," he said. "You wanna come?"

Did I want to come? I fell into a mode that I hadn't used since 1992, when I'd spent two weeks living in my friend's garage in San Diego.

"Hell, yeah, dude," I said. "Spark it up!"

For the next four days, I wandered, all afternoon and all night, down wide boulevards and piss-stained alleys, side streets and neighborhoods east of the highway, past what seemed like hundreds of bars, all of which disgorged rock music of every conceivable subgenre. The city was awash in beer, whiskey, and really good-looking people from all over the world, of both genders, squeezed into tight shirts. The few locals that I met told me that Austin wasn't always like this. It was usually even cooler, because there was no one from out of town around.

I stayed through Sunday night to check this hypothesis. The air felt hazy and thick; the town throbbed with a whopping collective hangover. Little dental instruments scraped at my sinuses. Where was that restaurant I'd eaten at three days before at three a.m. when I was drunk to the point of collapse? I only walked about three miles out of my way to find it. At some point, I sat on a patch of grass and began clawing at my eyes. I called a cab company on my cell phone.

The driver showed up about ten minutes later. I got into the cab. He didn't look at me. We drove away, and he continued to stare ahead. When we hit the highway, he whipped his head around and stuck out his tongue.

"AHHHHHHHHHH!" he said. "WATCHA WATCHA WATCHA!"

The force of his weirdness pinned me against my seat. I looked at his face. He was a guy about my age.

"Haw," he said. "I'm just fuckin' with you."

When I got back to where I was staying, I called Regina. She'd love Austin. I just knew that she would.

"Dude," I said. "We've got to get out here!"

"Don't call me 'dude.' "

"Sorry, dude. We should think about living in Austin for a while."

"Are you serious?"

"It's relaxing and sunny and the people are really cool," I said. "Don't you think we deserve that?"

"Maybe."

"I could start a band."

"You are *not* going to start a band."

"I might. Because I was born to rock!"

"Yes, dear."

"You have to check it out, though, dude. There are tons of families with kids here. I see kids in restaurants and bars. The people here are *just like us*."

"All right," she said.

"Really? Do you really mean it?"

"We have to live somewhere. Why not Austin?"

We went house-shopping in Austin on Memorial Day weekend. It didn't make my mother very happy.

"My first grandchild is going to be born in *Texas*?" she said.

This was quite a judgment from someone who lives in Phoenix. Using a phrase I'd repeat many times in subsequent years, I said, "It's not Texas, it's Austin."

"I'm sure it is," she said, "for some people."

We'd entrusted our search for a home in Austin to a guy named Milton, a friend of people we knew in Chicago. I'd never met a male Realtor who wasn't some twenty-five-year-old C-average chucklenut who wore bad cologne, but I checked my skepticism because we didn't have much time. Milton confounded expectation.

He was standing in the lobby of the hotel where we were staying. He was a skinny guy in his early fifties with a healthy tan and a haircut that said, "I ain't got time for any of that fancy shit. Let's go fishing!" He crouched, legs bowed slightly, and stuck out his right arm at a 90-degree angle. I took his hand. That posture gave his shake a lot of torque.

"Hey-hey!" he said. "Milton!"

Milton grew up in Waco, but he's lived in Austin since the late 1960s. This is a good combination. The fact that he left Waco for Austin at all makes him cool, and the fact that he grew up in Waco means that if a foreign army ever invaded Texas, he'd be a handy member, if not the leader, of the resistance. Here's a story he told us once:

Man, I was out in the woods this weekend, doing some hunting. I had me a shitload of Shiner Bock and a rifle. I musta killed something like a dozen deer. Then when it was time to go, I realized, I've got a dozen deer here, and they're gonna rot, and who the hell wants to leave a bunch of rotten deer in the woods? Ain't nothing like fresh deer meat cooked in a backyard smoker! So here's what I did. I dragged 'em all into a line, and cut slits in the back of all their necks. I found a bunch of rocks and put one in each slit. Then I took some rope and I cut it into twelve pretty long segments, and tied each segment to a rock. The other end of the ropes got tied to the bumper of my truck. I got behind the wheel, started it up, and drove . . . RIIIIIIIIP! The skin came off like that. *Shiiiiiit!* That's a lot of deer meat, I tell you what! I got some in my freezer if you want some . . .

Milton is married to a Yankee from Pittsburgh. They have two adorable little daughters. He describes himself as a "yellow-dog Democrat." "I'd vote for a yellow dog before I'd vote for a Republican!" he says. "I tell you what."

He was the perfect Austin guide, and he drove us around.

"I think y'all are gonna like it down here," he said. "I'll tell you what. I've lived in Texas my whole life, but Austin is special. I ain't never been anyplace where people are this friendly. I'm the luckiest sonofabitch in the whole world. There's something in the air here that makes people happy. What're those things called? Endomorphines."

"Endomorphines?"

"Yeah. Endomorphines. I tell you what. This city is something. And it's because of the endomorphines."

"Milton, I think you mean endorphins."

He paused.

"Nah. I call them endomorphines."

We pulled up to a boxy house on a corner lot. The yard was scruffy, with magnolia leaves in the beds and a sickly looking low-lying cactus near the street, but the building looked like it had never lacked for love. It had white vinyl siding, dark-green shutters, and new windows. There was a ten-foot-high windmill, stuck into a concrete block, in the middle of a flowerbed. I also noticed a porch swing, a mailbox decorated with the design of the Texas state flag, and a life-size silhouette of a cowboy leaning against the post, all of which looked like stuff you might find at the first highway knick-knack shop on the way to the lake. A jolly-looking guy with a crew-cut appeared at the doorway. Like everyone else we'd met in Austin, he was dang friendly.

"I'm so glad y'all are here!" he said.

We went inside. Every room had deep brown shag carpet, wood paneling on the walls, and acoustic tile on the ceilings. Until 1999, when the city opened a new airport south of downtown, the house had been directly across the Interstate from the main runway. The owner, whom I'll call Barry, had a laminated front page from the newspaper the day the airport closed. It showed a jet looming over the house.

"It's a lot quieter now," Barry said.

The kitchen looked like it hadn't been used in many years. A quaint Chambers stove with a broiler and original burner covers, but disconcertingly frayed wiring, took up most of the room. There was no pantry, and not enough counter space to chop a carrot. All available wall space was taken up by Barry's collection of Texas license plates, most of which appeared to be from the same time period. There were two bedrooms, one large and one decent-size, and an unspectacular bathroom with a dirty-looking porcelain tub. At the back of the master bedroom was a door. Barry opened it to reveal an empty apartment. That's when we got the house story.

It was built before the airport in 1941, one of the first in the neighborhood, when the area was a distant suburb of downtown, mostly transitional dry forest between hill country and coastal lowland. After a few years, the first couple that lived there sold it to a woman named Nola and her husband, who spent forty years there. They added the master bedroom along the way, which meant that the original house couldn't have been much more than 650 square feet. When Nola's husband died, she sold it to Barry and went to San Antonio to live with a niece.

A few months later, Nola called Barry.

"I'm being neglected," she said. "Please come get me."

Barry figured that Nola wouldn't appreciate his "friends." But he also felt like it was her house, even if he owned the title. So he built her an apartment in the back. Seven months later, she went into a nursing home and never returned, and Barry had a rental unit on his hands.

This apartment, born of generosity, made the house particularly valuable, because it meant there were two bathrooms, even if the second one had a moldy plastic seat screwed to the shower wall. It also meant a second kitchen, with its own refrigerator and stove and cabinet knobs, a ceiling fan, and a wallpaper runner over the cabinet decorated in flower patterns from the Laura Ashley remainders catalog. Out the back door were a patio area, a reasonably large one-car garage/junk shed, a covered carport, and some slivers of grass.

"I think y'all need to take a serious look at this place," Milton said.

We drove around for three days, seeing some places that were OK, and one that had a slate shower and four bedrooms and a large, open kitchen and really plush carpeting that would have been perfect for baby crawling. It was five minutes south of downtown, but it was also $199,000, and therefore not in our budget at the time. We had Milton make a limp lowball offer that got rejected in fifteen seconds.

The car was silent.

"I wanted *that* house," I said.

More silence.

"So y'all wanna go look at Barry's house again or what?" Milton said.

"OK," I said.

The next day, we loaded up a cooler of Shiner Bock, which I'd already grown to love. It's malty and slightly bitter, but it doesn't have the acrid tang of cheap corporate beers, even though it sells in Texas for about the same price. We took the beer over to Barry's to close on the deal. Barry gave Regina and me big, friendly hugs. "I knew it! I knew it!" he said. "This house feels right for y'all. You'll treat it like the lady it's meant to be!" His Realtors stood around looking nervous, swearing that they'd never sell a house outside the suburbs again. We didn't know at the time that the house had been on the market for nearly five years. Later, we found out why.

We all posed for a picture, beers hoisted, except for Regina, who had a club soda. I immediately sank deep into a sea of damp Texas kitsch. This would be, I realized, my first grown-up house, where Regina would go into labor, to where my son would come home from the hospital, where I would finish writing my first novel. My first boyhood house, in Memphis, Tennessee, had been about this size. There are family photographs of me standing waist-deep in a hole that my dad dug in the yard, of a little gray poodle licking my face, of me sitting in a blue canvas easy chair reading the newspaper, that serve as my only memories of my first four years, and yes, I was reading at four years old. Will my son, I wondered, have the same thin recollection of this house, his toddlerhood nothing more to him than an archaic folder of iPhoto documents, or can I somehow give him something more specific to remember? What will this house mean to him in the year 2037? Will he think I'm cool?

My life's timeline ran through my mind as I simultaneously signed the paperwork and drank a Shiner Bock. I felt good. With a little makeover, this house would be a fine place for us, in a relaxing town full of good people, a place that had some of the weirdness of Chicago but much better weather, a place that lacked the grit, the sadness, the corruption of Philadelphia. In my mind, Austin was already our home. We wouldn't have any problems in *this* neighborhood.

FIVE

We Shall Not Call Him Moses

August–September 2002

As we drove from Philadelphia to Austin, with Hercules in my lap and three crated-up cats howling in the back, Regina and I had a lot of time to think about our upcoming parenthood mission.

"We're gonna have a baby," I said. "Can you believe it?"

"Well, I *am* carrying him," she said.

"Right. But can you believe it in general?"

"Well, it's hard to imagine that I'm gonna be breast-feeding. And I'm nervous about whether or not the baby will sleep at night. Actually, I'm nervous about everything."

"It's funny, because I'm not nervous at all. Except about money. Then again, I've been nervous about money my entire life."

I actually craved the responsibility that fatherhood would bring. I liked the idea that people would be dependent on me. I'd felt like the employee, the son, or the clownish afterthought my entire adult life. It was time for me to prove that I could take the ship's tiller.

Somewhere along the journey, I wrote this in a notebook:

I've never appreciated those whiny, seemingly omnipresent essays about the difficulty of "coming to terms" with being an adult man. Sure, fatherhood is challenging. But so were, for instance, being tortured in a Chilean prison, fighting in various wars, and undergoing Stalinist interrogation. I wonder what Ariel Dorfman, Primo Levi, and Arthur Koestler, men who wrote memoirs about actual struggle, would think about the genre of whiny new-parent hand-wringing. Well, I guess Dorfman is still alive, but I'm not going to ask him. Would Aldous Huxley have contributed to *The Bastard on the Couch II*? Hell, no. He took psychedelic mushrooms in his mature years. Did Hemingway edit his paternal doubts out of *A Moveable Feast*? Of course not. He either didn't have those doubts or didn't feel the need to express them. That's not to say I'm comparing myself to any of these guys, but there was a time when writers didn't complain in their memoirs, and when men didn't complain about fatherhood. It was either something you did, or something you didn't do, and then you lived your life. We're biologically motivated to reproduce. If it happens to you, then it's your time. Just enjoy being an adult. You'll be dead soon enough.

Of course, from the moment our son was born until the moment I'm typing this sentence, I've done nothing but whine. But that's just because I'm generally a whiny person. Even if I'm incapable of adhering to it, I still hold fast to the principle stated above.

Meanwhile, Regina was feeling more ambivalent, and more scared, than I was. While fatherhood would change my routine, I wasn't exactly going to be giving up anything significant. I'd still be working full-time and I wouldn't be the sole source of nourishment for a helpless infant. Regina, on the other hand, had been more or less independent for fifteen years. Now she'd chosen to put her art, the most profound expression of her being, aside. She was willing and happy to do that, but what worried her was that she didn't know when she'd start again. It could be a year, it could be two years, or it could be forever. The reason that dads shouldn't whine is because whether you're a dad or not a dad, your life stays basically the same. It's just a matter of increased responsibility. But once a woman has a baby, she's a mom, and the world demands a lot from moms. Regina understood this, and it made her nervous.

Halfway through our drive, we stopped so Regina could have a baby shower. She grew up in Nashville, and her mother and best friend still live there. So of course that's where she got showered, not that it made the experience any more fun for me. While I believe that dads should actively participate in every aspect of their child's life and their partner's pregnancy, there's still something totally absurd about the idea of the "couples shower." Regina had the *Baby Bargains* book. She knew what she wanted and what we needed, and her judgment served as Talmud in our house.

As the bleats of greeting and the pastel-wrapped gift boxes began to accumulate around the pool, Regina's best friend assigned her husband, who, for the sake of this narrative, I will call Tim, to fetch some more chairs.

"Can I go?" I said to Regina. "Please?"

"OK," she said. "But come right back."

"Of course I will," I said.

As we pulled out of the driveway, Tim said, "You know, I've got some weed in the glove compartment if you wanna . . ."

"Oh. I wanna. Real bad."

Fifteen minutes later, we returned with the chairs. My mood had improved drastically. I gave Regina a fat kiss.

"Hey there, baby."

"How was getting the *chairs*?" she said with equal parts disdain and envy.

"You know," I said. "Chairy."

Tim and I approached the pool. "These people are crazy," I said. I soon found myself in a conversation with my sister-in-law, saying, "We have a great *plan* for the baby. I figured that if you have a plan, then planning is easy. All you have to do is stay *organized*."

"Uh-huh," she said.

Regina had a few friends in town, and they had all come to the shower, as had my mother. But the majority of attendees were women from Regina's mother's church.

"I've heard a lot of things about you," one of them said to me. "But I don't believe them."

Why, I wondered, do people always talk to me that way?

The conversation turned to the ice-cream social that the church ladies were planning, with all the proceeds going to charity.

"*Wow*," I said. "You all should come up with your own recipes for sundaes and then have a contest to see which one is best, and then you should call the newspapers and make sure everyone knows about it in advance. I think you have a *really* good chance. And you could get an ice-cream company to donate all the fixings. It could *totally be one of the society events of the year*."

"It already is, honey," said a church lady.

"Oh."

By this point, everyone was as festive as I. My sister-in-law had been making pitchers of margaritas all afternoon, de-emphasizing the mixer. There was merry clucking around the pool. The shower was about to begin.

They put Regina in an upright chair, the sun broiling above her. A sheen coated her face as though she were one of Vincent Price's prize possessions in *House of Wax*. Considering all the time Regina unwittingly spent radiating outside during her pregnancy, I'm surprised Elijah wasn't born with an apple in his mouth. But like a good Southern girl, she sat there politely.

"Hey, man," I said. "Don't you think Regina should get a little *shady*?" This got no response, so I had to add, "You know, like an umbrella?"

She opened her presents, which were pretty normal for a contemporary shower: Baby monitors, onesies, a Diaper Genie, booties, a hideous felt "growth chart" from the Lillian Vernon catalog. I overreacted to each one, burying my face in my hands, or raising my arms to the sky, subtly indicating to everyone that I found the gifts tacky by saying "*OH MY GOD!*"

The church ladies weren't amused.

Later, in a reasonably accurate preview of what ideal fatherhood is actually like, I chased my three-year-old nephew Westlund (not a Jewish name) around the pool, my arms in the air, saying "Rawwwrrrr!" while he shrieked to his daddy not to let the monster get him. If you can get past the initial infant-as-vegetable stage, suddenly fatherhood becomes a permanent role-play where you are either the monster or the monster victim. Sometimes you are also a bear or a lion or a dinosaur, but the principle of chase remains the same. If, like me, you have no actual skills to teach your children other than ranting at the news, you can at least come up with new ways to scare the hell out of them. Regardless, my skills at playing monster with my nephew impressed my in-laws, who were still in the process of assessing my worth.

"You were really good with him," my sister-in-law said.

"Children . . . ," I said, pausing for literary effect, "understand me."

After that, we left Nashville, arriving in Austin more or less on time.

"Just like Willie Nelson in the mid-seventies," I said.

"Yes, Neal," said Regina. "You're *exactly* like Willie Nelson."

The air in Texas felt like a dishwasher on rinse. Everything was steamy and moist. Regina staggered against the hood of the car.

"It's amazing I haven't passed out yet," she said.

Milton was at the house waiting for us with his friend Mike, whom he'd hired to rip out the shag carpeting, the wood paneling, and the acoustic tiles. I was under the impression that we were paying Mike with Shiner Bock until Regina showed me the checkbook months later. Hercules hopped out of the car. Within thirty seconds, he'd flopped on the concrete from heat exhaustion.

"You got one of them dogs, too?" Milton said. "There's two that look just like him right next door."

"That can't be true," I said.

"Hell, I ain't lyin'!"

We looked over the chain-link fence that lined the western edge of our small lot. Two Boston terriers came roaring out of the house next door, their eyes bulging, their mouths drawn back in that hideous happy-clown rictus that Bostons do so well. One was young, sleek, neurotic, and rabbit-fast. His name, we learned later, was Bruno. The other dog, Bruno's mother, Charlie, was shaped like breakfast sausage and was about as intelligent. Hercules stood and began to wiggle excitedly. I picked him up and walked over to the fence.

"Stop it, Neal," said Regina. "You don't know those people . . ."

I let Hercules go. He fell in slow motion, landed on all fours, and proceeded to run across the yard toward his two new friends in even slower motion, as "Born Free" played in the background. Bruno picked up a well-chewed plastic bottle, and Hercules got the other end. Thus began an orgy of snarling, drooling, wrestling, dog-butt-wiggling joy.

"Dang!" Milton said. "Moving to Texas is the best thing that ever happened to that dog!"

Though Hercules made friends quickly, we didn't have much wiggle room ourselves for socializing. We'd arrived at our new home deep into Regina's pregnancy. She'd grown more sluggish and had begun to move with less enthusiasm and efficiency. This meant that I needed to do more work, but I've never been good at painting within the lines and I've always had problems following written directions. I should be ashamed to say that my wife put the baby's room together mostly by herself, but you need to trust me when I tell you that it was better that way.

First, we had to order a crib and changing table; any relatives we knew who already had children were still using theirs. *Baby Bargains* said that one particular brand was a good deal, so Regina plucked the products off the Internet. The stuff arrived. She moved to open them, but I told her to sit down. I took the pieces out of their respective boxes and stared at them for a few minutes.

"I appreciate the fact that you want to help," she said. "But I think you should give me the screwdriver."

"Thank you for not making me do this," I said.

Most of our concerns were practical. But we weren't yet completely separated from the corrosive notion of child as hip, wacky fashion accessory. Since we'd moved to Texas, we thought it would be fun to decorate Elijah's room in a "cowboy" theme. Apparently, we weren't the only ones to whom this had occurred. Regina found a website called mycowboybaby.com. It led her to a vintage chenille fabric quilt with a cowboy design. After that, it was off to Moonshine, an online custom-lamp company, where Regina found a cylindrical cowboy-silhouetted lamp on sale that matched the room décor perfectly. And our friend Denise gave us the perfect little pair of cowboy boots. We'd also collected a few posters from the Hatch Show Print Shop in Nashville, one of a bucking bronco, one from an old Kentucky State Fair, a carnival scene depicting a "Freaks" tent, and a poster of Johnny Cash. This would be a room where *we* wanted to hang out. The Man in Black, guitar in hand, would somberly watch over our boy, in a room colored deep yellow. As the ever-practical Milton pointed out, "You ain't gonna notice if the baby pukes."

All of those items put together cost us about fifty bucks. Infant clothes, on the other hand, were expensive. We would pretty much rely on grandparental generosity and hand-me-downs from our nephew to keep our kid dressed, but that's not to say we lacked other options before his birth. Soon after we arrived, Regina hooked into something called the Coo de Tot Coalition. Coo de Tot was born when Katey Gilligan, an Austin mother, visited a sweatshop while on vacation in Hong Kong. She found the sweatshop quite louche and decided that she wanted to dress her lovely daughter Talia in clothes that didn't "symbolize blood, sweat, and tears." It was a lovely sentiment, but handmade baby clothes cost four times as much as the sweatshop-manufactured clothes they sell at Old

Navy. Maybe that doesn't occur to people who can afford to holiday in Hong Kong.

Some American children are being born into a world where everything is self-consciously "indie," extremely ethical, and pretty expensive. It's the world that David Brooks describes in *Bobos in Paradise,* his only good book. For instance, Brooks eviscerates the modern American wedding for having only one true purpose: To allow the couple a forum to show off its "uniqueness" and good taste. Nothing matters more than idiosyncratic consumer choice. Well, now that generation is having kids. Uniqueness is multiplying.

Coo de Tot, which Regina found through her La Leche League chapter, is a perfect example of this phenomenon, a successful floating marketplace that occurs in such locations as the beer garden of a Tex-Mex restaurant called Guero's and the outdoor section of an urban-pioneering garden-and-gifts center called Big Red Sun. The whole affair has that laid-back feeling that can only be supported by tenured or executive incomes. Regina and I went to a Coo de Tot bazaar soon after arriving in town and were overwhelmed by all the specialness. There were booths for GaGa Mondo, which sold bibs and placemats made from imported Mexican oilcloth; Wee Bitty Rag Top, specializing in "radical hats" for babies and toddlers; Daisy Dream Design's blankets made from 100-percent recycled Hawaiian shirts; and Rockit Baby's muscle shirts for six- to twelve-month-olds with the logo CHICKS DIG ME. The fact that all this stuff would be outgrown within a few months didn't seem to be a concern. Everyone at Coo de Tot seemed so happy and healthy, and they made their own cider from scratch. I felt insecure.

"This makes me *want* to go to Wal-Mart."

"Oh, be quiet," Regina said. "It's cute."

The one clothesmaker who really fit our aesthetic was Ramonster, which made "Swankwear for Kids." For only $52, we could get a Boys' Classic Gold Western shirt, and for $56, we had the option of buying a Pearl Snap Engineer Striped Jacket. We passed. But these seemed tasteful and sane when compared with the $24 "Pisher" snap shirt from Yid Kids. I thought, what self-respecting Jewish parent would put their kid in something like that? I spoke my thoughts aloud.

"Would an Italian parent buy their kid something that said 'Lil' Dago?'" I said. "How about a T-shirt for a black baby that says 'Darkie'!"

"Shhhh." Regina was more demure.

"Putawear. For the *chingada* inside us all."

"Enough!"

Regina had actually made a Coo de Tot friend online, a woman who designs handmade diaper bags and slings, "inspired," she later told us, by her darling daughter Zoe, who was doing very well at Montessori school. She agreed to barter a painting of Regina's in exchange for a sling, which was beige in color with some blue etchings of a guy playing a lute or some other goddamn thing. The barter economy actually works pretty well in Austin. I once got some plumbing done for a case of beer, and a guy gave me a bag of weed after I picked up his mail for the weekend. In any case, Regina liked the sling, though I could never figure out how the hell to use it.

For twelve bucks at our first Coo de Tot, we bought a little pillow that depicted rosy-cheeked baby cowboys and their pet horses. In the center of the pillow was a pocket, and inside the pocket was a cloth. We were supposed to write a message for our son, and then the designer would print out the message on the cloth, which the boy could then read when he was older.

I accepted the task of writing the message, of course, but first we had to figure out a name for the kid. For me, there was only one acceptable name. My first son would be called Moses.

"I am *not* naming him Moses," Regina said.

"But it's your maternal grandmother's maiden name!"

"No."

"Come on. It's perfect!"

"Why don't we name him Jesus, then?"

"Have you ever met a white kid named Jesus?"

"No, and I've never met a white kid named Moses, either."

"The name is majestic. It's from the Bible! Behold! Moses!"

"Mo Pollack. He'll sound like an old Jewish man."

"Someday, he'll *be* an old Jewish man."

"Absolutely not. What's your second choice?"

I thought about this for a second.

"Ezekiel."

"Oh, come on!"

"We can call him Zeke. Or EZ."

"I like Isaac."

"Uh-uh."

"It means 'he who will laugh.' "

"It also means 'he who was the bartender on *The Love Boat.*' "

The carousel went around. Finally, Regina and I came to a détente on Elijah. And so we came to give our son, like eight million other people of our generation, the same name as that of the actor who played Frodo in *The Lord of the Rings,* though not, I must add, because of that. Then we began to argue about nicknames.

"We could call him Eli," she said.

"We could. But we won't."

I explained to Regina that when I was a kid, we had some family friends with a son named Eli. This boy had some behavior problems. One night, during Passover seder, my father got fed up and locked him in the pantry. Many years later, Eli, now an adult, thanked my father for this. But the action had always bothered me, not because it had been ineffective, unwarranted, or even particularly cruel. It just seemed so random. I considered this an uncomfortable memory.

"We can call him E," I said. "That would be a cool nickname. Or Jah."

"Jah?"

"There is no God but Jah," I said, in a very bad Jamaican accent. "Jah Rastafari."

"Maybe he shouldn't have a nickname."

With that settled, I was able to write the message insert for Elijah's special pillow.

"Dear Elijah," I wrote. "The world is a horrible, horrible place. But I will try to make it as pleasant for you as I can."

Regina asked me to try again.

"But it's true!" I said.

"That's not the point. Say nice things to him."

I decided that I wanted to meet him first.

While we dithered over the superficial trappings of parenthood, the health-care industry continued to suck our marrow. Unicare was bilking us for $700 a month, but apparently that wasn't enough. In the phone book, we found a nice man whose job appeared to be finding the health plan that would destroy people's lives the least. He came up with something from Blue Cross for about $450 a month. But there was, as always, a caveat. Blue Cross wouldn't cover Regina under this policy until she'd had her six-week post-birth gynecological exam, because it's against policy to actually provide assistance to anyone with potential health problems. So I got the coverage, as did Elijah, but Regina had to buy into six-week emergency coverage until she passed the exam, and then she could join our regular health plan. So to summarize: An as-yet unborn person can get health coverage in America, but an expectant mother can't. It's almost as though the system were in the charge of for-profit corporations who have no regard for people's well-being.

We got Regina an OB/GYN appointment before we even moved to town. This time, we had a real doctor. He was short, fit, bald, and efficient, and he wore a crisp well-trimmed mustache. His name, seriously, was Dr. Love. Not all of Dr. Love's politics jibed with ours. He told us that he refuses to prescribe birth-control pills because he believes the hormones and steroids in the pill are bad for women's health. Fair enough, but he also advised his patients toward a family-planning center that promotes abstinence, or, barring that, the rhythm method. On the other hand, he was one of two OB/GYNs in all Central Texas who worked with midwives, and he took a lot of Medicaid patients. He was kind and competent and honest, so what did it matter that his children weren't allowed to celebrate Halloween?

Regina also wanted a doula. I'd never heard of a doula, so I looked up the word. Allow me to quote from a World Health Organization brochure that I found.

> A doula provides support consisting of praise, reassurance, measures to improve comfort of the mother, physical contact such as rubbing the mother's back and holding her hands, explanation of what is going on during labour and delivery, and a constant friendly presence. Such tasks can also be fulfilled by a nurse or midwife, but they often need to perform technical/medical procedures that can distract their attention from the mother.

Regina had some very specific ideas about how her "birth experience" should go, and she said she needed someone besides me to keep the bureaucrats and pill-slingers at bay. This was Regina's decision. I had one job: To nod and say, "Yes, dear," to whatever she wanted.

Regina had found our doula on the Internet before we moved to Austin. Her name was Lanell. About a week after we got to town, Lanell came over to our house. She was about our age, warm, straightforward, and mellow, but in an attentive way. This was a hard personality type for me to understand. I can be focused, and I can occasionally be calm, but never both. That's one of many reasons that I'm not a doula.

Lanell told us that she was a licensed massage therapist, and an active member of DONA, the official North American doula association. She gave us some fliers and showed us her rice sock. This was a fuzzy purple thing about the size of a small brick, and it was full of rice. She said that if you put the rice sock in the microwave for a minute, it stayed warm for a long time and was very soothing on the muscles. I went into the kitchen and tried this. The sock came out pleasantly sweet smelling, like a bag of warm rice pudding.

"Can I get a teriyaki chicken sock to go with this?" I said.

Lanell and Regina exchanged a contemptous look. Foolish man, they said to each other silently. Then our doula asked if we had any questions.

"Yeah," I said. "How much is this gonna cost?"

She told us.

"I see," I said. "That's more than we can afford."

"I'm willing to barter."

We ended up getting half off. In exchange, I would copyedit a doula handbook that Lanell was writing, and Regina would do the illustrations. It would be a lot of work, but we were going to get an important service at a reasonable cost out of the deal. Not everyone in Austin can be bought for a six-pack of Shiner.

Simultaneously, we started our birthing classes, for which we couldn't barter. Regina had chosen the Bradley Method, a kind of left-wing boot-camp program for expectant moms. When people talk about "natural childbirth," they generally mean the Bradley Method, which preaches that birth can happen without drugs for the mother. It also imparts biologically accurate, extremely detailed information about how the body works during labor and teaches techniques in how to reduce pain. According to the Bradley Method website (an unbiased source), 86 percent of the couples who use the techniques have spontaneous vaginal deliveries without medication.

"Are you sure you don't want drugs?" I said to Regina.

"Drugs are bad for the baby."

"Yeah, but . . ."

"Millions of women throughout history have . . ."

"If you're talking about history, then it should probably be billions."

"Millions, billions, trillions, whatever. They all managed to give birth without painkillers."

"Because they didn't have any other option."

"Look, Neal. An epidural is bad for the baby. It's not Demerol, but it still goes straight into his bloodstream. I would just like to try it without the drugs, OK?"

"OK."

I thought of a line from the Bill Cosby routine about natural childbirth: "The father, however, can have all the drugs he wants."

Regina wasn't open to discussion on the topic. She'd read an essay by the late Dr. Robert Bradley in which he described the reaction of one of his patients, before the official birth of the Method. The patient had experienced birth "consciously, without her mind clouded with medication or her body paralyzed by needles in her spinal fluid." Bradley writes, "The woman was exuberant, and she was so grateful that she grabbed me suddenly . . . I awkwardly fell on top of her as she kissed me."

"That's what I want," she said.

"You want to kiss Dr. Love?"

"No," she said. "I want to be exuberant."

"But you are exuberant!"

"I mean during birth."

"Oh."

Dr. Bradley subtitled his method "Husband-Coached Childbirth." He wrote, "To me, there is nothing more hideous than a woman alone in labor. But there is no better companion than the man she loves." A bit later, he continued, "We notice in animals that during labor they loosen all their muscles. Women need to be reminded to go limp in the same way . . . there is nothing more effective than the familiar voice of the husband whispering in his wife's ear the same love line of gobbledy gook he whispered in her ear in the moonlight that started this whole business in the first place."

For six consecutive murky Tuesday nights, we drove north up I-35 to a doctor's office in a strip mall that looked like it had been built about the time I was going through puberty. I questioned my original assessment of Austin. Up the highway, there aren't any weird punk-rock clubs. It's all Rudy Fazuli's and the Container Store. People in the northern suburbs experience South by Southwest no more directly than they do Carnival in Montevideo. Everywhere I looked, I saw generic tract minimansions and the retail supercenters that serve them. The magical Austin slacker fairyland seemed like a mirage.

Our instructor was a small, bright-eyed woman who reminded me of a better-looking version of my high-school drama teacher. She had five children, she said, and the last three had been born using the Bradley Method. The first two births were terrifying and horribly painful. One of them had ended in a Caesarian section because she'd gotten so tired early on that she didn't have the energy to push the baby out. The Bradley births, on the other hand, had been outstanding. Really, she was so tiny that I doubted she could have birthed five feline babies, let alone human ones.

"Either she can afford a personal trainer," Regina said. "Or I want to bottle her metabolism."

The other couples in the class were relentlessly uninteresting. Either they seemed to represent the Tim-McGraw-concert-going sector of American society or they wore sandals with socks and listened to Emmylou Harris on purpose. After the first two weeks, I stopped wearing ironic T-shirts because no one seemed to notice. Possibly, they had their minds on more important things.

"I don't have anything in common with these guys," I said.

"You don't think you have anything in common with *any* guys," Regina said.

Many years before, I'd attended Bradley Method courses for my newspaper story that never ran. Those classes were warm and intimate, in a dark room with oak beams and comfortable pillows. This class had all the charm of a pyramid-scheme seminar in a Holiday Inn conference room. I'd rather share intimate details about my life with strangers on public buses.

That said, the teacher imparted practical information, unpretentiously, about the stages of the birth process and ways to get the mother through each stage. This was a surprise. I'd expected a course full of New Age bullshit about chakras and the Goddess Within. Our teacher showed some videos that contained elements of this, but only because they were mostly shot in the 1970s, in Northern California. The videos showed birth. Lots of birth. There was no screaming or hair-clutching or any of the usual melodrama you see; it was just calm women working very hard, breathing heavily, and squatting into pools of water while flute music played in the background.

"Can you do that?" I said to Regina.

"I can definitely do that," she said.

Regina leaned into me. The instructor turned down the lights, giving the room all the ambience of a trucker motel at three a.m. I began to rub her back.

"Husbands," the instructor said. "Feel the rhythm of your partner's breathing . . ."

"Behave," Regina whispered. She knew me too well.

"Of course I'm gonna behave. I'm your birth partner."

"Make deep circular breaths with her. Two become one."

This made even Regina roll her eyes.

"Whatever," she said.

Still, we bought into the Bradley deal. With Lanell's help, Regina crafted our "birth plan," which I would give to the hospital staff upon arrival. The doula and I would make sure it stayed on course. It went:

We all desire a healthy outcome for mother and baby. To achieve this we respectfully request: the time to labor; privacy during this event; freedom of movement including in the shower; and positive encouragement at all times.

We chose to use Dr. Love and our Doula, Lanell, for our birth because we would like to try to have this baby using natural childbirth techniques. We would appreciate your assistance to achieve this goal. *Please do not offer pain medication during labor. We will request it if we decide to use it.*

Labor & Delivery

FETAL MONITORING & IV	Intermittent monitoring with external monitor or Doppler. No IV unless medically necessary, drink clear liquids instead. Heparin lock okay.
VAGINAL EXAMS	Limit the number of exams to allow Regina to remain relaxed.
AUGMENTATION / INDUCTION	Avoid using Pitocin for augmentation, try alternate methods such as walking and nipple stimulation.
DELIVERY	Self-guided pushing & choice of delivery position.
EPISIOTOMY	Regina would like to avoid episiotomy by using massage, hot compresses, slow pushing, and position changes.
BREASTFEEDING & CORD CUTTING	Place baby on Regina's chest immediately after birth to allow for bonding & breast-feeding. We prefer to wait for cord to

stop pulsing before cut. Give Neal option of cutting.

EMERGENCY   Discuss all procedures with us before they are performed. Please allow Neal to stay with baby should any emergency procedures need to be performed.

Few couples have ever gone into childbirth as educated as Regina and I. We knew every possible permutation and were prepared for all curves. This might just be the easiest birth in the history of humankind.

SIX

The Process

October 2002

O ur last act of pleasure as a childless couple, just before Regina descended into the not-being-able-to-move phase of pregnancy, occurred when we went to see Beck give an acoustic concert performance in the auditorium of Westlake High School. We drove twenty-five minutes from our house, south and west, into a land of swooping hills, oak, and cedar, an area so prosperous that it was almost beyond our imaginings. It was the suburbs. We weren't disdainful, but we still felt alien. We had our little house in the city and we would never live in a place like this.

The sign in front of the auditorium read TONIGHT BECK, in the same lettering that it would have used to say PEP RALLY 3 PM. GO COUGARS! Our seats were in the seventh row on the left side. The auditorium was larger, and had better acoustics, than some opera houses. A couple rows behind us, I saw another couple about our age. The woman was just as pregnant as Regina. I made eye contact, raising my eyebrows, as if to say, "Huh? Huh? Check it out! We may be having a baby, but we're still going to see Beck!" I pointed at Regina's belly. The woman turned away in disgust, as though I'd just tried to flash her. It was somehow comforting to know that women will respond to me in the same way no matter my situation.

Beck was touring to promote *Sea Change,* his lyrical, haunting breakup album. It's the testament of a guy who realizes, in his thirties, that life is long and hard and not so much fun. Though our lives were pretty easy, pretty fun, and totally breakup-free, Regina and I still considered *Sea Change* our soundtrack. While Beck played, Elijah swirled around inside Regina, soothed and melancholy. Or so Regina said. We both wanted to believe we were directing Elijah's musical taste, even before Day One. We realized this was probably our generation's equivalent of playing Bob Dylan records to kids who despised the music, or, worse, didn't give a shit. But who knew? Maybe we'd have one of the few kids who did.

The show moved along. Beck told a story about the first time he'd played in Austin, at South by Southwest, and how no one had come to the show and he'd made a big mess on stage, breaking a bunch of instruments. Afterward, a ratty-looking burnout came up to Beck and said that his show was the greatest thing he'd seen in twenty years. That, Beck said, was Gibby Haynes from the Butthole Surfers. As I listened to the story, I thought, this is the cultural nexus on which I want to place my son. He would start out indie, even punk, and then he'd have a breakout hit and get rich while still not becoming lame. Or he could end up like Gibby from the Butthole Surfers, which wasn't as glamorous a fate, but it was still an interesting one. Regardless, I silently pledged to myself that my son would not have a generic American childhood. My kid was going to be cool.

Our cool kid was due October 18. I sat around that whole day watching television, waiting for a sign, wanting the adult part of my life to begin already. Regina was even more impatient, and justifiably so. She'd been three centimeters dilated for several weeks, and had been having intermittent contractions the whole time. Technically, she'd been in low-level labor for nearly a month.

My symptoms of impatience were mental and emotional, but the baby had squished Regina's intestines and organs to the left side of her body. She could barely eat, and when she did, she'd get a horrible sharp pain in her side. Her diet was reduced to small amounts of rice and soy milk. She felt sharp pains whenever she stood up because the baby was pressing on her pelvic floor. We had to get that baby out.

Regina sat in warm baths filled with lavender-scented salt. We went for a three-mile walk by the river until she could barely breathe. We even had sex. One of our birthing books said that "nipple stimulation with orgasm" was the key to inducing labor. So we went at it, with special emphasis on me stimulating her nipples. I really enjoyed myself, as I was always looking for an excuse to have sex several times a day. I later found out that Regina didn't feel quite so enthusiastic.

"We're doing it out of necessity, not because we're horny," she said.

"I'm kind of horny."

"You're always horny."

"True enough."

"*Everyone* is having a baby but me."

"Now you know that's not true."

"Yes it is. Sarah Jessica Parker had her baby, and we were due at the same time."

"Sarah Jessica Parker is not everyone."

"It just feels unreal. He's never going to come out. It feels like we're in some kind of alternate reality."

I dealt with the stress like all men have throughout human history. I got drunk. After the first six false alarms, I started making plans to go out. Regina gave me her permission. As long as I stayed relatively near home and took my cell phone, I could party a little. I was pathetic, but she was forgiving.

One night I went out with a couple of guys whom I'd met on the Internet. They took me to a karaoke bar, and then to another bar, and then it was 3:30 a.m. and I found myself in some crappy apartment near the University of Texas that was supposed to have two bedrooms but had been turned into a five-bedroom through the strategic use of screens and curtains. It had been a long time since I'd partied in a place with a Jimi Hendrix poster on the wall and Tom Robbins books on the shelf.

My cell phone rang.

Shit! My wife was going to go into labor, and I'd been smoking schwag. The burden of my collective sins weighed heavily.

"Where *are* you?"

"Um, out."

"I'm having contractions!"

I turned to my companions.

"Guys," I said. "You have to take me home now. My wife's having a baby."

"Whoa," said one of them, who couldn't have been older than twenty-three. "That's heavy, dude."

I got home within ten minutes. My head was a little fuzzy, but the thought of immediately becoming a father had sobered me up quickly. Regina was sitting straight up in bed. I sat down next to her.

"How are you?"

"They stopped. I'm not having him tonight."

"Thank God. I'm a little drunk."

"Yeah, you smell like whiskey. Come to bed."

"Of course I will."

I stroked her hair.

"I'm sorry I stayed out so late."

"That's OK. I know you need to, for some reason."

"I love you."

"I love you, too."

"Can I go out tomorrow night, too?"

"No."

"OK."

The next day, we slept until eleven. That afternoon, Dr. Love gave Regina an examination. He was concerned about the condition of the amniotic fluid. We had to make an appointment to get induced.

This was exactly what we didn't want. Induction meant pitocin, and pitocin was the dreaded drug.

Pitocin is a synthetic form of oxytocin, the hormone that induces labor. The contractions it creates are double-backed, with almost no break in between, causing mothers to scream in agony for pain medication. The increased contractions also compress the umbilical cord, cutting down the baby's oxygen supply. Men have slender right to preach about how a woman should give birth, so with Regina's permission, I'm going to attribute the following statements to her.

She says, while realizing that her opinions are controversial, that hospitals use pitocin because they don't want patients lingering in a labor bed, particularly if it's a busy night. The drug also suits doctors' schedules. It comes in handy to know when labor's going to start. Just as important, labor also interferes with a mother's schedule. To some people—and it's their right to think this—labor is a hassle that needs to be gotten out of the way. Plus, if women get an epidural right away, they don't feel the pitocin. Finally, it's a major drug, made by a major drug company, and they make a lot of money off it. There's never been a drug company yet that didn't try to maximize its profits at all times. Occasionally there are cases for which it's medically necessary, but those are rare. For an overscheduled, impatient, drug-dependent society with an uncaring, bureaucratic health system, pitocin is birth's perfect solution.

The scheduled induction really threw off our natural-birth plan. The magic of birth, which we'd anticipated for so long, had gradually become something dread and horrible, and this was the capper. Dr. Love gave us until November 1.

After the sonogram, Regina was moping around the hospital when she ran into one of the women from our birthing class. Regina told this woman our troubles. She gave Regina the name of her acupuncturist.

We didn't have much time. Regina scheduled three acupuncture sessions on the three days leading up to Induction Day. The acupuncturist covered her swollen body with needles and she swore she felt something give right away. It was the Chinese version of pitocin. The first night, nothing happened, but at midnight after the second session, she started having contractions.

At three a.m., her water broke. She came in and told me. I shot up, ran to my dresser, pulled two pairs of socks out of my sock drawer, and threw them in a bag. It was Halloween.

"Hey!" Regina said. "If he's born today, we could call him Edgar Allen Pollack."

"Oh my God! That would be hilarious! It's perfect!"

"I was just kidding."

"No! I'm a writer! He has to be named Edgar Allen Pollack! Oh, please, please, please?"

"We'll see."

Our passage from the hospital's parking garage went slowly because Regina was having contractions, and also, she was trying to walk with a towel squeezed between her thighs. We passed a couple of nurses coming off the night shift. I don't remember their specific faces, but I do remember the looks they gave us, which were equal parts tenderness and pity. My mind was empty of doubt. This was my responsibility, my duty. I wouldn't be denied and I couldn't be replaced. I was a birth partner. She was 7 centimeters dilated and 100 percent effaced. It would be quick.

By seven a.m., Regina was settled in her hospital suite, which contained a large private room with a love seat and a rocking chair and a separate bathroom with a shower big enough for two. It was decorated in a homey way, if your idea of home is a Hampton Inn with an IV drip and a fetal monitor by the bed. Lanell got there just as we were checking in; she took her place by the birth mother, as doulas have done since the dawn of time, sitting on a large blue bouncy ball like the ones people use to do enhanced sit-ups at the gym.

"So is the birthing ball an ancient tradition, too?" I said.

She and Regina exchanged another contemptuous look. While they commiserated, I had time to make sure we'd put everything in the "labor bag," or "birthing bag." This is a relatively modern innovation. I don't have a record of what exactly was in our birthing bag, but I do remember that we packed Beck's *Mutations,* Willie Nelson's *Teatro,* and a collection of international lullabies, all of which Regina thought the baby would find relaxing during labor. Other than that, I think we stuck with the basics, like diapers and clothes for the baby. Our labor bag could have looked a little like that of our friends from Philly. I have their list. Let me share a few of the items: "Yellow toiletry bag with cosmetics, toothbrushes, hair gadgets, shampoos, etc. . . . swim trunks for George . . . food for George— pretzels, trail mix, nuts, fruit, yogurt, sports drinks, cheese, graham crackers . . . Altoids," and "Last Harry Potter." Before we packed our own labor bag, I told Regina that if she made me bring a Harry Potter book to the hospital, she'd have to find another dad for Elijah.

Dr. Love came to visit at 8:20 a.m. It was his day off and he was supposed to be with his children, or golfing, or both. Regina lay on her side looking very serious. The contractions were coming closer together and she needed to get through them. I held her hand and told her to breathe. Here it went. Our private birthing session, our deepest, most intimate experience together, the very core of human creation, the apotheosis of our biological imperative, had begun. A nurse came into the room.

"Would y'all mind if a high school student observed you?" she said.

"Regina," I said. "What do you think?"

"Whatever," she said. "Hnggggggggggg!"

"I think it'll be OK," I said.

When the nurse said "a" high school student, she must have actually meant "three" high school students, because that's what appeared.

"Hell," I said. "Why not just invite a whole grade-school class in to watch us?"

They all laughed nervously.

"How about a high school football team?"

I'd like to think the nurse regretted choosing us for observation.

The hours flipped along. Regina lay on her left side, then her right. She sat in the rocking chair and then on the bouncy blue ball. Another entourage of student nurses marched through the room. The doctor that was leading them pronounced our yet-to-be-born son "a good-sized baby." Regina's back started to hurt. I ran down the hall and put the rice sock in the microwave, returned, and held it on the small of her back.

"Mmm," she said. "That feels really good."

We were approaching a primal place. By noon, the contractions had become stronger. But our training kept her comfortable. I soothed her and told her to breathe, and Lanell massaged her left hip. It looked like this might wrap up soon.

At one p.m., Dr. Love examined Regina. The labor hadn't progressed much in the last three hours. The cervical walls were starting to thin. We had to decide immediately whether or not to use pitocin. He recommended it.

This was exactly what we hadn't wanted. All ambitions of a normal childbirth would cease the second they hooked up the "pit drip." Regina and I looked at each other with fear.

"I have to get this over with."

"OK."

At that moment, a bureaucrat walked through the door.

"We were wondering how you intended to pay for this visit," she said.

"You've got to be joking," I said. "We have health insurance."

"We don't have any record of that. If you could just come to my office."

She left.

"Calm down," said Regina. "I need you to stay calm."

I did, but here was what I was thinking: *Goddamn shithole mother-fucking dickhead fascist fucking health-insurance system designed by a bunch of goddamn cocksucking donkeys. I'd like to stick a pitocin drip up the CEO of Blue Cross's bunghole and leave it there to fucking rot until his intestines explode.*

Instead, I said. "Give me five minutes. Lanell, you're in charge."

When I got back, it was 1:30. A nurse was installing the IV. Regina looked pale; she'd chosen this over a C-section. She trembled. And then the pit drip unleashed hell.

Lanell's notes from after the pitocin drip started like this: "Neal @ bedside very concerned re: pain." Actually, I stood there desperately rubbing my face. You would, too, if suddenly your wife's body arched in agony and she screamed: "AAAAAAAAAAH! I can't stand it! Oh no! Please make it stop! No! No!"

The contraction let up for a second.

"It's trying to explode out of my back," she said.

"Everything will be OK, dear."

"Uh-huh. AWWWWWWWWW! OOOOOOOH! Oh God!"

This went on for about an hour. Dr. Love came in to check on Regina. She looked like she'd been hanging on the rack for about a week. I was terrified. It looked like my wife was going to explode and die, just like John Hurt in *Alien*.

"We might want to consider an epidural," said Dr. Love.

This was also exactly what we didn't want. Epidural was pain medication taken to the highest degree, a combination catheter and spinal tap. Any last vestige of a natural childbirth would be gone.

"WHAAAAAAAAAGH! Please make it stop!"

"Sounds like a good idea," I said.

By three p.m., Regina was sitting up in bed, propped on pillows. A long, thin tube ran down the length of her right leg, pumping sweet chemical relief into her quivering veins. I dabbed her forehead with a washcloth.

"How are you?"

"Mmmmmm. Everything's fine. No worries. Ahhhhhh."

"Can I get an epidural, too?" I asked.

A new nurse came on duty. Her name was Donna. She was stocky and in her mid-fifties, and she'd presided over more births than everyone else in the hospital combined. It had been nursing school until she showed up.

"The woman is tired," Donna said. "Let's get this baby out already."

Regina lay there and pushed. She sat up and pushed. She gripped the sides of the bed, straining and huffing. Donna put a "squat bar" over the bed. It formed a metal arch. Regina gripped the top. When that didn't work, Donna brought in a sheet and had Regina grab one end. They did a tug-of-war, with Regina pushing the baby out while she pulled on the sheet. The crown of the baby's head appeared. After that, the baby didn't move.

Dr. Love had gone for the day. His partner, a South African guy named Polon, came in for a consult. Regina continued to push. The doctor took Donna, Lanell, and I aside.

"There's no way the baby is fitting through that pelvis," he said.

We told Regina the news. She looked exhausted. I started to tear up, just a little.

"It's OK."

"We didn't want it this way."

"It's OK."

The doctor told us that he wouldn't allow Lanell in the operating room. She was pretty indignant, and I imagine that she felt insulted. But there was no time for disputing the doctor's word at this moment.

"You need to let *me* in," I said.

He agreed to that. The nurses started unplugging Regina's pit drip and her epidural. I walked down the hall to get a drink of water. My head buzzed, my hands shook, my chest felt full. Life suddenly seemed comprised of decisions I didn't want to make. Would all of fatherhood be like this?

When I got back to the labor room, it was empty, like we'd never been there at all. Regina was already in the operating room by the time I found it. She had a shower cap on her head. They were lathering her belly down with a disgusting brownish-yellow liquid. I took a seat by her head. It was 7:10 p.m.

She was quivering, but that was more from the anesthetic than from fear. I tried to keep her eyes focused on mine, but she was elsewhere. Her calmness had gone away.

"I can't breathe," she said.

The doctor had already started to cut.

"She said she can't breathe!"

"She can breathe," he said.

I looked at him, which was a mistake, because my gaze went over the sheet that was shielding Regina's face from the surgery. I saw a bulbous mess of organs and blood and white globule-like things. Guts may be funny or thrilling when they appear in a zombie movie, but they're just nauseating when you're trying to get your wife through the birth of your first child. My heart shattered.

"I still can't breathe," she said.

Ten minutes passed, and then fifteen, and still the baby hadn't appeared.

"He's stuck in her pelvis," the doctor said.

The doctor walked to the other side of the operating table, put his hands on Regina's pelvis, and pressed down, hard. He pressed again. Nothing. Two more presses. Nothing. A nurse pressed on the other side.

My mind swirled into the void; I saw the great tragedy of my life taking shape. I was going to lose both of them. I'd be alone, in Texas. Hercules would be all I'd have left. And the cats. But they didn't count.

Then my son was out, screaming. My nine-pound, ten-ounce son. He'd been gestating a month too long already. He didn't even look like a newborn, except that he was covered in mucus.

They put Elijah into my arms. My face was a mess of snot and tears. Lanell came in then, and she took a picture.

"He's a moose," I said.

"Look at that," a nurse said.

She pointed to his chin dimple.

"He's definitely yours."

Holy shit! He *was* mine! That's when I really began to weep.

The nurses took him away for washing. Regina was asleep. Lanell and I went out into the hallway.

"That was horrible!" I said. "How could they put Regina through it all?"

"It's the process."

"Fuck the process."

In front of the newborn room, I ran into the doctor.

"That woman is never to have a vaginal birth," he said. "Ever. If she does, it will kill her."

The uterus walls, he said, had been too thin and tore when he made the incision. Her uterus could have ruptured.

"Oh."

"It was the most harrowing birth I've ever presided over. Make sure it doesn't happen again."

"No problem."

I went into the nursery. Elijah was lying placidly in a little plastic bin, all washed off. His eyes were wide open. When a newborn is like that, they say he's "aware" or "taking it all in," which I doubt. But if he was taking it all in, he was probably wondering if every room in the world was decorated with black-and-orange cardboard witches, cats, and pumpkins. I poked his little belly.

"Hey there, little man. Hey there, fella. Are you ready to rock? Are you ready to party? Are you ready to have a good time with Daddy?"

Meanwhile, Regina lay in her recovery bed, her mind misty with anesthesia. She was barely aware that she'd given birth. Her face was waxy and sallow, like she'd been drained of all blood. Lanell handed Elijah to her.

"Hey, bay-beeeeee," she said. Her voice was thick and slurry. "Hiiiiiiiiii."

It was feeding time. Regina and Elijah were very intent on each other. I was deeply moved by the sight of them together, but I was also kind of dizzy. I staggered against a wall.

"You should get something to eat, Dad," said Donna the Super Nurse.

Just east of the highway from the hospital, about three blocks away, was Star Seeds, an all-night diner in the lobby of a Days Inn. There were punk-rock band stickers all over the walls, and you didn't want to touch anything in the bathroom, but the food was cheap and pretty good. This would almost certainly be, I thought, the coolest place that a guy had ever chosen for his first restaurant meal after witnessing the birth of his son.

I was a dad now, and I really needed a patty melt.

While I ate, I was finally able to compose in my head the message that would go on Elijah's special pillow that we'd purchased at Coo de Tot. "Elijahroo," it went, "you have made Regina and me so happy. We have no way to judge you objectively, but we think you are the cutest, smartest, funniest, sweetest baby in the world. Our lives were wonderful and full before we had you, but you have made everything so much better and brighter. You are our greatest joy. We're going to have so much fun together. Love, Daddy."

2

AFTER

SEVEN

To Snip or Not to Snip

November 2002

A couple of weeks before Elijah was born, I was doing something very important on my computer when Regina entered.

"I was curious about something," she said.

"Sure."

"I wanted to know if you had any feelings about circumcision."

"Nope."

"I was doing some research . . ."

With Regina, that's always a dangerous clause.

"The American Pediatric Association doesn't recommend circumcision anymore. It *used* to be medically recommended, but now they're neutral."

"I would say that I'm neutral on the topic as well."

"They don't use anesthetic, Neal. They cut off nerve endings and it decreases sexual sensitivity. In two words: It's barbaric. I can't do it to him. I just can't."

"You must leave me to think on this question for a while," I said, and yes, I do talk like that sometimes.

I went to the usual source for village elders who are trying to solve a tough ethical problem: An article in *Mothering* magazine. Regina had helpfully supplied the link for me. It said that Western cultures, until the nineteenth century, had no tradition of circumcision. The Greeks and the Romans passed laws forbidding "sexual mutilation" after coming into contact with the cultures of the Middle East. It became more common during the anti-masturbation hysteria of the Victorian era. Doctors claimed that circumcision cured everything from epilepsy and tuberculosis to headaches, eczema, and bed-wetting. At this point, the article became truly interesting and relevant, if a bit didactic and terrifying. It called circumcision a "radical practice" that didn't begin until the cold war era, "part of the same movement that pathologized and medicalized birth and actively discouraged breastfeeding." Until the 1970s, hospitals didn't even have to seek parental permission to perform the surgery.

The foreskin, the article continued, is a natural part of the human anatomy, and there's no reason it should be removed. And then the kicker: "Parents should enjoy the arrival of a new child with as few worries as possible. The birth of a son in the US, however, is often fraught with anxiety and confusion. Most parents are pressured to hand their baby sons over to a stranger, who, behind closed doors, straps babies down and cuts their foreskins off . . ."

That was about enough. The article was actually shrill beyond measure. I knew there was a reason I hadn't taken women's studies classes in college. Still, I thought, maybe circumcision is wrong after all. Maybe everything I'd always thought about my penis, and, by extension, the world, is also wrong. For the first time in two decades, I'd been forced to stare my Judaism right between the ringlets. I'd arrived at my first Reb Tevye moment; I was no longer the tailor Motel Kamzoil.

On the one hand, I thought, Jewish men get circumcised. It's what we do, or what gets done to us. I've been circumcised my whole life, and my dick works fine. Hell, I thought. It works better than fine.

On the other hand, maybe Regina was right. Maybe circumcision really did decrease sexual sensitivity. Was that something I wanted to deny my son? Wouldn't his life be painful enough? Wait a second. My son wasn't even born yet, and I was already thinking about the quality of his future orgasms. Something felt improper.

This was a very hard decision for me, so I did what any good Jewish boy would do in such a situation.

I called my mother.

"Hey, Mom," I said.

"Neal! Honey! It's wonderful to hear your voice! How are you?"

"OK."

"And how's Regina feeling?"

"She's hanging in there."

"Poor thing."

"Yeah. Listen, Mom, I wanted to talk to you about something."

"Of course, honey."

"Regina and I were thinking about not circumcising Elijah . . ."

It's hard to describe exactly what my mother's voice did at that moment, but "convulsed" is probably the closest word I can find.

"No, oh, no no no Neal. Don't say that to me. We're prepared to take anything. But you *have* to circumcise him."

Prepared to take *anything,* I thought. What did that mean?

"Regina did this research. And . . ."

"I don't care about Regina's research. She's not Jewish."

"But we were thinking . . ."

My mother began to openly weep on the phone.

"Oh my God, Neal! I can't believe you're doing this to me! You have to circumcise! You have to!"

"My wife . . ."

"Your wife is immaterial here. You can't betray six thousand years of Jewish tradition."

Suddenly, my generation's sin of intermarriage lay fully on my back. The fate of the entire diaspora rested on my decision. I saw a God I didn't particularly believe in waving an angry finger at me. An innocent medical inquiry had turned into Sophie's Choice.

"You can't forsake your people," my mother said. "Promise me."

I began to quiver.

"I promise, Mother," I said.

"And please don't tell your grandmother about this. She wouldn't understand."

"Yes, Mother."

I sounded like Norman Bates, saying, "Yes, Mother" like that. When I hung up the phone, I went into the bedroom, where Regina had propped up her feet.

"Well?" she said.

"My mother says we'd betray six thousand years of Jewish tradition."

Regina had been ready for that answer.

"Oh, does she, now? We'll just see about that! I will *not* circumcise my son! I will not put him through that pain! I can't bear it!"

"Yes, dear."

Now, just as my mother had five minutes earlier, my wife began to weep.

"You can't make me do it, Neal! You can't! Promise me!"

"Yes, dear."

"Hold me."

"I need some time to think."

I went to the back of the house and closed the door. My parents had said some other strange things to me during the pregnancy. On one family visit, they'd been teasing me, saying that Elijah would probably end up being a "Republican engineer," whatever that was. I said that I'd love him no matter what he became.

"Now you know how we feel," said my mother.

Nice.

Regina pounded on the door.

"Neal! I'm furious with your mother! I'm not Jewish and she's going to have to deal with that! We have to talk, *now*!"

At that moment, I wanted to buy a plane ticket to Uruguay and never come back. I've always wanted to go to Uruguay because I know that if it got boring, I could be in Brazil or Argentina by lunchtime. But there I was instead in Austin, Texas, and my rational brain had ceased functioning. Something deep, primal, and lizardy emerged. I clawed at my face and pounded my head against the door. What the fuck was wrong with these people?

I subsequently waged a subtle family campaign that mostly involved calling my sisters and saying, "You won't believe what Mom said to me." Regina told some friends, who were suitably appalled, but powerless. My parents were more systematic. They called every member of the family and all of their friends, no matter how distant, to tell them of my potential betrayal. Aunt Estelle e-mailed me to say something like: "We have no idea what's going on with you and your parents. If it were up to us, we'd probably circumcise, but we support your decision either way." That was sweet of her, but the message indicated that my parents were near hysteria. Regina's family, meanwhile, was politic. My sister-in-law said that it would probably be good if Elijah "looked like Daddy," but went no further than that. They were good Protestants and they stayed out of our affairs.

A week went by. I couldn't bear talking to my parents. My brain was a fetid goulash of guilt and resentment. Through a sister, I learned that my mother had said, "I guess I never thought about the fact that Regina wasn't Jewish before."

It's not as though my parents are super-Jews themselves. They go to synagogue, but only occasionally. When they do, they usually complain that everyone there is old and that the dinner they went to with friends afterward was "just OK." I was Bar Mitzvahed because that's what Jews did, not because of some familial covenant with God, or so I thought. Regina's mother, on the other hand, is a devout Sunday churchgoer who prays before dinner and plays in the church handbell choir. One afternoon before Regina and I were married, her mom blurted out poolside, "Neal, how Jewish *are* you?"

I said, "Um, ahm, I had a Bar Mitzvah and my family, um . . . we don't go to temple all the time, but . . ."

Regina later explained to me that this was the wrong answer. I'd had my anti-Semitism antennae up, but her mother didn't care what my religion was, as long as I *was* religious. For her, devotion trumped sect. She didn't particularly want to see her daughter with a devout hedonist; the grandson of Rabbi Menachem Schneerson, on the other hand, would probably have been fine.

Our wedding had been deliberately, almost absurdly secular. My mother said, "I will not set foot in a church," to which I replied, "What are you, the Bride of Dracula?" But honestly, I didn't want to get married in a church, either, so a lawyer friend of Regina's family married us in her mother's backyard. The ceremony featured a brief denomination-neutral Scripture reading, a testimonial by one of Regina's bridesmaids that mentioned Kahlil Gibran in defiance of my wishes, a Roy Orbison song, and a recitation of *The Owl and the Pussycat*. Faith wasn't part of our lives, and it was off the table at the wedding. But with Elijah's birth pending, our secular chickens came home to their secular roost.

My father called. I was in no mood to hear from him.

"We're very upset by this," he said. "Your mother hasn't slept."

"Tough. I've got other problems."

"You listen to me, young man!"

"No. You listen to *me*!"

"We've decided that if you don't have him circumcised, he won't be our grandson."

There is no other hand!

"Are you out of your fucking mind?"

"We demand it."

"You're in no position to demand anything."

"We haven't said anything about you moving to Austin, of which we disapprove, or about that terrible house, or about the kid's stupid *name*. . . ."

That was it.

"Stupid name?" I said. "Fuck you . . . Bernard!"

And then I hung up. More face-clawing, head-pounding, floor-pounding, and Cro-Magnon yowling ensued. Meanwhile, Regina was already a week overdue, and going on about how the stress of Peeniegate would harm Elijah's brain chemistry. That was baggage I wished she hadn't carried on.

She and I lay in bed and talked seriously. What I felt toward my parents went far beyond anger, past resentment, veering toward something close to temporary hatred. This was our first major decision for our child, and my own mother and father were trying to completely take it out of our hands, based on arguments that we found superstitious and naïve. But I also had a larger family to consider, aunts and uncles and cousins and sisters, and, beyond that, a generation of nieces and nephews and second cousins to come, not to mention "six thousand years of Jewish history." If we decided not to circumcise, it might very well rip open a wound in my family life that would take decades to heal (though by writing the previous five pages, I may have just done that anyway).

"We have to," I said.

"I know we do," said Regina, and she began to cry.

That evening, I called home.

"We've decided to circumcise," I said.

"Good," my father said. "I feel like that will connect him to my father. And my grandfather before that. And down through the generations."

He was sincere, and I almost found myself touched. But I must have missed that lesson in Hebrew school. Our traceable family goes back to rural Germany in the eighteenth century whether or not I let someone cut off the cover of my son's *glans*. After the argument was settled, my mother sent me an e-mail that read, in part, "I hope you will always remember how you treated your parents."

I chose not to reply.

The earliest days of Elijah's life were full of decisions, not as emotionally overwrought as those brought on by Peeniegate, but still difficult. I started to wonder when the "fun" part of fatherhood would kick in. That first night in the hospital, Regina was immobile on camel tranquilizers. I slept, or was supposed to sleep, on a mat on the windowsill of her room, which would have been the perfect size for me if I were Billy Barty. But there was to be no sleep. I spent most of the night trying to figure out how to clean up the steady stream of black tar-like poo that was oozing out of Elijah's asshole. The nurses were sympathetic, since they deal with dozens of new dads every week who cry for help when the defecation starts. They're used to seeing a wastebin full of goo-smeared paper towels.

To my parents' infinite credit, they'd landed in Austin by ten a.m. the day after Elijah was born. I saw them out the window of our room. They had silly grins on their faces, and my dad was carrying an enormous mustard-colored teddy bear with a red bow around its neck. By the end of the day, the bear was on the windowsill, Regina was sitting up, and we were all taking turns holding this sweet-smelling sack of wheat on our shoulders. I took special pleasure in rocking in the chair the hospital had provided, singing a song of my own devising to Elijah. It went like this:

"He's Elijahroo/He's a piece of poo/Watcha gonna do?/Whoop-de-whoop-de-whoo!"

Elijah seemed to like that. He also liked it when we all sang his "theme song," to the tune of the theme from *Bonanza*. It went: "Dum dum dum dum dum dum dum dum dum dum . . . Elijah! (Ba-ba-ba-ba) Dum dum dum dum dum dum dum dum dum dum dum dum. Dum dum dum dum dum dum dum dum dum . . . Elijah! (Ba-ba-ba!) Dum dum dum dum dum dum dum dum dum dum!" And so on.

Elijah began to wail for no discernible reason.

"Oh, Elijah," I said. "Don't be such a goddamn baby!"

For me, all was happy cell-phone calls and merry e-mail. I've always been fond of occasions that force people to talk to me nicely whether they want to or not. By those standards, this was the pre-eminent moment of my life. One e-mail, from someone with whom

I hadn't been in touch lately, said, "We love you and we love your baby!" Now that was how people *should* talk to me, I thought. I was a man now and I'd earned respect the hard way, so I definitely deserved a nap.

After forty-eight hours in the hospital, Regina was up and lurching about. Elijah hadn't malfunctioned. I have no idea when it's appropriate for the father to leave the hospital, but I knew that I'd be of much greater use to my family if I got a good night's sleep in my own bed. Regina didn't protest much. "I'd rather have you refreshed and helpful than grumpy and insane," she said.

I picked Hercules up from the neighbor's and let him give me a big long stinky slurp, while I said things like "You've got a new wittle baby brother, yes you do, yes you do . . ." The house was empty and quiet. I sat in my blue easy chair and reveled in my domain while watching Turner Classic Movies. I made myself a cup of peppermint tea. I took a bubble bath. I treated myself so well you'd think *I'd* just given birth. By ten p.m., I was in bed with the dog, fresh cotton sheets, and a genre novel. This would be the most peaceful night of my life.

At midnight, the phone rang.

"The nurses are in here," Regina said.

"OK."

"They say he's lost weight."

"That's normal. He's a huge baby."

"They want to supplement with formula."

"Ridiculous. Just tell them no."

We'd done some reading that said formula, while containing all necessary nutrients, didn't have the same disease-blocking attributes as mother's milk. Regina was determined to make Elijah the world's healthiest child.

"They're going to do it unless our pediatrician tells them otherwise," she said. "And he's out of town."

"Oh."

"It's gonna hurt his immune system," she said.

"One dose of formula is going to hurt his immune system?"

"What should I do?"

This was a snap decision that required wisdom I didn't possess. I tried to think of a smart Jewish man from history, like Solomon, and what he would advise. Let's see. Offer to cut the baby in two, and the person who protested the loudest would . . . that one didn't work.

"I'm not sure."

Thus, Elijah got supplement he didn't need, and we'd once again learned that the whole point of the world was to unintentionally conspire against its inhabitants. Everyone else, the postpartum nurses at St. David's Memorial Hospital in particular, was trying to destroy our family. For that last twenty-four hours Regina was in the hospital, they became our enemy. First they made our healthy child eat out of a formula tube. Then they said they wouldn't let us check out of the hospital unless we agreed to take him to the pediatrician the next day. After we agreed, they still wouldn't let us check out, because we'd forgotten to record the last time Elijah had urinated.

Amazingly, he did pee, and the next morning, we drove to our pediatrician's office. We'd chosen a nice guy named Rivas, who was about our age. It was sobering to realize that doctors were no longer older authority figures. Rivas bounced into the room.

"How are we all feeling?"

At that moment, I felt about as mentally sharp as a mushroom, but I said, "Fine."

"He didn't mean you," Regina said.

"Right."

We laid Elijah on a cushioned table. Rivas leaned over him.

"Why are you here again?"

"The nurses told us to come," said Regina.

"This child is healthy. I'll see you in three months."

Now, with other health issues out of the way, circumcision loomed. More than two years later, we learned about a guy from

Houston called "Max the Mohel," a pediatrician from Houston who performs pretty much every bris in Texas. Since the vast majority of these ceremonies occur within three hours from his home, that's not quite as big a challenge as it sounds. We didn't learn about Max the Mohel in time, but we wouldn't have used him even if we had. Strangely, my parents didn't want a bris. All they cared about was the surgery. It's not like we knew anyone in town to attend a bris anyway; we'd only been living there two months. Also, perhaps I mentioned earlier that Regina didn't want it done at all.

Our pediatrician refused to perform the operation. He recommended a urologist to us. Eight days after Elijah was born, we went to the urologist's office. This is how it works, he said. He would put Elijah on a board and strap down his hands and feet. Then he'd slide a metal ring over the top of the penis, which would cut off the circulation to the foreskin and gradually kill the nerve endings. Over the next week, the foreskin would gradually turn black, and then it would rot off, and then Elijah would be permanently connected to his ancestors.

When Regina called about the procedure, they told her that the doctor used topical anesthetic. That made her feel a little better. When we were actually in the doctor's office, we asked him about that.

"Of course we don't use topical anesthetic," he said. "Everyone knows that stuff doesn't work."

We wouldn't put our son through pain without anesthetic! But by then, it was too late. The doctor took our baby from us and told us to wait in the hall. A few minutes after the procedure, he said, he'd let Regina in to nurse. I went into the waiting room, sat with a six-month-old issue of *Sports Illustrated,* and tried to remember a time when I wasn't an adult.

Regina and Elijah came out. He was screaming. She was bawling.

"Babe . . ."

"Let's just go!"

And so I drove us home, which was strange enough considering that Regina usually does all the driving, but even stranger because my newborn son was in the backseat howling because someone had just lopped off the tip of his penis, and my wife was holding him, weeping as though her soul was being ripped from her body, and my heart and throat and face felt clogged with sorrow and grief and mucus and shame, and I could barely see the road through a film of tears and I thought, Oh, this is just fucking great.

About an hour later, my parents, who had since returned to Phoenix, called to see how Elijah was doing, both on the line at the same time.

"How's Elijah?" my mother asked.

"He's asleep. He cried a lot."

"He'll be fine. It didn't hurt at all."

EIGHT

Ooh, Baby Baby

December 2002–February 2003

We soon found we were less exhausted than people had told us we were going to be. Elijah didn't have colic, though we seemed to be able to get him to fall asleep only by sitting him upright in his car seat. After that, he slept normally, which allowed us to develop a routine: Regina fed him, and I did everything else. I cooked, walked Hercules, did laundry, and scrubbed toilets. The responsibility was oddly satisfying, like I was proving to myself that I could be a man, though the only proof I really needed was sitting in his bouncy chair a room away.

One afternoon, two weeks after Elijah's birth, I went into the bedroom. Elijah lay on the bed, wearing his little yellow-duckie jumper. Regina stood over him.

"Look."

He had his eyes open. The fetal squint was gone. This time, he *definitely* was taking it all in. He looked directly at us and made a little noise, and I quote: "P-poo!"

It wasn't as though I didn't love him before. But in every parent's life, there comes a point where your child captures your heart and sends you down a permanent path of joy and misery, worry and triumph, and all the emotions in between. I thought:

Elijah, you beautiful little shit. I'm yours now.

Soon after that, Regina was recovered from surgery, and she went about the business of mothering while I went back to work, albeit only in the next room. Regina embraced this temporarily full-time position. For the first three months of your child's life, you're basically taking care of a plant. You feed it, water it, and change its soil. Infants make a lot of demands on their parents, but the demands aren't specific like they'll become later. It's easier to deal with a wailing, hungry infant than a two-year-old who's throwing a tantrum because you're out of strawberry popsicles. And if your infant is healthy and sleeps normally, as ours was and did, the experience can actually be liberating, particularly for the mother who's managed to avoid the dread spectre of postpartum blues.

So while Elijah suckled at her elixir-producing teat, Regina watched the entire run of *Xena: Warrior Princess* in the mornings, and the entire run of *Buffy the Vampire Slayer* in the evenings. She also read a six-volume series of historical pulp fiction about Ramses the Great and spent an extraordinary number of hours mastering Morrowind, a fantasy role-playing video game, learning in the process that it's not hard to breast-feed while playing Xbox. At night, we sat together and watched the first three seasons of *The Sopranos,* which took us about a week. It was, Regina says, the most awesomely satisfying period of mindless pop-culture consumption in her life, because she didn't have to feel guilty that she wasn't doing something else. As long as Elijah fed properly, she could watch as much *Buffy* as she wanted.

The first few months of Elijah's life were really pleasant for us. Regina and I didn't fight at all. Our roles were clearly defined. I worked, she breast-fed the baby, and, in between, it was family time. She'd chosen to completely set aside an indeterminate number of months so she could give Elijah a good start. Meanwhile, the restrictions of her last trimester were lifted; Regina could suddenly walk a mile in less than an hour and a half. She could turn over in bed. Best of all, Elijah fell asleep anywhere, regardless of situation, time of day, or noise level. Our tiredness may have been transcendent, but at least we could go out wherever and whenever we wanted. So we took Elijah to the movies, loud ones like *X2: X-Men United,* and he slept. We took him to low-impact parties where people were only allowed to smoke outside, and he slept. He slept through an entire professional basketball game. We spent a lot of time at restaurants, drinking iced tea and ogling him as he twitched atop the table in his car seat, and we began to make offhand comments about how he was a "miracle baby." Through our early-parenting fog, we only vaguely realized that the rest of the world was there. The plant got watered, and it grew.

The only parent-related tension in our lives emerged from Regina's inability to find a bra that fit her. After Elijah was born, Regina's breasts, which had been largish to begin with, grew absolutely enormous while the rest of her stayed more or less the same. While this means little to me, and probably will mean little to other men reading this, Regina assures me that women everywhere will gasp when I say that she started looking on the Internet for a size 36G bra.

Every couple of weeks or so, a soft light-brown padded envelope would get dropped at our front door. Regina would scoop it up and run into the bedroom. A few minutes later, I'd hear "ARRRRRRRRRRGH!"

"What?"

"My boobs are too big for every fucking bra in the world!"

"Oh," I'd say, as I tiptoed away.

Because Elijah was so portable, we traveled a lot. When he was two months old, we took our first family vacation. My father was having his sixtieth birthday party in Phoenix, and we decided we should drive. It was a seventeen-hour trip, so it needed to be split up.

My vacations may not always be good, but at least they're original. It's fairly typical of us that instead of stopping halfway in Santa Fe, or Albuquerque, or somewhere even remotely memorable, we'd choose a place with no nightlife, mediocre restaurants, and bad hotels. At this stage in Elijah's life, it was actually perfect; a ten p.m. bedtime is equivalent to an all-night kegger when you have an infant. Las Cruces, New Mexico, is an exceedingly mellow place, home to the second-largest university in one of the least populous states, and proud of the fact that former astronaut Frank Borman has chosen to live there. I booked us a room at a bed-and-breakfast that was on its way to being transformed into an inn with condos at the back. It's always less expensive if you stay at a place that's under construction. The hotel was also an "art gallery," which meant lots of blankets, Remington knockoffs, and paintings of little kneeling Native American girls with flowers in their hair. There weren't many guests. We got a two-story room that hadn't seen its final coat of lacquer more than two weeks earlier. The extra bedroom wasn't necessary, and neither was the extra bathroom, and the many pastel-colored coyote lithographs certainly weren't, but large quarters are always nice, and this spot wouldn't qualify as a dump until at least 2010.

Hercules was with us, and he was still a puppy. That morning, while I was in the shower and Regina was nursing, Hercules had gone into the suitcase, pulled out a pair of my dirty boxers, licked them until they were soaking, and then, when he'd absorbed as much residual odor as possible, shredded them to bits. He needed a walk.

Both White Sands National Monument and Carlsbad Caverns are within a two-hour drive of Las Cruces, but even though we had our special infant-hiking backpack with us, Regina didn't want to go to Carlsbad because she was afraid Elijah would inhale some prehistoric mold spore and die. For some reason, White Sands seemed like a lot of work. So, on our first morning, we drove twenty minutes out of town along an unpaved road, to the Organ Mountains. I'd read about a hiking trail that led to an abandoned turn-of-the-last-century hotel that had become a sanitarium. Unfortunately, the building had been looted and now it was just a useless shell.

Regina dropped Elijah into the backpack, which had more straps on it than an upside-down roller coaster at Six Flags, and we hoisted him onto my back. My little family and I approached the trailhead, where we encountered a park ranger.

"No dogs."

"The sign says allowed on a leash."

"There's ice on the trail."

Hercules looked ready to hump something. Regina and I studied a city map, which we'd picked up at the hotel, for other options. Las Cruces seemed to have some public parks.

"How about this one?" I said. "Burn Lake. It sounds nice."

We drove back into town and found ourselves on a road by the highway. This was a land of down-market fast food chains that jack up Native American cholesterol levels for profit. We passed Whataburger, Roy Rogers, Hardee's, and Popeye's. The smells of fried meat, boiled meat, and melted cheese wafted through the car, tempting us toward a fresh hell. We drove up and down the road several times and saw several parking lots, but no parks.

"There's a sign!" Regina said.

We made a turn. Burn Lake soon appeared, an oblong concrete shell the size of two football fields, wedged among a rusted-out sewage-treatment plant, a used-car dealership, and the interstate. It contained maybe three feet of silty brown water. Though we should have turned around instantly, we parked and got out to stretch. At the far end of a gravel path sat some beleaguered playground equipment. I saw a fat little girl at the lake's edge, stirring mud with a stick. Next to us, in a van, two bloated behemoths who I assumed were her parents coughed madly. A sweet cloud of marijuana smoke floated out the window.

When I was a reporter in Chicago, I would probably have hung out in that van and smoked up with those large people, quickly scribbled down what I remembered of the scene afterward, and pounded out a piece full of salty local color for the next week's paper about the "authentic" lakeside culture. Now I didn't really want to talk to those people. They probably didn't have good weed anyway.

Regina and I front-loaded the kid into the Baby Björn. This situation, apparently, didn't call for the hiking backpack, because there weren't going to be any uphill climbs; it was just walking in regular shoes. I often asked Regina why we needed three separate devices (the sling was the third) in which to carry the baby, but she just looked at me incredulously, as though I were asking why the baby needed to wear diapers.

Hercules strained at the leash. He really wanted to walk around Burn Lake. I ran with him for a few feet. He whipped along, doing his best imitation of a rabbit at a greyhound track. We stopped to talk to a toothless old dude who was baiting a hook with some cooked chicken.

"What's in there?" I asked.

"Catfish!" he said. "Lots of tasty catfish!"

We moved past him quickly. Earlier, on our way to the mountains, we'd seen a prison work crew picking up garbage by the roadside. Now they were sitting in the picnic area, manacled together in their orange jumpsuits, eating their lunch.

One of the prisoners asked, "Hey, what kind of dog is that?"

"Just a little dog," I said. "Nothing special."

As I headed back to our Passat, carrying my son in the Baby Björn and walking my purebred Boston terrier on the leash, I was full of genuine shame. Class guilt oozed from my every pore. I wanted to say, as if anyone cared, "These are but the trappings of yuppiedom! It's not who I am in my soul!" But I was no longer cool, and all the water in Burn Lake wouldn't wash that away. I swore to myself that this needed to change.

Our early experiences with Elijah caused Regina and me to develop a "parenting philosophy," an oxymoronic phrase if there ever was one. We would be cool parents. The fact that we had no idea what this really meant didn't stop us from deciding it. We did know it had little to do with our disciplinary plans for Elijah, or our feeding and sleeping strategies; of course we wanted him to be healthy and to have a good education. In those respects, we weren't cool. We were just parents. But we weren't going to be people whose interest in popular music, or not-so-popular music, died the day our first kid was born. There would still be movies in our life, and they wouldn't all feature talking cartoon animals. If there was a concert we really, really wanted to see at midnight on a Wednesday, we, or at least I, would try to be there.

Upon his arrival, Elijah immediately became the most important thing. Of course there would be changes. But we were here first, and we invited him. We would not succumb to the cult of child-rearing; our kid was not going to be our excuse to retreat from the wider world. He would be our passport, and we would be his.

Thus, actual passport in hand, I went on my first business trip as a father. I'm guessing it was unique in the history of first business trips taken by fathers, because I can't imagine a situation where such a trip could be duplicated. Still, it was, technically, a business trip, and therefore relevant to this narrative.

I was invited by the John Adams Institute of Amsterdam to be the American representative at Dutch National Poetry Day, an annual celebration. Because I'd never actually published a poem in English, I was a somewhat odd selection for this honor. In my home country, I generally performed my spoken-word-poetry parodies in front of a dozen people or fewer in the back rooms of independent bookstores, but in the Low Countries, several thousand people had witnessed my act in grand opera houses and cavernous, acoustically generous concert halls built to house acts like Oasis and Blur. Oscar, my Dutch publisher, thought that he might be able to cash in on this situation.

When I say "Dutch publisher," it sounds like I have publishers in many countries, which isn't the case. My first book had been published in Spain, and was supposed to have been published in Italy, but the Italian translator absconded with the only copy of his manuscript and apparently he's yet to be found. In the Netherlands, the only other country to fall for my act, Oscar and I decided to try something different. We packaged together pieces from the book, as well as some political satire that I'd done and about a dozen poems (all translated into Dutch), and sold it under the title *Neal Pollack's Undying Love for the Citizens of Holland (And Also Belgium)*. The cover of the book featured me in my Homestead Grays cap, Allen Iverson jersey, $5 sunglasses, and goatee, arms crossed, making me look like a failed auditionee for a Beastie Boys tribute band. I'm still not clear as to why the John Adams Institute invited me, as opposed to, say, John Ashbery, or any other person in the United States who actually writes poetry, but it was a free plane ticket and a free opportunity to achieve my lifelong dream of becoming huge in the Low Countries.

"Do you have to do this?" Regina asked.

"It would be a great insult to the John Adams Institute if I didn't," I said.

"We have a three-month-old baby," she said. "Don't you care about him at all?"

"Of course I do," I said. "I care about him more than anything in the world. But I still want to go to Amsterdam. It's a fun opportunity for me."

"You just want to go to Amsterdam so you can smoke pot," she said.

"That's not true," I said.

She looked at me, arms crossed.

"OK," I said. "It is true. But that's not the *only* reason."

I felt a little guilty, not so much because I was going, but because I'd be going without her. Though I was going to be gone only four days, she'd be taking care of the baby by herself. She definitely got the short end of the transaction.

For twenty-four hours in Amsterdam, I was a responsible representative of my country. Oscar had set up some interviews for me with such high-powered outlets as a monthly Jewish newspaper from Rotterdam. Also, as part of the National Poetry Day celebration, I and the other participants had each been assigned to write a fable and to teach a workshop about fables to a class of high school students. I hadn't written a fable since I was eight years old, and it showed; in a couple of hours, I slapped out a lame animal parable about tolerance, based on the recent assassination of Dutch prime ministerial candidate Pim Fortuyn, about whom I knew nothing. Then I taught my class, and chose, as the organizers had instructed me to, the "best" student from the class to give a presentation that evening. My student would compete against the other students from the other classes. If she won, she'd receive a prize. Up until fifteen minutes after the lecture ended, I was sober.

As I walked out into the late afternoon, I had three hours before I had to present my poetry in a public performance. Now, I decided, would be the perfect time to get high. Amsterdam's coffee shops held no mystery for me. I'd visited many times and knew all the neighborhood spots, not just the places for Australian backpackers. Since I basically did nothing else when I was in Amsterdam, other than visit art museums or eat cheese, I'd more or less memorized a stoner's walking tour that would be the envy of the most experienced Cannabis Cup judge.

When I next looked at my watch, two hours and fifteen minutes had passed in a magnificent haze of high-octane legal weed and herbal tea. I'd enjoyed conversations with a one-armed Nigerian taxi driver and an anthropology professor from a low-rent Midwestern community college who'd just emerged from a two-day mushroom trip in his hotel room. I stepped out onto a major thoroughfare, full of confidence in myself both as a professional and as a dad. I pulled a picture of Elijah out of my wallet and thought clichés that were still true:

I love my son so much. Look at him! He's so beautiful. Life with him is going to be a wonder. I'm the luckiest man in the world. Now what happened to the Keizersgracht?

To my right, I saw one of Amsterdam's many "smart shops." These are less famous than the coffee shops, but their wares are more powerful, more obscure, and just as quasi-legal. I walked in, briefly pondered a display of homegrown peyote, bought a packet of some sort, and swallowed two pills with a gulp of water. By the time I arrived at the venue, my lips felt like sausages. Oscar gave me a conspiratorial grin.

"How are you feeling?" he said.

I couldn't tell him that at the moment I was imagining that my eyes had popped out of their sockets, shot forward ten feet attached by thin ligaments, wrapped themselves around my head, and reinserted themselves in new sockets that had opened up just above my eyebrows. He wouldn't have understood. So instead I said, "Oh, fine."

I was second on the evening's program. My opening act was Gerrit Komrij, the poet laureate of Holland. As befitting his position and nationality, he was stern, angular, and slightly bemused. He wore mostly black and read in Dutch. This gave me a lot of time to ponder the fact that my legs were slowly melting into the floor. I wondered how I'd make it up to the podium without them, particularly since the rest of my body was slowly filling up with oatmeal. When the poet laureate of Holland cut his reading short because he had a train to catch, the emcee introduced me as our "distinguished American visitor." A film of dripping sweat plagued my entire body. When I took the podium, I was hot.

"Good evening, people of the Netherlands," I said. "My name is Neal Pollack. And I am the Greatest Living American Writer."

With that, I lifted a pitcher of water off the podium and dumped it over my head.

Oscar and his friends seemed to think it was funny, even if the rest of the crowd didn't. This gave me encouragement to continue. We were on the eve of the Iraq invasion; as I'd sat there not listening to the poet laureate of Holland, I'd decided to deliver a monologue of pure patriotic bluster to parody the misguided war fever that was currently gripping the United States.

"I stand here representing," I said, "the greatest country in the history of the world, the beacon of democracy to oppressed people everywhere. Our enemies tremble in the face of our awesome military might and our international system of secret prisons that are accountable to no one. Our allies feel safe and comfortable under our broad protective wings. All hail the United States of America, where literature kicks big ass!"

A man in the back of the hall rose, shouted, "You will be punished!" and stormed out of the hall. I later learned that he was the Iraqi representative to National Poetry Day. Apparently, they don't teach irony at the International Institute of Poetic Exiles.

The rest of the evening was a mix. My student from the fable class gave a great presentation and won the prize, but then later, on a panel, I compared a German poet to Hitler and accused the moderator of asking the "stupidest questions of all time." When someone in the audience asked me what advice I'd give to young people who wanted to be writers, I said, "It doesn't matter what you say. If you say it loud enough, and for long enough, eventually people will pay attention."

"Well," the moderator said, "I'm certain we will now all live our lives according to Mr. Pollack's wise advice."

Afterward, my prizewinning student came up to me with her parents.

"Thank you," her father said. "You've really inspired my daughter."

"I have a son," I said. "So I understand."

Then it was three a.m. and I was in my hotel room. My breathing

117

was raspy and shallow. I'd ground my teeth down at least an inch. I called home.

"How'd it go?" Regina said.

I told her.

"Oh, Neal."

"Why does this always happen to me?"

"I don't know. Don't you want to hear how your son is doing?"

"Of course I do."

"He's sleeping pretty well and he ate peas today."

"That's great."

Soon after, I was coming down the escalator at the Austin airport, feeling not much worse than I had when I'd left. Regina looked just as tired as me, if not more.

"Daddy's home."

"We're glad to see you."

I'd brought back a box of Belgian chocolate for her, a purple elephant with googly eyes for Elijah, and a $337 long-distance bill that my publisher wasn't going to pay. In addition, the committee for National Poetry Day was making me exchange e-mails with the Iraqi poet to try to heal the rift, but it only got worse. He wrote, "You are complicit in the crimes of your President, as are all the American people." I replied, "Don't blame me, I didn't want this war." That ended a historic epistolary exchange.

"I'm glad to be back," I said.

And I was, too. I was thrilled to see my family. But I think I ingested some sort of evil hipster seed in Amsterdam that would soon threaten us all. The earliest days of fatherhood had been a surreally enjoyable trip. But as routine began to set in, I began to strain at the limitations of my role. I still had more than two full years left in that coveted eighteen-to-thirty-four demographic, and I was determined to ride my youth into the ground. Brandishing that noble attitude, Daddy started a rock band.

NINE

Escape from Dangerous Mountain

March–October 2003

S oon after I moved to Austin, I went to a party with some people I'd met at a show. This guy Mark, who was into motocross racing, was talking excitedly. He'd really gotten good at guitar, he said. He was ready to go into the studio.

"You know what the best thing is?" he said.

"No."

"I'm gonna be in a band with Dickie Moist!"

"Who?"

"You know. From the Moistboyz!"

He said it in this tone: *Everyone* knows Dickie Moist! And the thing was, whenever I told this story, people looked at me incredulously. They implied: How could you not have heard of the Moistboyz? So I Googled "Dickie Moist," and here's what I found: Dickie Moist, a guy whose real name is Guy Heller, had recorded an obscure side-project album with one of the dudes from Ween, and he said things in interviews like "Rock and roll is the song of sex, savagery, and pride, a beast from the past that has no plans. It can kill or shit gold. It is for those who stand tall, toothless and broke."

Such, I realized, was the lingua franca around town. This was a completely alternate cultural universe where the sneering visage of Johnny Rotten occupied prime billboard space in the downtown party district and where frat-boy piano bars turned punk rock because that's what the market demanded. Only in a universe like this would a guy like me even think about starting a band. I told Regina of my plan, even before Elijah was born.

"You can't do this now. We're having a baby! Please!"

"But I'm writing a book about rock 'n' roll. It'll be research! And besides, this is *Austin*. You *have* to have a rock band."

"I'm not going to be able to stop you, am I?"

Immediately upon arriving, I'd become friends with a guy named Ben, who'd sent me a sycophantic e-mail several months before. Ben had many tattoos and piercings, but he also held down a relatively respectable tech job. He owned his own house and worked there. When work was slow, I went over to his place and we made plans. He was the only person in town I knew who was under thirty. In fact, he was twenty-five. I decided that he'd be my conduit to help me reclaim the youth I thought I'd lost, and he'd also be able to help me start a band.

On August 31, 2002, the Neal Pollack Invasion made its debut. We knew six songs, five of which had been written in the previous month. Ben had shoehorned us into a show he was promoting at an outdoor venue called Club DeVille. That day was also the season's first University of Texas home football game, which had occurred during the afternoon, so Austin's downtown party district was full of drunken ex-jocks in burnt-orange shirts. They were the types of people who had been beating me up, or threatening to beat me up, my entire life, except that they were also Texans. If I'd thought about this in advance, perhaps I would have worn a different T-shirt than one that read IMPEACH GEORGE W. BUSH.

After my sound check, which had gone smashingly, I went to the bar for a drink. I had a squirt bottle of water in my other hand. On the way back, I passed a group of UT people who were heading for the exit.

"Nice shirt," said one of them.

"You think so?"

"No. I think you're a traitor."

Before they could walk too far away, I popped open my squirt bottle and sent a stream down his back. Totally punk rock! He turned around like a red-eyed devil horse snorting fire.

"I will KILL you!"

He champed at his bit and clawed his hooves into the ground. His friends were sober. They held him back, and they even managed to get him out of the bar before he made good on his promise.

"I'm coming back for you, fucker," he said.

When I was done trembling, I sat down and I trembled some more. I called Regina, who was coming to the show later. And I told her what had happened.

"Why do you always do this to yourself?"

"Do what?"

"Oh, Neal."

The show went off reasonably well, though there weren't many people there to see it, because the opening band that Ben had booked, Alfalfa Male, had been so bad that they'd driven away three-quarters of the audience. Even more frustrating was the fact that Alfalfa Male, made up of four of the scrungiest-looking, longest-bearded, grumpiest middle-aged men in Texas, *knew* they were bad. They had a papier-mâche "Suck Meter" set up in front of the stage so the audience could tell them exactly *how* badly they sucked. By comparison, the Neal Pollack Invasion was Iggy at the Fillmore.

After I was done with my mind-blowing twenty-minute set, I went back to Regina, who was sitting far away from the stage in a lovely maternity sundress. Standing next to her were two friends of ours who had never seen me perform. They looked at me in shock and horror.

"It was interesting" was all Regina would say.

The guy I'd squirted chose that moment to come back into the bar. His eyes were barely open and his face drooped down to his knees with drunkenness. But he still had muscles.

"I've been thinking about you," he said. "And I really want to beat you up."

The fact that I was now shirtless and slathered in sweat hadn't dissuaded him, apparently. I positioned myself behind Regina and put my hands on her shoulders.

"You can't beat me up. I have a pregnant wife."

He got up in my face and pointed a finger into my chest.

"You shouldn't wear that shirt!"

"This is America. I can wear whatever shirt I want."

His face scrunched, as though this was something he'd never considered before.

"OK. But you shouldn't squirt someone with water if they say they don't like what you're wearing."

"Fair enough," I said, and I extended my hand. He shook it, turned around, and walked away looking very confused. Regina regarded me with something far beyond resignation.

"Neal, Neal, Neal."

I spoke to her belly.

"You see, son. That's what rock 'n' roll is all about."

My little womb-lesson must have worked, because after Elijah was born, I spent his first year entertaining him at all times, and he didn't call my performance amateurish once. He thought that everything I did was hilarious. I responded by giving my adoring public what it wanted. One afternoon I cleaned his butt and put him into a clean duckie jumper. He seemed to be aware of me, so I started bouncing my hands lightly on either side of him. He bopped up and down on the bed and I started humming "Lester Leaps In," an old Count Basie standard I remembered from my brief mid-nineties jazz-dork period. I definitely caught him smiling during that, so I took it to the next level, and quoted from a different jazz standard:

"Salt Peanuts! Salt Peanuts!"

Elijah gurgled with glee, so I did it again.

"Salt Peanuts! Salt Peanuts!"

Fun was our first priority, but with the initial months of parenthood successfully completed, Regina began to want some of her pre-motherhood life back. It was a rough thicket for us to negotiate. The scheduling conflicts began. I was around most days after five p.m., when we'd feed, bathe, dress, and get the baby to sleep together. But before then, we had "Mommy Time," which was most of the time, and then "Daddy Time." Initially, Daddy Time was from three to five p.m. on weekdays, with longer shifts on the weekend. Some days, that was fine. But on other days, three p.m. would nearly arrive and I'd realize that I'd been sitting in my underwear at the computer all day but that I hadn't actually written anything. On those days, I'd come out of the back room that served as both my office and Regina's painting studio, which was an OK arrangement because we never got the chance to work at the same time.

Regina would be watching some terrible thing on Animal Planet like *Amazing Veterinary Rescues*. Elijah slept or swatted at mirrors and twirly things while on his blanket. She looked at me with desperation tinged with hope.

"Is Daddy Time early today? Oh, please let it be so."

"Not today. I need until three-thirty."

She sighed, deeply and exhaustedly.

"OK. You get *one more* half hour. But you have to keep him until six."

"No problem," I said, playing the only card I had. "I'll give him a bath by myself."

There were many advantages to our self-employed life, the foremost being that, ideally, we got to retain some sort of freedom and individual identity and could work more or less anytime we wanted.

Suddenly, though, every activity was subject to a negotiation. There weren't set times for anything. I enjoyed the randomness, because I mostly reaped its benefits, but it was hard on Regina, who'd been forced to put her art, and her teaching, on hold. It wasn't, she explained to me, like she was desperate to rejoin the workforce. Her painting was based on something deeper than the need to be productive. She'd been painting since she was a little girl, and that was how she expressed her best ideas and her deepest emotions. Her paintings were more than a job, they were a part of her, as vital as her organs.

With the initial buzz of motherhood gone, she felt adrift and uninspired. During Daddy Time, she'd go into the back and stare at an empty canvas. Or she'd check her e-mail, or take a shower, or pay bills, or, on rare occasions, do her nails. It was her time, her only time, so it didn't matter what she did. Often, she'd hand the baby to me, say, "I'm going out," and disappear in the car. If she stayed out way longer than two hours, I called her.

"Where are you?"

"I'm doing things."

"What things?"

"Just things, Neal. It doesn't matter."

"What things? Come on, just tell me."

"I'm trying on shirts at Ann Taylor, OK?"

She was very defensive.

"I didn't want to tell you. Because I thought you'd judge me."

"I'm not going to judge you. Except that I think you could have found something cooler than an Ann Taylor store at the mall."

"Don't be a snob. I'll be home in a little while."

"How long is a little while?"

"A little while, OK? I'll be home in a little while."

Mostly, we were glad that we both got to be at home with Elijah all the time. We felt like we really knew our son, even if the extent of our knowledge was that he laughed at funny faces, got butt rashes sometimes, and enjoyed eating applesauce. Some people we knew had to leave their infants in day care eight to ten hours or more every day. Few of them were happy. At least we got to create our own brand of frustration.

I started moving the parameters of Daddy Time, usually announcing the changes when Regina and I went to bed the night before. Some days, it was nine to eleven a.m., so I'd have the rest of the day to work. Some days, I promised eleven a.m. to one p.m., but that often transmuted into 11:30 a.m. to one p.m. If a couple of phone calls came in the morning, I pushed Daddy Time back until one to three. This created problems around the house, largely because we were all home together, all the time, and familiarity breeds contempt. As with all negotiations, sometimes things just broke down.

Regina: "I don't want to take him right now! I had him all day yesterday!"

Neal: "Oh, yeah? Well, if I don't work, then we don't eat!"

Regina: "Your work will not suffer if you watch Elijah for two hours on a Friday morning."

Neal: "How do you know?"

Regina: "I know."

Neal: "Why don't you stop trying to hold me back?"

Regina: "Oh, go ahead. Blame me."

These kinds of arguments, and occasionally worse ones, were pretty common. But so were the simple joys of watching our child grow up. One day, we were lying in bed as a family. Elijah was between us and Hercules was at our feet. The boy looked at me, reached up, touched my cheek, and said, "Da-da!"

He was only six months old, and he could talk! His first word was my name! What a wonderful son he was! Regina waited for the "Ma-ma" to come, but first, Elijah had to say "dog" and "cat" and "chair" and "TV."

"He hates me," she said.

"No. He just hasn't said "Mama" yet. This isn't a competition."

"Thank you."

"Though he obviously likes me better."

"Right."

But Regina got the best word of all. One afternoon, she took Elijah walking around an outdoor mall because she needed the air and also wanted to look for a new pair of eyeglass frames. Elijah saw the cardboard cutout of what was, apparently, a familiar figure to him. He pointed.

"Spider-Man!" he said, and immediately turned his attention elsewhere.

Later, Regina said to me, "Neal, how did he know who Spider-Man was?"

After all, she thought, neither of us had ever introduced him to Spider-Man in any way. But here's where I had the upper hand on her in understanding our child. I was incredibly proud of the first brand name that Elijah could recognize, but not particularly surprised. I knew that boys are genetically predisposed to understanding that nothing is more awesome than Spider-Man, except possibly Batman, the Thing, and Wolverine. I was only surprised that Spider-Man wasn't Elijah's *first* word.

As the days progressed, other milestones fell. One day, we were all hanging out in the back with a Baby Sartre video or something like that. Elijah rose up, his hand on my shoulder, let go, and lurched toward the television. He'd been feeling his way around the coffee table lately, so at first we didn't notice.

"Holy shit, Regina," I said. "He's walking."

"You know, you're right. He *is* walking."

He moved toward the TV, his arms out in front of him, Frankenstein's Baby.

"TV!" he said, like the American child he was. "TV! TV! TV!"

Because Elijah was now mobile, we could no longer take him with us everywhere. We still tried to get out, to reduce the odds that we'd strangle each other. Our social life as a couple had more or less ceased when Elijah reached the crying-in-restaurants phase. We continued to go to the movies, though. Regina would take in the five p.m. matinee, drive home, and hand me the keys, and I'd get to the theater in time for the seven p.m. show. Sometimes she'd do the seven p.m. and I'd do the nine p.m. Then we'd talk about the movie later in bed. Occasionally, we'd get a sitter, and we'd consolidate, paying for one movie, hiding in our respective bathrooms for a few minutes, and then sneaking into another. We weren't proud of this, or at least she wasn't, but it saved us some money, and thus we were able to see *School of Rock* and *Intolerable Cruelty* all in one evening.

We found another couple, with more or less our sensibility, who also didn't want to pay for babysitting. Once a month, one of us would go over to Shannon and Lacey's house to make sure that Emmett, their adorable little butterball, didn't get his head caught between the slats of his crib. As repayment, one of them would come by our place a week later. This was generally an effective strategy, though they took better advantage of it than we did. One night, we had them co-op us, and we decided to go bowling. It was a half hour before I threw out my knee. Another night, we went to see a late show of *Ray*, and that was the Sunday that some guys decided to simultaneously set off stinkbombs in every theater in town to protest "corporate moviegoing."

They would often stay out until 1:30 or 2 a.m., which would cause Regina and me to stagger home after enduring a long night of their Australian zwieback, which had really stinky farts. Once, I mentioned to Lacey that sitting for Emmett was a pleasure, "except for your annoying dog."

"Oh, you're one to talk," she said.

It had never occurred to me that someone might find Hercules annoying.

Meanwhile, Regina found a "drinking group" that called itself Tequila Tuesdays. I put "drinking group" in quotes because they usually had one or two drinks and were home by ten because everyone had to work the next day. However, Regina also joined a book club that was only marginally about books. Several of the women in the club did things like fix dinner for the Drive-By Truckers when they came to town, and they all liked to drink. I was so proud of Regina. When she stumbled in at one a.m., redolent of wine, it was hard not to love her.

Usually, though, I did the going out. Regina barely protested, because she was too tired to protest. She continued to understand that I needed to exorcise my shallow party demons. I was living in a town where going out, and hanging out, seemed to be the primary industries. I've never been one not to take advantage of my surroundings.

The Neal Pollack Invasion moved forward quickly, without some of the usual requirements of a rock career, like rehearsal or songwriting. I'd taken some singing lessons from an opera singer when I lived in Philly, which meant I could kick out an acceptable version of "On the Street Where You Live," from *My Fair Lady,* but that song has little currency in the world of punk. There wasn't time to learn anything more; I had a book to promote. I loaded Elijah into the Baby Björn, put Hercules on the leash, and walked around Austin's various party districts, staple-gunning band posters to bulletin boards and telephone poles. My son was already learning the principles of indie marketing.

The South by Southwest music festival arrived. They booked us at someplace called Tequila Rock, which sounds like a bar in Cancún that caters exclusively to Europeans but was actually one of the many clubs in Austin that appears for SXSW weekend and then vanishes forever. Tequila Rock had a capacity of about 500 people, two tiers of floor for the audience, a full complement of colored lights and disco balls, a smoke machine, and an unadorned back office where a guy with greasy hair was fingering thick wads of paper money.

Before the show, Regina predicted disaster. But I assured her that all would go well. I'd persuaded my friend Jim Roll, a legitimate singer-songwriter from Michigan, to anchor the band, and he'd brought in two professional musicians, Neil Cleary and Jon Williams, who weren't capable of playing an off-key note if they tried. When they combined with Dakota Smith, who'd written the songs for the original, pre-professional Invasion, we were undefeatable. Our show was at 8 p.m. Around 6:30, I went up to the light-board guy and made some requests.

"I want you to go completely crazy with the lights during every song," I said. "I really don't care what combinations you use. And also, set off the smoke machine whenever I yell out 'Smoke machine, motherfucker!' "

"OK," he said.

We played a twenty-five-minute set, which was all we had in us. Every one of the forty or so people in the room seemed to enjoy themselves, except for the sound guy, but that was understandable, since I'd spit water all over his equipment. I even signed a couple of autographs. The indie-record-label people that I was trying to con into releasing an album came over to me.

"Pleasantly surprised" was their verdict.

Then Regina approached.

"Pollack. You are the luckiest sonofabitch in the world."

"I told you these guys were good."

"They were like a real band."

"*I told you.*"

A few hours later, we came home. The college student we'd hired to babysit was sitting on the couch looking a bit shaky.

"Any problems with the kid?" I said.

"He slept the whole time," she said. "But . . ."

"But what?"

"There was this terrible accident outside. This car wrapped itself around that telephone pole . . ."

She pointed out the window.

"It took them all night to get the people out of the car. Everyone just left."

"Weird. Did Elijah wake up?"

That was her last night in our employ. As it turned out, she'd just viewed a typical day in the neighborhood, whose evil secrets had not yet become clear to us. Great dangers lurked on the highway access road.

But what did I care about living on a street where near-fatal car accidents were de rigueur? My modest SXSW triumph had caused me to think that this rock thing could actually end up being a side career. I didn't let the facts that I was thirty-three years old and that I'd never been in a band before quash my fantasia. There was no way, I decided, that I could put my youth to bed without a rock 'n' roll phase.

"Please give it up," Regina said. "You're not a rock star."

"I know that."

But did I? At night, after Elijah's last feeding, I'd lie in bed or sit up watching *SportsCenter*, imagining myself as the newest member of punk rock's pantheon. And I meant real 1970s punk rock, not the fashion-model Strokes-led genre revival. No! I would be authentically punk: broke, unpopular, and pathetically desperate, though I doubt Johnny Thunders ever drove a Passat wagon or carried a kid around in a Baby Björn. It was time to go on tour.

I spent the summer getting ready, doing the usual things one does to prepare for a rock tour—renting a Ford Econoline van, mapping out driving routes, trying to find an amp for my bassist—and some unusual things, like asking people for money on my website and accepting a $1,000 check from Music for America, a nonprofit left-wing political organization, in exchange for serving as their "spokesperson." I think they overestimated the Invasion's draw, but I wasn't about to tell them that. My guys weren't going out on tour with me for the love of the music, or at least not only because of that. I had a payroll to meet.

The only way that would happen, according to my math, would be if we stayed on the road for three and a half consecutive weeks, playing a show a night, with maybe one night off. It would be a true rock grind, because I was a determined warrior.

I also scheduled things precisely so I could be home to help Regina get ready for Elijah's first birthday party. This was my only real priority. I may have wanted to rock, but I was a *dad* who rocked, and not in some Dan Zanes folk-revival way, either. Someday I wanted to show Elijah a picture of me shirtless and screaming in a dark Baltimore cavern and say, "Boy, this is how I spent your first year."

My right knee hadn't been the same since someone had smashed it with a whiskey bottle in Ben's hot tub a few months before. As I was doing a local show the night before I was to leave on tour, it gave out. The emergency-room doctor told me that I'd strained my meniscus, and maybe I even had a minor tear. This wasn't particularly good news. The meniscus is a little C-shaped bit of cartilage just under the knee joint, but it doesn't usually heal after an injury because it has no blood supply. Also, the meniscus tends to deteriorate with age anyway, so damage probably would never completely repair. Middle age had arrived.

"It should probably feel better if you stay off it for about a week," the doctor said.

"Yeah. But I have to go on a rock tour for a month."

He considered this for a moment.

"Well then. You might have a problem."

Three hours later, my knee was immobilized in a stiff brace with royal-blue padding, and I was on crutches. I also had a month's supply of Vicodin, which I cracked immediately. Already, my tongue had grown thick.

I lay in bed with Regina. She cradled me.

"Why did this happen?" I said.

"I don't know, baby," she said.

"I worked so hard . . . I just wanted . . . I wanted . . . It's like I'm being punished!"

I sobbed out of proportion with my problems. The drugs had taken full effect.

"Oh, God! No! No! No! No! No!"

By 7:15 the next morning, we'd loaded the van and it was idling in the driveway. I was the last one in. I hobbled out of the house on crutches, having slept three hours, and popped two Vicodin.

Regina came out in her nightdress, with the baby in a sling on her hip. I kissed her and felt my throat gum up. She mussed my hair.

"Be brave, superstar," she said.

"I can't do this."

"You have to."

As the van pulled out of the driveway, I looked at my family through the dirty back window. How would I survive without them? Regina was letting me go on a monthlong rock tour when she was at home with an eleven-month-old. And I wasn't even a musician. That is the living definition of a good woman.

Elijah wagged his hand. His eyes looked bright and alive, and I was leaving him. I wept as we drove down the street and hit the I-35 on-ramp. There was no escape. I clutched my bottle of Vicodin to my chest, lay down, and closed my eyes. When I woke an hour later, my family was gone and I was on tour.

Every tour has at least one Long Drive. Most have several. But I tried to limit them. I knew that if my guys were to put on a good a show for me every night, then at least I wanted to give them several hours a day to watch TV. With that philosophy established, and after I got my temper under control, they started calling me a "good boss," particularly because I was paying them on time. Still, leaving Providence, Rhode Island, on a Tuesday morning more than two weeks into the tour so we would spend a night in Pittsburgh was an unappealing prospect.

We were five hours into the very wide state of Pennsylvania when it began to rain. Fifteen minutes later, it began to sleet. A film of dirty porridge blew over the windshield. Then came rain again, an unrelenting downpour. Passing trucks sprayed puddle water over us in broad, dangerous sheets. I called the show promoter to make sure that everything was OK.

"Are you in the weather yet?" he said.

"Oh, yes," I said.

Still, we expressed a fine collective mood. It wasn't yet sundown, and we were only an hour outside of town. We wouldn't be going on until midnight.

A sign was flashing orange: ROAD CLOSED. We pulled up at the checkpoint. Jim was driving. A very wet police officer met us.

"What happened?" Jim said.

"Spill," said the officer.

"How long until you reopen?"

"Not tonight."

"Well, how do we get to Pittsburgh?"

"Pray."

Apparently, a tractor-trailer carrying a cargo of magnesium sulfate tablets had overturned. The Pennsylvania Turnpike was on fire. We pulled off at the exit, stopped at a gas station, and consulted our map.

"We're screwed," Jim said.

Our only option, if we wanted to get to Pittsburgh in time for the show, was to take a five-hour detour through the Cumberland Gap in West Virginia. We had no choice; it was always possible that lots of people in Pittsburgh wanted to see the Neal Pollack Invasion at midnight on a Tuesday. And so, as a truckload of Epsom salt burned the Pennsylvania Turnpike in the midst of a terrific squall, we descended into the abyss. I called home.

"Do you want to say good night to your son?" Regina said.

"Sure."

"Elijah, say good night to Daddy!"

"A ga!" Elijah said. "Ba!"

"Hey, buddy. Are you being a good boy?"

My phone chose that moment to run out of juice.

I wanted nothing more than to be home, to put my child to bed, and to cuddle up on the sofa with my wife to watch whatever she wanted, which, knowing Regina, was a rerun of *Stargate SG-1*. I'd been coming around to the idea of fatherhood, tiring of the struggle over schedules and duties. It was time to settle. But that was still a few weeks away. Instead, we were in West Virginia, driving into a dark torrent.

We saw the sign.

BEWARE, it said. DANGEROUS MOUNTAIN.

The mountain was definitely steep. A rock slide seemed likely. But considering what we'd driven through in the last three hours, it was no more intimidating than anything else. We crawled up Dangerous Mountain slowly, but almost arrogantly, as though we were beyond defeat. Indeed, we ascended, and to celebrate, Dakota turned his iPod to a song that none of us liked. At the top, we looked into a valley, where there was a town. It didn't appear to be raining anymore.

Soon, we were unloading our gear into the backstage area of an abandoned movie theater. We played in front of eight people and earned thirteen dollars. Why, in the name of God, was I here?

Out of the fog walked five men in black leather, their hair in either Mohawks or pompadours. They looked like they'd been lugging gear for fifteen years straight.

"Oi," said one of them. "Is this Pittsburgh?"

They were called Gold Blade, and they were from England. This was their first American tour. They'd been two hours behind us on the turnpike; otherwise, they would have been the opening band. From their first note, I realized how absurdly out of place that order would have been. The room shook with an explosive crush of sweat and strength. It was as though the Clash had stepped through a time portal, minus political pretension.

Gold Blade sang the title song to their latest album, *Do You Believe in the Power of Rock-n-Roll?* Their magnetism was undeniable, their sound a weird fusion of the Stooges and AC/DC. In other words, it was the real thing, hard guitar and drum-mashing ground out by angry professionals with nothing to prove or lose. Also, their lead singer, John Robb, is a British television host and fashion model. Now *this* was a band. The lyrics went, well I don't know exactly how they went, but the chorus certainly went: *"Do you believe / do you believe / do you believe / in the Power of Rock-n-roll?"*

Then I understood: Gold Blade had stepped out of the fog to teach me a lesson. Rock 'n' roll has no purpose or meaning other than to perpetuate itself. You have to put on a show whether people come to see you or not, and you'd better do the best you can. Maybe I could apply that lesson to my life, to fatherhood, which, after all, was about perpetuating the species and trying to do it well. Maybe being a dad was all about the effort. The tour would slog on for ten more days, but my mind had drifted elsewhere, to seeing my wife and son again. Gold Blade kicked ass, but I was just a dad.

My family and I had been apart for nearly a month. We'd arranged to have our touching reunion at the Four Seasons Hotel in Atlanta. I realize that this flies somewhat in the face of the portrait I've been trying to paint of us as ordinary people just trying to get through the next bill-paying cycle. But a friend of Regina's was getting married in Atlanta, and they had good rates at the Four Seasons for guests, and, you know, what the hell? How often do you get to stay at the Four Seasons? The plan was this: Regina would leave Elijah in Nashville with her mother, and she'd meet me for a couple of nights at the hotel, and then we'd drive back to Nashville and I would get the special treat of seeing my son without other business to distract me from him.

"Mmm, baby," I said to Regina, on the phone from the van. "I am gonna make such sweet love to you."

"OK, dear."

A week before we were supposed to meet, she called me.

"I can't leave him, Neal. I just can't."

"Sure you can. It's just for the weekend."

"We haven't been apart for a day since he was born! It's too hard for me!"

This was obviously not up for debate. The next day, we talked again.

"Here's what's going to happen," she said. "I found my mother a room at the Marriott. It's only ninety-nine dollars. She can stay there with Elijah. That way, I still get to see him every day but we can be alone."

"Well," I said. "There goes our hotel discount."

I was waiting for a cab at the Atlanta airport when I realized that I'd misplaced my gift bag. Elijah was particularly into pigs at that point, and I'd purchased a really nice pig puppet for him at a toy shop in New York. Regina was waiting for me at the hotel. I called her. I'd slept about fifteen hours that week.

"I can't find the pig puppet! Where the hell is it? Someone stole the pig!"

"Wait. What are you talking about?"

"I lost Elijah's present! At the airport! I am such a bad father!"

"Calm down. It's probably in lost-and-found."

"No! It's gone!"

A half hour later, I walked into a hospitality suite at the Four Seasons, without my pig puppet. Regina gave me a chaste kiss. Her friends were all watching, as was her mother. Good Protestant girls don't show emotion in public.

"I'm glad to see you. You can walk!"

"I've been walking for a while. Now, where's my boy?"

On cue, Regina's friends parted to reveal Elijah sitting on the carpet playing with some toy. It was a week before his first birthday.

"Elijah," said Regina's mother. "Look who it is!"

He turned. His eyes were as wide as one of those kids in the *Love Is* . . . cartoons. God, he was beautiful.

"Ah ha ha!" he said.

He crawled toward me. I ran toward him. And I scooped him up. Never have I hugged anyone for as long or as hard.

"Hey, little man," I said.

"Awwww," said Regina's mother.

I put Elijah down and ran toward the other side of the room. He started crawling toward me, cackling with joy. I put my arms in the air and said "ROWRRRRR!" We resumed the endless monster chase, ignoring everyone else around us. Two days later, the pig puppet turned up at lost-and-found.

Immediately upon returning home, Regina went into Hipster Homemaker mode in preparations for Elijah's first birthday party. She baked chocolate cupcakes and decorated them to look like the face of Frankenstein's monster, prepared cookies shaped like black cats, brewed a bowl of green punch that contained a translucent glove filled with red Jell-O, and ordered a mess of retro decorations from a website called oldfashionedhalloween.com. She painted a miniature spot-on copy of one of those decorations—an adorable picture of a top-hat-wearing, tap-dancing cat—onto a handmade invitation, and ran off color copies. I wrote the inside copy for the invite: "Batty batty batty! Wings don't fail me now!" The fact that only my brother-in-law Lloyd caught the reference from *Hollywood Shuffle* didn't make me think it was any less clever.

The party was smashing. For the grown-ups, we stocked the larder with Shiner Bock, a deli tray, good-quality fruits and cheeses, and fresh-baked bread with olive oil. There were some children as well, most of them actually younger than Elijah and therefore even less willing to participate in social life. There was a lot of crawling, grasping, and drooling. Usually that doesn't happen at my parties until the end. Some of our single friends came, but they mostly had a beer and left, not really interested in talking about the salutary qualities of the Diaper Genie.

Meanwhile, we'd begun to coalesce a little group of like-minded parents. My job at the party, other than to feed a cupcake to Elijah for the inevitable chocolate-all-over-the-mouth photo, was to entertain the dads. I did this by playing records. Good records. My records.

Two dads were more interested than the others: Shannon, from our babysitting co-op, who had a daytime copywriting job but refused to let his six-month-old son, Emmett, get in the way of doing avant-garde improv comedy and voice-overs for independently produced *anime* movies, and my neighbor Jennings, who'd been in a popular indie-rock band in Iowa and had an SST Records sticker on the back of his Subaru station wagon. Jennings claimed that his son Eamon's favorite band was Devo. Eamon was two and a half. To prove his point, he said, "Hey, Eamon!"

Eamon was dressed as a flying monkey from *The Wizard of Oz,* which he informed me was his "favorite costume ever."

"Yes, Daddy?"

"Are we not men?"

His son replied, "We are Devo!"

On the one hand, it was absurd to think that a two-year-old could have a favorite band, and even more absurd to think that the band could be Devo. Then again, most of Devo's music was weird and peppy. Who's to say that a kid couldn't have the taste to like it better than Raffi? I considered the fact that making kids listen to Devo was actually kind of square, but then I remembered that my parents' record collection contained one album of quality, *Let It Bleed,* but it didn't leave its shrink-wrap until I was sixteen. The rest of the records, which took up about half a shelf in our linen closet, were comprised of Broadway cast albums, a Beatles greatest-hits collection, the Beach Boys' *Surfin' USA,* and my father's favorite single, The U.S. Army Marching Band playing "And the Caissons Go Rolling Along." By comparison, my music collection was Kurt Loder's. This *was* the right approach! Our children deserved cultural guidance from us. Wasn't that our job? They needed Devo.

Elijah opened his presents. Among them was a special gift from Dad. Regina unwrapped the package.

"Oh, Elijah. DVDs!"

"Oh, no," I said. "Better than DVDs. *Muppet Show* DVDs."

"He's too young for *The Muppet Show.*"

"You're never too young for *The Muppet Show.*"

When the gifts were done, I bragged to Jennings and Shannon that Elijah really appreciated the music I played for him. To prove this, I put on Sly and the Family Stone's *Greatest Hits* album. They approved.

"That's a great idea," Shannon said. "Stevie Wonder would be good, too."

"Elijah really likes 'Stand,' " I said.

"Cool," they said.

There would be no more rock touring. I didn't want to leave home for extended periods. And now I'd begun exerting cultural control over my son; I was going to shape his mind until he was exactly like me.

From now on, it would be Daddy Time all the time.

3

DURING

TEN

Yucky Fu

January–April 2004

*W*huhhhhhhhhhhh! *Mmmmmm! Whuhhhhhhhh!*

If you didn't hear the sound every day, you could easily think it was a distant siren, or a wounded animal seeking a crawl space under the house. But for us the sound heralds no fresh emergency. It just signifies the beginning of our day. In many ways, it also signifies the end.

Whuhhhhhhh. Whuhhhhhhhhh. Ahmmmmmmmm.

Sometimes the sound begins at 6:45 a.m., sometimes 6:30, or 5:30, and occasionally, mercifully, a random minute during the seven o'clock hour. We always note the precise time. Martyrdom takes many forms. Human beings, even sixteen-month-old ones, weren't created to wake up this early. If they were, whoever created human beings was wrong.

The sound gains energy.

Whuhhhhhhhhhh! Whuhhhhhhhhh! Ahmmmmmmmm!

As it drifts down the hall to our bedroom, the sound slowly begins to take the form of human language, a primitive Esperanto primarily concerned with the consumption of peanut butter, the magical qualities of sea animals, and the lyrics to "The Wheels on the Bus."

It has a weird singsong accent like the ones deployed by actors playing Italians in Olive Garden commercials.

"Ma-ma! Ma-ma! Ma-ma! Daaaaaaaaa-deeeeeeee!"

"The beast has awakened," I say. "It summons us."

Regina pulls a pillow over her head.

"Oh, God."

"I know."

Though I'm drowsy, I also feel secure. I can ignore this sound, much like I ignore the morning's first backfiring truck or construction noise. My eyes won't open for good until around 10:15 a.m. or so. I love sleep. I love it so much.

"Your turn," she says.

"Bullshit!" I say.

Regina's tone isn't pleading, nor is it desperate or angry. Rather, her voice bleeds a combination of exhaustion and justified sacrifice. It's the precise tone adopted by Montgomery that led to Rommel's surrender at El Alamein.

Evenly but cruelly, she says, "I take him every morning. Today, I'm going to sleep in. And I'm going to do it as late as I want. You *will* give me my day."

"But I smoked pot last night!"

"That's your problem."

The sound has now become fully distinctive.

"Li-jah up! Yaaaaaaaay!"

Regina gets out of bed, not bothering to put on her bathrobe. She tucks two pillows under one arm and the dog under the other. Without speaking to me, she walks through the door to the back room, which contains a futon and is basically soundproofed from the rest of the house. She stops, and I feel a rare, warm ray of hope. Maybe she'll turn around.

"Go!"

She doesn't turn around.

The door slams.

All right, already.

My boxers sit saggy and low on my hips, like a ratty curtain in the front window of an abandoned house. The mirror shows a bit of a belly, better than it was six months ago but never again in full retreat; too much forehead; and eyes rimmed with telling dark crescents. Hair has begun its irreversible creep up my back, destined to culminate in nothing good. It's a cliché, but it's nonetheless true. Mr. Pollack is no longer my father.

I'm the daddy now.

Elijah is in his crib, wrapped in the fuzzy green blanket with pictures of sheep on it that he, adorably, calls his "Baa bo."

"What's up?"

"Mommy!"

"Mommy's sleeping."

"Mommy seeping. Uhhhhhhh. Da-deeeeeeeeeee!"

"Yes, son. It is your daddy. And he bids you good morning."

I open the shutters. Elijah sits up and holds his blanket in front of him.

"Baa bo! Baa bo!"

"Yes. That's your sheep blanket."

He holds up his other blanket.

"Bo!"

"Blanket."

Next, he reveals, as he does every time he wakes up or whenever else he gets a chance, his special purple elephant with the googly eyes.

"Fant!"

"Correct. That is, indeed, your elephant."

In proud succession, Elijah shows off three different bears ("Bah!"), a horse ("Sah!"), the pig puppet I bought him after my tour ("Puh! Oink! Oink!"), and, finally, the ceiling fan ("Fa!").

"Thank you for introducing me to all your friends. Plus the fan."

He stands in his crib, lifting his arms.

"Ta da!"

"Ta da!"

"Ah! Ah! Ah! Ah!"

"Are you a monkey?"

"Ma-tee! Ma-tee! Ba-boon!"

"OK, baboon. It's time to change your diaper."

"Che da-per!"

I stagger into the kitchen. My hands shake as though they were palsied. My head feels heavy, shriveled, and dehydrated; it's a giant prune. Hadn't I pledged to never again drink beer *and* smoke on the same night? Austin is a bad town for moderation. The teakettle goes on the burner.

In the living room, I turn on the television. The American Pediatrics Association says children under two should watch no television at all. I agree, in theory, but theory doesn't mean jack at 7:30 on a Sunday morning. I also think the APA made those recommendations before the birth of Noggin, the MTV of every American child under the age of four. Elijah chooses *Connie the Cow,* a British cartoon about an exuberant bovine and her wacky animal friends, who include a hedgehog that wears a sock on his nose. Later, Regina and I will ban Connie from our house after Connie begins hosting a "milk break" sponsored by Kellogg's Cocoa Krispies. Still later after that, we allow Connie back into the fold when we realize it's the only way we can keep Elijah from destroying the bedroom blinds while Regina checks her e-mail.

Elijah runs circles around the living room.

"Sa! Sa! Sa!"

That could mean "sock," or "horse," but at this time of the day, it usually means "cereal." So, at Elijah's command, I sprinkle a handful of Cascadian Farms Purely O's on the coffee table.

"Noooooooooo! Nana truh!"

The last time she visited, Regina's mother, Elijah's nana, brought him a pastel-colored plastic cement mixer. One morning, Regina began putting cereal in the mixer. Since then, Elijah will only eat his cereal from there.

"Sorry. I forgot."

Elijah has already seen this episode of *Connie the Cow,* which is not surprising, as there are only about six episodes. They air over and over again. Over and over and over. I want to drink my tea and read the Internet. Elijah has other agendas. He runs into the kitchen and points at the refrigerator. Shit. He's doubly hungry today. I'm going to have to cook him breakfast.

"Milk! Milk!"

"Who's up for some milk, then? Do you also want to eat?"

He jumps up and down, flapping his hands. I taught him to do this at mealtimes. It's one of my proudest innovations as a dad.

"Eeeeeeeeeee! Eee! Eee! Eee!"

"Do you want eggs?"

"Ah!"

"Do you want cheese?"

"Chee! Chee!"

"Do you want . . . pineapple?"

"Pa! Pa pa pa pa pa pa! Ahpul!"

I scramble a grain-fed cage-free egg and mix in a few chunks of Tillamook medium-sharp cheddar cheese. The pineapple, which I serve in a separate dish, has no special brand qualities as far as I can tell, but he eats it anyway. By the time we finish breakfast, *Sesame Street* is ten minutes old.

Elijah and I often watch *Sesame Street* together. I've established certain rituals. For instance, Cookie Monster presents the letter of the day in skits that have a classically neat three-part structure unchanged from my own boyhood. Cookie Monster looks at the letter and struggles with his eating addiction. Another character ambles along and informs Cookie Monster that he's holding the letter of the day. Cookie Monster then gives in to his addiction, consuming the letter in an orgy of ecstatic munching.

I tickle Elijah and munch him all over while saying "Um num num num num!" Elijah seems to enjoy that.

Another prominent feature of this era's *Sesame Street* is the "Journey to Ernie" segment. Ernie always gives away his hiding place to Big Bird, and then they sing the "Journey to Ernie" song together. I find the narrative a bit simplistic and repetitive, but Elijah likes it. The segment comes on. During the song, I hold Elijah's hands, and he shifts back and forth on the balls of his feet.

I lift Elijah by his armpits and swing him around when the Count reveals the number of the day. If that hideously unfunny lisping abortion of a character Baby Bear appears, I say to Elijah, "Always remember, son, that Baby Bear sucks."

"Ba-bee Ba Suh!"

"That's right."

Then comes Elmo's World, a special time of the day.

"AHHHHHHHHHHHH!"

After this initial expression of joy, he sits for approximately twenty brainwashing minutes. I hop around and say, "Look, Elijah! Look! I'm just like Mr. Noodle!" But his trance is unbreakable.

Sesame Street ends. I turn off the TV. Elijah shrieks because he likes to dance along to the closing credits. I turn the TV back on.

"Ah ha ha!"

"Let's put on your shoes!"

"Shooo! Shoooo!"

"Who wants to go to the car?"

"Ca! Ca!"

"And who wants to go to the store?"

"Sta!"

"And what's next to the store?"

"Pa pa! Pa pa pa! Pa?"

"The park! That's right!"

When I have Elijah in the car, I tend to listen to college radio so I can expose him to bands whose music I don't know. But that day, I listen to NPR.

A wave of monstrous self-loathing overwhelms me. I'm a thirty-five-year-old white guy driving a Volkswagen station wagon, going to the gourmet grocery store, with a child seat in the back. What next? Should I call in to the pledge drive? Maybe I'll get a *Car Talk* coffee mug! Maybe I should renew my subscription to the lecture series at the 92nd Street Y, or feel guilty about racism but do nothing to stop it.

I soothe myself. Fine, I think. I can listen to NPR, but I don't have to like what I hear.

A reporter is doing a story on private contractors in Iraq. One of the contractors says he took the job because he's $40,000 in debt back home.

"That's a big chunka change!" the reporter says.

"Goddamn stupid faux-populist bullshit," I say, while my Volkswagen Passat idles at a stoplight. "No one says 'chunka change' . . . You wouldn't know *real* debt if it crawled up your ass at an Arcade Fire concert . . ."

"Daaaaa-deeeeee!"

I realize that I've once again retreated into grouchy middle-aged-man territory. When did I become that guy who complains that the world is going to hell in a handbasket? The fact that the world actually *is* going to hell in a handbasket is no excuse. I'm with my son. I should enjoy these precious moments.

"Who wants to see the ducks?"

"Duh! Duh!"

"And what sound does the duck make?"

"Dahk dahk! Dahk dahk!"

Together, we make a quacking chorus.

"Dahk dahk dahk dahk dahk dahk dahk!"

I look at Elijah in the mirror. He's kicking his legs and smiling goofily. What a lovely creature. We have so much fun together at the playground. I must celebrate these magic hours, though I'll need a pot of chai with soy milk if I'm going to see noon. I'd say coffee instead, but I'd be lying; sometimes I drink chai with soy, and I hate myself because of that.

Goddamn stupid NPR.

"Dahk dahk!" Elijah says.

That kid is so happy I'm his dad. Most of the time, I'm happy, too.

We arrive. Next to the grocery store stands a playground with separate areas for toddlers and for older kids. A little coating of dew dapples the grass and the plastic slides. The moms with their pink jumpsuits, burnt-orange visors that declare a lifelong devotion to their U-of-T sororities, and overfed Dylans usually don't show up before ten, so this is a good time.

There's also a park with an artificial "wet pond," where a variable number of ducks troll for bread. To most people, and even to most children, ducks are among the most quotidian of creatures. But to my son, they might as well be fire-breathing unicorns. The mere sight of one duck sends him into peals of ecstasy of the type not heard since the mid-1970s public appearances of Steven Tyler.

This morning, either Elijah has scared the ducks away with his enthusiasm, or an informant has warned them in advance that he was coming and they snuck out the laundry entrance.

"The ducks aren't here today," I say. "They went to Branson, Missouri, on vacation."

I laugh at my own joke.

Elijah flaps his left hand.

"Bye-bye, duh."

"Bye-bye, ducks."

Elijah and I go to the store, Central Market, which has a whole section devoted to the vegetables of Holland, a cheese section divided both by geography and type of farm, and a deli counter that features six different kinds of capers. A display advertises Japanese *panko* bread crumbs as a "customer favorite." The store's recent remodel added a "spa bar" and a gourmet-tea tasting booth. Customers get free tastings of chipotle-herb marinated pork loin and enoki mushroom ragout. I sometimes find myself carting around a kid who's begging me to feed him, specifically, clementines.

Elijah behaves quite pleasantly at Central Market as long as I'm continually shoving samples into his mouth. In short order, he slurps down pieces of honeydew melon, watermelon, Valencia orange, cherry tomato, regular tomato, cheese Danish, apple Danish, fat-free tortilla, whole-wheat tortilla, and butter tortilla. This gets me to the deli counter.

I take a number. To distract Elijah, I play peek-a-boo, hiding behind the red balloon I tied onto the cart at the entrance. The balloon cuts loose and drifts upward.

Elijah shrieks. I'm ten seconds from being that guy with the baby who ruins everyone's day.

"Now you're in for it," says a woman next to me.

"Let me try something," I say.

I look up at the ceiling, flap my right hand, and say,

"Bye-bye, balloon."

Elijah stops shrieking. He also looks up at the ceiling, flaps his right hand, and says, "Bye-bye, boo! Bye-bye, boo!"

We flap together.

"Bye-bye, boo!" we say.

Victory!

Long live Alternadad!

But such successes are fleeting and intermittent. A year later, when Elijah is two and a half, I find myself in the same store, only this time, for some reason, I've let Elijah walk next to me, out of the cart. He's running just beyond my grasp, sticking out his tongue, and licking the glass of the deli counter. I stop him, so he runs over to the olive bar and starts flinging cipolines. My expert parenting skills steer him away from that, and back to the deli counter, which he licks again. The guy behind the counter looks at me with the scorn he usually reserves for bands he doesn't like.

A woman walking by says, "That's terrible."

"I'm really sorry."

"Oh, no, I didn't mean it that way. I meant it's terrible for his health."

Everybody's a goddamn parenting expert! *You* try dealing with this kid every day, I want to say. He didn't have his nap. He's tired. He's off.

He's not usually like this.

There's an Italo Calvino story in which a guy is looking at the stars through a telescope and a sign appears in the cosmos. It reads I SAW YOU. But what did they see? he wonders. Did they see me at my best moment, or at my most embarrassing? How can I get them to see what I'm *really* like? I often feel exactly the same way about my parenting. Don't judge me, people, I want to say. You should have seen me at this time last year. I was the best dad in the whole wide world.

It was like we'd taken on a new roommate, except he didn't pay rent, he hogged the TV with his crappy shows, and we had to wipe his ass at least three times a day. On the plus side, he could sing "The Itsy Bitsy Spider" on cue and was very soft and cuddly. But the fact that we loved Elijah unconditionally didn't stop him from flying into rages for no reason and from breaking things all the time, on purpose. He continually distracted us. Our house degenerated into total filth.

This was hard for me. Before I was married, my apartments had always been extremely clean. I'd scrubbed my toilets once a week and cleaned my showerhead with a Q-tip. No magazine or CD was ever out of place. In my one concession to bachelor stereotype, I didn't make my bed, because I figured there's no point in making your bed when you sleep until one p.m. on the weekends and when the only guests you have are already drunk by the time they get to your house.

I realized that marriage would mean some concessions. But I didn't realize that I was marrying an adult female Pigpen, a woman who seemed to have a genetic penchant toward sloppy surroundings. It didn't take long before I started to complain. For instance, Regina's bras were hanging from every doorknob.

"I'm airing them out," she said.

"There's a great strategy I have for airing things out. It's called laundry."

I began to realize that Regina employed an odd household logic. It had only a little bit to do with her not wanting to do chores, because I was more than willing to split the work with her. Slowly, it occurred to me that, for psychological reasons, she really didn't *want* things to be clean, that she preferred for things to skirt the near edge of vile before she went on a massive bleach rampage.

"You may be neat," she would say. "But when I clean, I *really* clean."

"That's one way to put it."

I tried to do laundry, but I ruined a couple of her sweaters and shrunk a couple of T-shirts. This led to disagreements.

"Did I *ask* you to wash my clothes?" she said.

"They were piled by my side of the bed. And they were starting to smell."

"I was going to wash them eventually."

"When?"

"When I wanted to."

"Why don't you just clean as you go?"

"My mother has been saying that to me my entire life."

Ah. Now I understood.

"Just don't do my laundry. It makes me feel like you're criticizing me."

There was, apparently, no convincing my wife that I wasn't her mother. Maybe, I thought, I should just start wearing bright-red lipstick, playing in a church handbell choir, and watching movies on the Lifetime network without realizing that they'd been made in the mid-'80s. Then the prophecy would truly be fulfilled.

These conflicts trebled once Elijah toddled into the scene. We'd managed to get the roster of cats down to two, but there was still Hercules. Baby made four living creatures that would excrete anything, any time, anywhere. While cleaning up a pile of steaming cat vomit, I'd discover a smudge of human poop on the floor. On humid days, Regina would get down on all fours and start sniffing.

"What are you doing?"

"We need to take Hercules out more often. I think he peed on the rug."

Sometimes I did push-ups on the living-room rugs, so I was used to clumps of cat fur getting stuck to my lips. But this was too much.

"I'm going to vacuum. The floor is filthy."

"You can't. You'll wake the baby."

"OK, then, I'll do it tomorrow when he's awake."

"Uh-uh. The vacuum scares him. And besides, we'll have to clean up his toys first."

Regina wasn't employing this near-insane circular logic because she was lazy. She actually liked her house this way. And she always had. Would Elijah inherit her penchant toward foulness? It was quite possible. Then I realized that one of the reasons I loved her was because she was a slob. It was wrong, but also intrinsic and unshakable. She wouldn't have been Regina if she'd been neat. So she won.

Our home life was pretty much defined by Regina's garbage-can philosophy. If something was near a garbage can, or piled atop an obviously full garbage can, then it was officially in the garbage, even if it was actually on the floor. She figured that someone, meaning me, would eventually empty it. But she hadn't counted on my change of attitude. When I caught Elijah running through the house with a filthy tissue or sanitary-napkin wrapper, I knew there was nothing I could do, because he'd just find others. When he dropped food on the floor, I stopped cleaning it up, because I figured the dog would get to it eventually. It no longer bothered me when I caught him playing in a pile of my dirty boxer shorts.

We raised our son as a hog and sow would their offspring. I used Q-tips only for my ears, and I cleaned the toilets only when I started sticking to the seat. I found myself saying things like this: "Son, please put Mommy's vaginal-itch cream back in her drawer." But I didn't say it because I really meant it. I just thought it sounded funny.

One day, I transcribed this conversation as soon as it happened.

"Neal, did you wash your hands after changing Elijah's diaper?"

"Oh. I forgot."

"But you're feeding him dinner!"

"And?"

"You could have poop on your hands!"

"Oh. I hadn't thought of that."

Regina, who routinely ignored dust balls the size of grapefruits, was nonetheless terrified that Elijah's health would suddenly and inexplicably fail. He was never allowed to eat something that would compromise his "development." She monitored me when I unpacked after coming home from the grocery store. I got lectured sternly for buying vanilla soymilk instead of unflavored, or for choosing luncheon meat that contained a hint of nitrates. One day, I returned with a bunch of bananas.

"I told you to get *organic* bananas!" she said.

"No way. I'm *not* paying ninety-nine cents a pound for bananas."

Her body tensed with excited fear. She looked concerned for her child, but in the way Naomi Watts was concerned for her child in *The Ring*.

"Neal?"

"What?"

"Do you want him to get cancer?"

"Yes, Regina. *I want him to get cancer.*"

Still, Regina and I were proud of Elijah's diet, which was undoubtedly the most nutritious and most balanced of any child's in the world. We learned that if you don't expose a child to candy, fast food, or soda, then he doesn't want candy, fast food, or soda. If the TV was on, Elijah was in the room, and a fast-food commercial appeared, we turned the TV off. We made an exception if the commercial featured a talking animal because Elijah loved talking animals and if we denied him talking animals he threw a fit. Regina taught him to identify the McDonald's golden arches, which he was attracted to anyway because they often hovered above a colorful playground. But she cleverly flipped the bill on him. *Super Size Me* had horrified us, particularly the stuff about child obesity.

"Do you see that M?" she said.

"Uh-huh," he said.

"That means there's yucky food."

"Yucky fu?"

"That's right."

"Jah no go yucky fu."

"Good boy."

In Elijah's first eighteen months, we taught him to like carrots, peaches, lima beans, green beans, tomatoes, peas, nitrate-free turkey dogs, ham, cheese, bread, Bearitos all-corn organic tortilla chips, lamb vindaloo, Chinese barbecued pork, tangerines, apples, grapes, grain-fed hamburger, salmon, apricots, raisins, udon noodles, free-range chicken breasts, edamame, corn, homemade pizza, spaghetti, beets, sweet potatoes, mashed potatoes, and approximately ten varieties of lettuce. But it wasn't all beets and suffering. We also fed him pancakes, albeit whole-wheat ones, and he got to pour his own syrup out of a little ceramic elephant that we bought for a dollar. When we took him out, and one of us ordered French fries, he got French fries. For snacks, he had something called "Cheddar Bunnies," which were organic, and "Fruit Leathers," (also organic), and all-juice popsicles. Later, we added pretzels to the mix, though he didn't like them any more or less than he did asparagus or avocados.

Elijah was a very healthy child: He didn't have a sick moment in his first 500 days alive. Perhaps his daily surroundings caused him to build up resistance to diseases that children in more sanitary environments didn't meet until it was too late. Or maybe his mother's seemingly wacky holistic-health practices actually worked.

Eventually, though, baby's first fever arrived. Elijah started running a temperature one night, and it carried over into the next afternoon. He was whiny and listless, whereas he was usually whiny and energetic. Regina left me alone with him for the afternoon. She was out of her soy creamer and had to go on an emergency store run. When did goddamn soymilk become such a big deal? I thought. Enough with it already!

I was sitting in my big blue chair, watching the weather radar for signs of impending moisture. Elijah whimpered over to me. I picked him up. He opened his mouth. Out came a sluice of bright-yellow vomit. I looked down at my shirt. It was covered in his puke, which was flecked with little chunks of tangerine. I hadn't seen anything like it since the last time I'd been in the bathroom at Emo's.

"Oh, no," I said. "Oh, God."

I went into Elijah's room and did triage, tearing off his jumper, while still stroking his hair and talking kindly, and wiping off any extraneous goop. Only then did I remove my own shirt. It smelled sour and old. I'd earned my first fatherhood medal. The phone rang. Regina was on the line. I'd already handled the situation and was more or less prepared to deal with anything else that came up, but I asked her to come home anyway. It was nice to have a partner in these situations. Besides, she really needed to see the puke, which was delightfully gross.

When she got home, we determined that Elijah needed to go to the doctor. We'd originally chosen our pediatrician because we'd liked the snug, homey feel of his office, which was tucked away in a far corner of the hospital complex where Elijah was born. Two months into Elijah's life, Dr. Rivas's office took some water damage. He moved to a place called Northwest Pediatrics, which was located in a corporate "wellness" park far north of downtown, where the Texas Hill Country had once stood.

We admired Northwest Pediatrics on first glance. Everything was so shiny. On the wall was a cartoon mural of Godzilla rampaging through downtown Austin. The doctors had accumulated impressive collections of Beanie Babies and superhero action figures, though they kept them behind glass. A television showed cartoons, and there were toys and a nice fish tank.

But the day Elijah entered the vomitorium I realized that something was a little rotten in that pediatric-themed environment.

"It's an emergency!" I said to the receptionist. "My son is burning!"

"We're not seeing patients today," she said.

"Of course you are. You're a doctor's office!"

"We're having a toxic chemical problem and we don't want the children inhaling them."

"A toxic *what*?"

"Chemicals."

"Who the hell lets toxic chemicals into a family-care practice?"

"They were stripping the floor this morning."

"My son could be *dying*!"

"We might be able to see him tomorrow afternoon."

Within an hour, we had Elijah at the office of the closest family practitioner, a slim, unassuming man with a fishy handshake. He quickly prescribed flu medicine so strong it could bliss out an entire suburban high school for a week. Elijah was cured, seemingly within minutes.

Later at home, after Elijah had fallen asleep, Regina got on the Internet.

"I think that doctor gave him twice the dose he should have."

"How could you possibly know that?"

"I found a website that talks about appropriate dosage."

Sometimes, the Internet drove Regina a little bit mad with its readily available health information. Still, she was correct that this doctor seemed trigger-happy with the drugs. I've always thought it's handy to know a doctor like that, particularly if you're going to go on a long plane flight and you want some Xanax. There are doctors you go to for actual health care, and then there are doctors you go to for the drugs. A few months later, when I decided I needed to go on antidepressants but didn't want to go through actual psychiatric screening, I knew who to call.

We also had a sleep philosophy. It was mutually beneficial to us and to the kid. In fact, Regina was even more dogmatic about sleep than she was about food. I put up no resistance; I liked sleep, too. So Regina got a book called *Healthy Sleep Habits, Happy Child.* It suggested that we put our child on a "sleep schedule." Elijah needed to get used to going to bed at the same time every night; we would determine this bedtime.

He slept in the room with us, in his Pack 'N Play, for the first five months of his life. For three of those months, he slept sitting up, in his car seat. Then he started sleeping in the crib in his own room. Eventually, his natural "sleep pattern" began to emerge. We determined that he got tired around 7:30 p.m. Totally by coincidence, this pattern coincided with the time of day by which we'd had just about enough of parenting, and it was also more or less when the stuff we liked on TV started.

He was about fourteen months old when we started putting him down at a regular bedtime. He cried a lot. It was painful for us, particularly that first night, because he was obviously confused. I went into the back of the house and put on my headphones. Regina paced outside his door and bit her fingernails down to their nubs. But we wouldn't give in to Elijah's demands, no matter how sad or sincere. This wasn't a hungry cry, a sick or injured cry, or a cry of fear. Obviously, if he were hungry, ill, afraid, or getting eaten by a giant snake, we'd go to him. But this was an I-want-to-hang-out-with-Mommy-and-Daddy-while-they're-watching–*Queer Eye for the Straight Guy* (which was, at the time, still in its novel phase) cry. He needed sleep and we needed a break. This was better for all of us.

By the third night of the schedule, he stopped crying when we put him down, and he went to sleep happily, babbling to himself.

Bedtime, as the book had predicted, had become something reliable that he could trust. The penance for our relatively child-free evenings was that Elijah woke up early in the morning. Eamon, the three-year-old down the street, slept every day until 8:30 or nine, then watched TV for half an hour, and then woke his parents. Now *those* were lucky people. We found ourselves praying for the day when Elijah, and, by extension, we, could sleep until noon without compunction or difficulty. As it was now, we considered ourselves rested if he slept past 6:30.

We often had to choose between sleep and fun. For instance, going to bed at ten p.m. wasn't an option, because *The Daily Show* starts at ten p.m. (eleven Eastern and Pacific). On nights when I thought I might want to have sex, I waived *The Daily Show* or told Regina it was a rerun. I always compared unfavorably, in her mind, to Jon Stewart.

Sometimes I eschewed the TV completely and went to late-night rock shows for "research." Occasionally, I would persuade Regina to join me, saying, "We are not going to be those people who stop going to rock shows just because we have a kid." I could sacrifice only so much.

R: What time does the band go on?

N: Probably twelve-thirty or so.

R: Twelve-thirty! That's late!

N: No it's not! That's rock 'n' roll!

R: You don't understand. I have to get up with the baby in *six hours.*

N: So go to bed early tomorrow night.

R: I hate going to bed early.

N: So do I. But we have to sleep sometime.

As Elijah grew older, the schedule became more difficult to maintain, but we kept 7:30 as a target time, stretching it to eight or 8:30 as the days grew longer. For a fine example of our ever-evolving getting-ready-for-bed process, we turn to an evening just after the end of Daylight Savings Time, 2004.

First, as we changed Elijah's diaper, we needed to keep him distracted and entertained. On that night, I dredged up "Frère Jacques" from my own boyhood, improvising lyrics for something called "The Diaper Song" that I made up on the spot. It was amazing how easily childhood songs came back to me, as though they'd been frozen when I'd hit puberty and had been waiting for the proper moment to thaw. The Diaper Song went:

> *Change your diaper*
> *Change your diaper*
> *Full of poop*
> *Full of poop*
> *Gonna take your pants off*
> *Gonna take your pants off*
> *Ding dang dong*
> *Ding dang dong*

Elijah loved that. Then it was time for pajamas, which required "The Pajama Song." This was a tune that Regina and I had been using for a while. It consisted of the word "pajamas" being sung over and over again in a lilting voice. After that came story time.

We actually gave him four books that night, though two or three were the norm. Unfortunately, they weren't books I liked. In fact, they were some of my least favorite. But we'd begun to realize that we couldn't control his taste. As hip as we tried to make Elijah, he was still a toddler, and toddlers can like some pretty lame things.

That night's first offering was an insipid softbound thing called *Learning with Teddy*. Regina claimed it helped Elijah learn the important skill of counting apples, but I suspected she favored it because it had been a gift from her mother. Next, I cringed when *The Polar*

Express came out, mumbling something about "pseudo-nostalgic white Middle American wish-fulfillment fantasy," but Regina said, "Just let him look at the pictures of the reindeer."

She and I agreed, however, on the third book, *Look and Find Elmo*, a repugnant *Where's Waldo?* ripoff that has the furry red cult figure searching all over Sesame Street for the source of some mysterious music, with side trips to find a strawberry sundae and a rubber duckie wearing a Viking helmet. Elijah, on the other hand, loved *Look and Find Elmo*, to the point where we eventually had to hide it for a few weeks at a time to save us the agony of reading it to him twice a day, every day.

As I slogged through *Learning with Teddy*, *The Polar Express*, and *Look and Find Elmo*, I longed for the days when I'd controlled Elijah's reading material. Under my watch, we'd done *Hand, Hand, Fingers, Thumb*, or any Sandra Boynton book, *Barnyard Dance* in particular. As Elijah grew older, there were happy days when he picked *Are You My Mother?*, or *One Fish, Two Fish, Red Fish, Blue Fish*, or *Sally Goes to the Beach*, or *The Charles Addams Mother Goose*, or a charmingly illustrated version of *The House That Jack Built*. Also acceptable, though not several days in a row, were *Clarence and the Purple Horse Bounce into Town*, *Who Is the Beast?*, and a strange book about a girl who rides a giant cat to the place where the streams are full of milk and there is a scratching-post forest.

The most puzzling books of all were by Richard Scarry. I don't know if anyone really understands what goes on in Busytown. It's a place where a pig drives around in a pickle, a policeman talks on his "motorcycle phone" and has a bathtub for a sidecar, a fox flies a "bratwurst balloon" that is seemingly powered by mustard, and all anyone else seems to do all day is put out fires and eat doughnuts. The strangest Richard Scarry book I've yet encountered is *Miss Honey's Busy Day*. Miss Honey, a female bear, lives with Bruno, another bear, in an indeterminate relationship. They sleep in the same room, but in separate beds. She makes him breakfast and then he drives *her,* in his "ice-cream truck," to school, where she teaches. Later he calls her at work to see how she's doing. After school, he picks her up and brings her a flower. There's every indication that Bruno is a child, and that Miss Honey is his mother, yet they also appear to be dating. Perhaps something got lost in translation across the Atlantic.

Certain books got one viewing, then immediately went into the far reaches of Elijah's closet, to be forgotten and hopefully never found. Paramount among these was *The Little Baby Snoogle-Fleejer.* When former president Jimmy Carter passes away, I hope for his sake and the sake of his family that none of the ceremonies mention this book, which he wrote and I assume forced his daughter, Amy, to illustrate at gunpoint. Amy works in muted and blurry watercolors, and she likes to paint amorphous blobs that are distinguished from the muddy background only by the fact that they have eyes. Her art is equivalent to that of an eight-year-old in the "special" classes, though Jimmy's writing isn't much better. His story involves a lonely little boy who befriends a sea monster. The boy's mother requires an operation but, fortunately, the sea monster has access to buried treasure. There's a reason Jimmy Carter won the Nobel Peace Prize and not the literary one.

But even *The Little Baby Snoogle-Fleejer* would have been better than the fourth book Elijah picked that night: *Puppy Songs,* a truly horrible thing that one of our neighbors had given him for his birthday. The "book" worked like this: You touched one of four buttons, and one of four songs played this terrible tinkly music off a microchip. Over, and over, and over again we endured "B-I-N-G-O," "Do Your Ears Hang Low," and "Oh, Where, Oh Where, Has My Little Dog Gone?," while Elijah rocked from side to side, mouth wide in glee.

"This is not a book!" I said. "It's an abomination!"

"I know," said Regina. "But he likes it."

Once we got his teeth brushed, we encountered stalling tactics as the night proceeded. Elijah wanted his night-light on. He wanted it off. He wanted a pillow. He wanted a different pillow. He wanted a blankie or a different blankie. He heard a "strange sound" and got scared. He said he'd pooped himself but he actually hadn't. And he always needed a song.

For months, Regina had sung him to sleep with a ditty about our cat Gabby, to the tune of the Winnie-the-Pooh theme. He loved this song:

> *Gabby the cat*
> *Gabby the cat*
> *Skinny little scrawny little*
> *Gabby the cat*

She switched to "Do Re Mi" from *The Sound of Music,* much to my objections, because I naturally blanch at anything related to Rodgers and Hammerstein.

Then it was my turn. I sang him a lullaby that I'd learned from Sandra Boynton's *Snoozers* book, with a tune that I made up:

> *Go to sleep my zoodle*
> *My fibblety-fitsy foo . . .*

The song ended, and then he was down. I came out of his room and jerked my thumb upward like an umpire calling someone out at the plate. Regina had already lost herself in ostensibly grown-up TV.

"Freedom," she said. "At last."

Fifteen minutes passed. We longingly turned our gaze toward Elijah's room.

"I miss him," she said.

"Me too."

"He's such a pookie."

"Yeah."

"He's my special pookie wookie ookie bear."

"Hey! I thought I was your special pookie wookie ookie bear."

"You're my *other* special pookie wookie ookie bear."

"Oh, good."

A pause.

"Regina?"

"Yes, pookie?"

"Can we *please* not watch the Sci-Fi Channel?"

ELEVEN

A Good School Is Hard to Find

April 2004

lijah, now fully a year and a half old, was becoming harder to control. He began to take on Mowgli-like qualities. The cats sometimes jumped on the coffee table to lick up crumbs. Elijah did this as well. At least once a day, we had to stop him from perching on the back of the sofa. Teacake, by now an old cat with an encyclopedia of exasperatingly stupid habits, had decided he only wanted to drink water from the bathtub faucet. One day I walked by the bathroom to find Elijah on all fours, licking the faucet and making slurping sounds.

Another afternoon, I heard Regina say this: "Elijah, what are you *doing*?" I went into the bedroom to behold my son humping a large yellow stuffed bear. This was a habit of Hercules' that Elijah had obviously picked up on.

We pulled him off and gave him a lecture.

"Elijah," I said. "Hercules is bad when he humps the bear. You're a boy and you can't go around humping things."

"Li-Jah no hump ba?" he said.

"That's right," said Regina. "You don't hump the bear."

This lesson was hard learned. Over the next month, we had to utter the following phrases:

"Don't hump the pillow!"

"Don't hump the chair leg!"

"Elijah. Do NOT hump Teacake!"

In bed one night, Regina said, "What are we going to do? Elijah is a humping machine."

"Just like his old man."

"The other day, I caught him with his diaper off in front of the television. He was playing with himself."

"Like I said."

"Right."

"He's little. This is normal."

Still, it was becoming clear that we'd been wrong when we'd characterized the boy, early on, as mellow. We began to realize that from here on, days with him would be difficult. He was smart and funny and was developing charm, but he was also easily bored. We liked Elijah a lot. We just knew that it would be a lot easier for him to like us if we didn't have to take care of him twenty-four hours a day.

A nanny wouldn't make any sense. For one thing, our schedules were so flexible that having someone else around would seem frivolous, not to mention cramped. The house was small and Regina and I were sharing a room in the back, my desk in one corner, her easel in another. Also, nannies were expensive. Despite our penchant for yuppie foodstuffs, or maybe partly because of it, we didn't have a lot of extra money. Regina had started teaching classes at the local community college, which should have helped with the bills. But because of that, I was watching Elijah nearly two full days a week while she was teaching, and that was taking away from my own work time, so it wasn't really worth it for her to teach in the first place. The old Daddy Time and Mommy Time roles were dissolving.

Day care seemed like the only real solution, but we were terribly conflicted. Elijah was only eighteen months old, and we were already considering sending him to "school." I didn't remember kids going to school at that age when I was a kid. You started kindergarten at five. Maybe, the year before, you went somewhere to play with clay a few mornings a week. There seemed like an inordinate amount of cultural pressure to educate your kids early and often.

Then again, Elijah didn't really have any friends. There was one adorable little girl named Mia, whose parents we'd met in the airport. Regina even got along with the girl's mother, who was more obsessed with organic food than she was. But they lived across town, and they were only one family. The other kids we knew were in day care all day, or they were infants. Elijah was cautious at the playground and didn't make friends that way. The fact was that we no longer felt able to provide him with everything he needed. So we started looking.

There aren't a lot of reliable day-care guides, especially if you're not that familiar with the town in which you live. The places that *do* have websites usually feature a generic "mission statement" about respecting your kid's individual needs, accompanied by a photograph of a kid at an art table. Internet bulletin boards, while they can occasionally prove useful, are also notorious dens of lunatic crankery. Regina looked in the Yellow Pages.

"There are like a million churches," she said.

"I don't want my son going to a church school."

"Come on. We're not going to send him to a Promise Keepers academy."

"It doesn't matter. There will still be Jesus lessons."

"What do you care? You don't believe in God."

"Neither do you."

"That's not true. I'm just not sure."

"Right."

"So I guess Jewish schools are out, too."

"Not necessarily."

"That's kind of hypocritical."

"Not at all. At a Jewish school, he'd learn a different language. Plus the food is better at holidays."

We compromised. On our first day, we went to a Methodist church. We got a little tour of the day-care center. The director was perfectly nice, but I balked at the schedule, which involved nothing more than snacks, diaper changing, naps, and, yes, chapel. Also the décor was very brown-paneled and revealed that the congregation had probably peaked around 1975. The half-day price was about $260 per month, the cheapest we could find anywhere, and that's pretty much what the place was worth.

"No more churches," I said.

"They're not all like that. My mom's church has a really nice day care."

"Perhaps. But your mom lives in Nashville. That doesn't really help us."

Next we went to Temple Beth Israel, which was nestled in a sylvan little grove across a creek wash from our dentist's office. We had to get buzzed through security, which really disturbed me. Security hadn't been necessary when I'd attended temple regularly as a kid, but I guess I hadn't been around many synagogues since September 11. Once we made it through the doors, though, we beheld paradise. The classrooms were enormous, brand-new, and ridiculously clean, full of art supplies and guinea pigs and all manner of book and toy. The walls were covered with student-made paper cutouts. There was a kosher kitchen with stainless-steel appliances.

We got shown around by the school's director. "You're in luck," she said. "It's song time."

In the school's main foyer, all the kids were gathered in a circle. A female cantor, who was short, dark-haired, and adorable, sat among them with a guitar. They were singing.

Mayim mayim mayim mayim (clap!)
O mayim besason!
Mayim mayim mayim mayim . . .

"What's this song about?" Regina said.

"Something about water," I said.

The song took me back to my days in Hebrew school; I'd actually hated them, so I returned my focus to the present. Now they were singing *Oseh shalom bimromav . . . Hu ya-aseh shalom . . .* , and my mind went back to Jewish camp, which I'd also hated. One day the rabbi had sat down at the piano and I'd seen his butt crack, and that had been about it for Jewish camp and me.

"These kids are so *cute*," Regina said. "I love this school."

A parent was walking past us.

"Don't even bother sending your kid anywhere else," she said.

"I won't," I said. "This place is the best."

We went into the director's office.

"Sign us up!" I said.

"We have a bit of a waiting list."

"That's OK. We want to send him here."

"Where would we be on the waiting list?" Regina said.

The director looked at a heavily scribbled-on piece of paper.

"Right now, you'd be about sixty-fifth."

"Oh."

"You should try the JCC. They have a really nice school."

They did. And we were even lower on the waiting list there. To add to the torture, the kids were all running around in their adorable Purim costumes.

"We would have had to put him on the waiting list before he was born," I said.

"Who knew?" Regina said.

There were other schools on our list. We went to one, called the Children's Discovery Center, that several people had recommended because it had a very loose "play-based" philosophy. Inside the room where Elijah would have started, there were at least twelve kids running around only in their diapers, in a room the size of our kitchen. We had a small kitchen. It was a scene, to my eyes, of near-Dickensian squalor. We rejected the Children's Discovery Center—far too quickly, as it turned out.

We went to another neighborhood school. The facilities looked like they hadn't been painted since the 1960s. Splintered wood was everywhere. Elijah would have been educated in a shed at the back of the property along with a dozen companions. A man in dirty coveralls was leaning on a merry-go-round toy that also hadn't been painted since the 1960s.

"Who's that?" I said to the woman who was showing us around.

"Oh, that's Leo. He does maintenance around here. We just let him wander in and out whenever he wants. Isn't that right, Leo?" she said.

Leo cackled toothlessly.

"THAT'S RIGHT!" he said.

In the car, Regina said, "It's sure not Temple Beth Israel."

The temple had spoiled us. By comparison, every place we saw looked like the slums of Rio. We found ourselves briefly charmed by a Montessori school, which was having a science fair on the day we went in; but that waiting list, too, would open up sometime in 2007. We were running out of Yellow Pages entries.

One afternoon we drove up to a little house framed with blue-painted wood in a neighborhood that was a lot like ours, only better. It was part of a chain that seemed to prey mostly on the offspring of hospital employees and people who worked in suburban office parks; that's where most of the schools were. But this one seemed to float free of excessive corporate influences.

We had an appointment with the director, a tall, lovely young woman whose nametag read "Miss Nikki." The school seemed pretty nice. Each room was large enough, and Miss Nikki introduced us to the lunch lady, who had been cooking at the school for twenty years. For some reason, Regina and I took this as a sign of community and stability. Miss Nikki discussed the school sweetly, but without overselling. A little girl ran up to her, and Miss Nikki ruffled her hair.

"My daughter," she said.

Elijah pointed at the window.

"Sah! Sah!"

"Outside," said Miss Nikki. "That's right."

We were charmed.

"What's your waiting list like?" I said.

"We'll have an opening very soon."

"Do you take checks?"

A few weeks later, before Elijah was supposed to start, I called the school to make sure everything was in order.

"May I speak with Miss Nikki?" I said.

"Miss Nikki doesn't work here anymore."

"Where did she go?"

"She went somewhere else."

"My son was supposed to start next week."

"We don't have any openings right now."

I gave her our name. She put me on hold. A few minutes later, she got back on the line.

"We have no record of your existence."

Behind the door stands the law.

"We paid money!"

The woman didn't budge. I was indignant, and also out my $200 deposit. So I called corporate headquarters to complain.

"They had a spot for us!"

"There's nothing I can do, sir."

"It's so hard to find day care."

"I understand, sir."

"In fact, maybe I can get one of my journalist friends to write an article about exactly how hard it is, and he can feature your organization."

An hour later, I got a call. A spot had opened up for us at the Montessori school after all. They apologized for the trouble. But we'd have to come back in and fill out the paperwork again.

We went back the next day. Regina did the clerical work. I went into the toddler room with Elijah, where he would now be spending twenty-four hours a week.

"This is Elijah!" I said.

The teacher, who didn't look older than twenty-two, was sitting by herself in a corner. She nodded sullenly. There were seven children in the room. All of them had runny noses. The kids also didn't really appear to be doing anything.

"Do you have activities for them?"

"They like to go outside and look at the flowers," said the teacher.

Elijah moped off to a cubbyhole and poked at a toy that was missing most of its components. I'd seen him look more stimulated at the hardware store. An adorable little girl came up to me with a book. She looked at me with pleading orphan eyes. I began to read to her.

Within two minutes, all the kids were sticking to me like puppies that had been denied their mother's teats. Did anyone ever read to them? The teacher slowly got up from her chair and came over. She started reading to the kids as well, like it had never occurred to her before. Regina entered the room.

"Let's get the hell out of here," I said.

We lost the deposit, but it was almost worth the relief we felt at having saved Elijah from spending time in a place like that. So it would be a few more months until he started day care, I said. So what?

Regina looked mournful.

"I have to do my art! I'm just getting started again . . ."

That night, I looked at the paintings Regina had been working on.

She was using wallpaper patterns from the 1950s as backdrops. In the foregrounds were images of women, bound at the hands and feet, trapped inside floating bubbles. Most of the women were headless; when they did have heads, their mouths were gagged.

"They're about what society expects from women, both before and after motherhood," Regina said.

"I can see that."

We really needed to find a school for the boy.

TWELVE

Don't You Be My Neighbor

May–June 2004

O ne Friday night around eleven p.m., I was sitting in my dark-blue leather recliner happily watching a Netflix DVD of *Dirty Pretty Things*, a movie about unscrupulous businessmen who harvest the organs of desperate immigrants. There were some noises outside. I looked out my window. Two guys were kicking the crap out of another guy on my front lawn. There was a white Cadillac parked at the curb. A woman got out.

"Ramon!" she said. "I told you to leave him alone. He didn't do nothing!"

The victim got up and stumbled farther into my yard, dragging his left side. The other guys followed, knocked him over, and resumed booting him in the kidneys. I opened the window.

"Get off my lawn, goddammit!"

They looked up for a second, and then started into the guy again. He rolled away from them, across the lawn, until he was in the flowerbed directly under Elijah's bedroom window.

I closed the window and bolted the door. Regina lurched out of the bedroom in her nightgown.

"What's going on?"

"Stay away from the windows."

"Are you serious?"

By the time the cops arrived, there was no one around for them to arrest. I explained to them that the white Cadillac often idled on the street corner. Sometimes women would get out and walk down the street toward the apartment complex two blocks away. Sometimes men would get into the car and it would drive away. A few hours later, it would return to pick up the women who were getting off their shift.

"Just be sure to call us if there are more problems," the cops said.

"Don't you worry. I will."

Suddenly, I was the nosy neighbor who calls the police when there are "suspicious characters" about. Since I'd become a dad, I no longer found seediness charming, except for brief bursts in controlled situations like, for instance, a fight at a dive bar many miles away from my house. But this was too close for me. If three guys are fighting over a hooker under your little son's bedroom window, then it's time to clean up the neighborhood.

We'd been in the house only a few days before we realized that the neighborhood had problems. Several days in a row, we got knocks on the front door and opened it to find guys who looked like the pictures on the cards the police send you when a registered sex offender moves into your neighborhood. These guys weren't registered sex offenders, as far as we knew.

"Is Barry here?" a guy said.

"No. He moved."

"Do you know when he's coming back?"

"He's not coming back."

"Can I ask you a question?"

"*What?*"

"Could you help me out with five or ten bucks?"

I tried to retain a shred of tolerance.

"Man, I wish I could. But times are tough, you know, and we've got a kid on the way . . ."

We didn't move to Austin to get away from the problems of a big city, precisely, but we also didn't expect to find them there. Our neighborhood was across the highway from the site of the old municipal airport, which had closed a few years before we moved in. It was officially called "The Harmon Triangle," because its main throughway was Harmon Avenue, and because it was wedged into a few square blocks among three major thoroughfares, one of which was the Interstate. As such, it had always been considered a way station to the airport. But the old airport site was about to undergo a big "mixed-use" redevelopment, including a children's hospital, and this would cause a boom in our property value. All this we knew in advance, and the redevelopment was moving forward. A few other things slipped under the radar.

First, the neighborhood had been home, until quite recently, to the Rio Motel and the associated Club Rio, which, in 1999, Texas State Attorney General John Cornyn called "a haven for illegal criminal activity." The motel had once been a Best Western and a Travelodge, and then in the 1980s Club Rio became popular with cops and pool sharks. By the time it closed, though, it had witnessed the capture of a murder suspect, several crack busts, a lot of gun complaints, more than 300 arrests, and a rash of bloody mattresses tossed into the alley. The neighborhood behind the motel—my future neighborhood—played host to wasted partiers and drug addicts, who wandered the streets all night long. That problem was considered solved by the time we arrived. The motel was now in the hands of a responsible owner, and no one in the neighborhood complained about it anymore. But they did spend a lot of time complaining about the First Workers' Day Labor Center.

In 2000, the city announced that First Workers would move from its downtown location onto the highway access road that abutted the neighborhood where I would later buy property. This would be

Austin's only official day-labor site. People in the neighborhood were worried about who this would bring in, and were also angry that the city hadn't consulted them before making the announcement.

Unfortunately, the most politically active man in the neighborhood also headed up a more-or-less racist group called Texans for Fair Immigration and hosted a weekly Tuesday night anti-immigrant cable-access show. He formed a neighborhood association as an outpost of his extracurricular interests. After the city announced the moving of the day-labor site, he took to showing up at city-council meetings to protest, doing such politically subtle things as wearing a toilet seat around his neck and saying, "Our neighborhood is going down the toilet." A local documentarian made a movie about the "struggle" to open the day-labor center, called *Los Trabajadores*. You can guess which side she favored. The movie aired on PBS in the spring of 2002.

If I'd been watching TV then, a documentary that accurately depicted my future neighbors as virulent bigots, job-starved immigrants, and sketchy ex-cons might have persuaded me to look for a house somewhere else. But when Regina and I arrived in the Harmon Triangle, there were few signs of conflict or danger. Our street was comprised of wood-frame houses built in the 1940s. They were all between 800 and 1,300 square feet, on modest-sized lots, and mostly in good condition. All our neighbors, at least the ones we met, were warm and friendly and welcoming. It seemed like a peaceful little patch.

Two weeks after we moved, we went to a meeting at a low-lying brick building down the street that rented itself out to itinerant churches and various branches of the recovery movement. Six people came to the meeting. It was presided over by the only remaining officer of the association, a nursery-school teacher about our age who lived catty-corner to us. She was nice and smart and well-meaning, but the struggle with the city had obviously made her tired and nervous. The first agenda item came up.

"We're thinking of having a lawyer write a letter," she said.

"To whom?" I said. "What about?"

"We want to threaten the residents at the apartments down the street. If they think the INS is coming, maybe they'll stop patronizing the Day Labor Center."

Regina and I looked at each other.

"What Day Labor Center?"

That's when I got the story, with special emphasis on how the city had treated the neighborhood in bad faith. Still, I didn't like what was being said. When I'd lived in Chicago, I'd written articles advocating the rights of immigrants to live their lives free of hassle. In particular, I'd crusaded for justice for Mexican street-cart corn vendors whom the city was trying to harass out of existence. I was a liberal, dammit. A friend of the dispossessed.

"I don't know about the rest of you," I said. "But I am *not* going to be party to calling the INS on my neighbors."

The small-scale xenophobia of years past clung to the neighborhood like a used bandage, but it was obvious that demographics had shifted; no one, including the woman who presided over the meeting, really bought into that program anymore. That was the last-ever gathering of the Eye-35 Neighbors Association.

On our walk home, Regina said, "What the hell kind of a neighborhood did we move into?"

"I don't want to talk about it."

Across the street from us, two doors down, there was a little house. On the day we moved in, we saw a bunch of dudes hanging out on the front porch drinking beer. They were pretty noisy. But I found it charming. People drinking beer on a porch in Texas: It was just like *King of the Hill!*

The house's official occupant was a Vietnam veteran named Al. His parents had once owned the place, but they were long gone; the deed now belonged to Al's nephew, who lived in Colorado. Al had a thick gray handlebar mustache. When he walked by our house drinking from his paper-bagged bottle of Wild Turkey at nine a.m., he always said hello to us. In previous years, he'd been an habitué of Club Rio, and much of that club's culture had migrated to his house. Women came in and out at all hours. There were always cars pulling up to the house, including the neighborhood madam's white Cadillac.

As the months crept along, the little house grew less charming. We got to know Al's next-door neighbors, Mikki and Jennings, and their son, Eamon, the kid whose favorite band was Devo. Little Eamon was always asking his parents when the "scary men" were going to go away. They had to put up a bamboo fence because they were tired of watching people defecate in Al's backyard next door. Al's house didn't have plumbing or electricity.

Early one evening, around the same time that I caught the guys fighting over the hooker in my front yard, I was in the back of the house, pretending to work. Regina barged in.

"Something crazy is going on at Al's house! These four women just pulled up in a car."

"This goddamn neighborhood," I said.

I looked out the front window. The women were on Al's lawn, screaming at him. One of them picked up a white metal porch chair and hurled it. Blood spread across Al's forehead.

My next-door neighbor Scott, a semi-professional weight lifter who I'd never seen raise his temperament above placid, came roaring out of his house waving a silver-plated .45. He charged across the street, gun in the air, shouting, "Get the hell out of here . . . NOW!"

"Call the cops," I said to Regina.

By the time the police arrived, the situation was over. The women had left. The cops lectured Scott, who sat sheepishly on the curb. His wife, Kathleen, was making relentless fun of him:

"Who do you think you are? Michael Douglas in *Falling Down*?"

I was starting to feel like that myself; it didn't seem right to me that we had to live in the middle of all this crap. Scott had bought into the neighborhood when jets still roared overhead eighteen hours a day and when Rio Motel crackheads parked their cars in front of his house on Sunday night. He'd earned the right to a peaceful life, yet *he* was the one getting into trouble with the cops. I knew that it didn't have to be like this.

The neighborhoods where I'd lived in Chicago were home to more than 100 languages, spoken by people from five continents. It had been a little noisy sometimes, occasionally I had to shoo ancient Eastern European witch-hags from picking through our stuff on the back porch, and there was gang graffiti on every mailbox. But I'd never felt danger like I did in the Harmon Triangle. Our neighborhood in Philadelphia had, admittedly, been rougher than this, but if all you can say about your neighborhood is that it's not as bad as Philly, then you're using the wrong scale of comparison.

No one in the Harmon Triangle had dared attempt anything political for years. But I had the naïvely progressive idea, born of watching community groups succeed in Chicago and from reading Saul Alinsky's *Rules for Radicals,* that things could get done. I'd met our state representative, Elliott Naishtat, at the Texas Book Festival a couple of years before. He was a liberal New York Jew adrift in the Texas House. Admittedly, he had grander concerns, like trying to stop the state government, which Molly Ivins always referred to as the "national laboratory of bad ideas," from canceling all public-health funding. But he was technically my representative, so I made an appointment. Jennings and I went down to the capital. We told our state rep about the situation, making sure to emphasize that the crime and degradation were making it hard for our neighborhood's hardworking immigrant families to realize the American dream. Our struggle was theirs, we told him.

I guess he had some power, because the next day, I got a call from our "district representative" at the Austin Police Department.

"You should come to us if you have problems," he said.

"Well. You're here now. Help us."

A week later, ten of my neighbors were in my living room, along with two representatives of the police department, who sat in two of my dining-room chairs. I offered them each a Shiner Bock. They said they couldn't drink on duty.

Our district rep was a square-jawed linebacker type named Crumrine. He was only a couple of inches taller than I am, yet it seemed like he was twice my size. I couldn't decide if those were chest muscles or a bulletproof vest. Either way, I had a feeling that he would be able to get things done. We filled the cops in on the specifics. I told them that our neighborhood had been given a bad rap in the past, but that things were different now. This wasn't an anti-Mexican immigrant gambit. No one wants a dangerous abandoned house on the block, and most of the people in Al's house were white or black, in equal proportion.

The police gave us a bunch of fliers and pamphlets and other police effluvia. Most important, they gave us their business cards. But they declined my second offer of a Shiner Bock.

I kept a steady, suspicious eye on Al's house, taking care not to talk to anyone except Al, who still passed by our porch most days. He seemed like a victim of these people, rather than the instigator, so I didn't bother confronting him. The rest of the cast of characters was constantly rotating. I didn't want any of them to know I was spearing the drive to shut the house down, in case they were revenge-minded. One morning a couple of weeks after our meeting, I looked out my front window and saw a little girl playing in an abandoned shopping cart. She was school-age, and this was the middle of a school day. I called the police. They showed up fifteen minutes later.

They found that this girl and her sister were living in the house with their mother and two dozen other people. The mother turned tricks on a dirty mattress in the back bedroom while the kids watched. The police called Children and Family Services, who opened a case on the mother but let her keep the kids on the conditions that she'd put them in school and that she'd get her own apartment.

Over the next month, my neighbors and I called the cops on Al's house every day. The police got other city departments involved. The Water Department slapped Al with fines. The power company warned him to stop poaching electricity from city lines. The building inspector didn't like what he saw, either. The house got condemned. Al and his friends kept living there. The police contacted Al's nephew in Colorado and told him that he'd better sell the house, and pay the fines, now. He wouldn't get any money if the county seized his property.

The house went on the market at a low price. One morning, we saw Al loading his belongings into a pickup truck. I went over to talk to him. I didn't really feel guilty that he'd been forced out. The lives of a lot of people were better now. He also didn't seem very upset, though that's probably because he had no idea that I'd been the one in charge.

"It's sort of a relief," he said.

"What's happening?"

"They got me a room at a nursing home. There's a smoking lounge and I'll have my own shower. It's been a long time since I've had three meals a day."

But for now, he was gone, and so was his house. A half dozen people tried to slip into Al's house through the back door that first night Al was gone. Jennings called the cops on them. A few days later, a tow truck came and pulled the abandoned pickup out of the driveway. There was a man sleeping in it. A few days later, the man returned with the pickup and told Jennings, "You'll never get rid of us. We'll be here forever."

The truck got towed again, and we were flush with victory. A couple of weeks after shutting down the combination neighborhood crackhouse/brothel, we celebrated National Night Out, flush with victory. This is an event where all of America's functional neighborhood watches make a public show of strength by throwing lawn parties. I was to host the Harmon Triangle's. I went to the police station and picked up an NNO packet, which included fliers, bumper stickers, and Austin Police Department trading cards, which featured photos of Austin's favorite cops as well as vital information such as how many years they'd been on the force and what their favorite movie was. The most common answers to the latter were, perhaps predictably, *Gladiator, Predator,* and *Death Wish.*

Mikki and Jennings rented a card table for three bucks from a friend of theirs who was a caterer. They made tasty chicken quesadillas, and brought store-bought vegetables and a bag of hot buffalo-wing-flavored corn chips, which I was tempted to complain about rudely. I don't believe that chips should be flavored. They should taste either like potatoes, or corn, with no flavoring but salt. There are no cool-ranch flavored potatoes, and therefore there should be no cool-ranch flavored potato chips. Corn doesn't taste like sour cream and onion.

They also made a couple of salads and bought some cold cuts and cookies at H.E.B., our local grocery chain. Astrid, our neighbor two doors down, brought some banana bread. She mentioned that she'd made *chiles rellenos* using chiles that she'd brought back from her mother's in New Mexico. She'd breaded them and stuffed them with Mexican cheese. I begged her to bring them over. Regina and I had purchased Shiner Bock, some cola, some water, and a twelve-pack of Fanta.

The whole block came by. There were about twenty of us, renters, homeowners, Anglos, Latinos, but we were all neighbors. We ate and drank and shot the shit. It was the usual 101-degree Easy-Bake Oven outside, but my magnolia tree provided shade. The police came by, and not just our district representative. We got the *district supervisor.* He talked to me like I was an actual adult, with friendliness and respect. "Mr. Pollack," he said. "We've heard about you." It was hard to believe that he was referring to me, but my dad definitely wasn't around. I was Mr. Pollack now.

This was my neighborhood, and I was glad to represent my friends, like John, the guy who rented the house across the street. There were few people in town I liked as much. He was a Ph.D. candidate in philosophy, worked as a brilliant substitute when the ponderous host of our local NPR midday show went on vacation, and was a member of a local comedy troupe that made fun of bad '80s movies. Some afternoons, I would take Hercules over to John's house—he was usually playing Pong on an original set from the '70s—and I would always leave with a gift. Sometimes he gave me a mix CD. Other times, if he was in the middle of a depressive episode, I left with a bag of weed, because the weed only made his depression worse.

On National Night Out, John decided it would be a good idea to turn on my garden hose and point it at Eamon and Elijah. And then he turned it on Jennings and me. Eamon took the hose away from John and squirted him. Soon, we'd made a big mud puddle in the middle of our yard. Elijah ran about, shrieking, his hands in the air. His diaper had ballooned to quadruple its normal size. So I took it off. And there we all were, wet and happy and, in Elijah's case, naked. Where there had once been despair, now friends and neighbors frolicked in the mud together. This, then, was my legacy to my son.

Later, some folks from 48th ½ Street stopped by. They told us that kids had been going up and down their street, shining flashlights into parked cars, seeing which stereos they wanted to steal. Also, someone had been going onto people's porches and setting couches on fire.

"Is there anything we can do?" they said.

"I'll take care of it," I said. "Shouldn't be a problem."

Six months later, Al's house had been completely gutted and rehabbed. It sold for $179,000. Al moved back to the Triangle, sharing a nearby one-bedroom apartment down the street with most of the same people as before. For now, someone else had to worry about them. But my jurisdiction was about to expand.

THIRTEEN

Ride the Brown Pony

July 2004

That summer, to give Regina a break, I took Elijah to the park several times a week. The closest one to us was called Shipe. It was a lovely little neighborhood place, with old shady trees, a kiddie pool and a grown-up pool, basketball courts, a soccer field, and a bridge going across a little creek that was mostly filled with Wendy's wrappers and algae. I humored Elijah and agreed with him that the creek contained many green frogs and, if he insisted, purple frogs. But though Shipe was little more than a mile away from our house, it occupied space in a different demographic.

Shipe was located in a neighborhood called Hyde Park, which had long ago organized to the level of historical preservation status. Every road had speed humps and circle-exchanges with flower planters in the middle. It was home to several politicians who made sure that kind of stuff would get done. There were several nice cafés and restaurants. It was the opposite of my neighborhood, whose main retail strip contained a beauty school, a pool hall, several used-car dealerships, a drive-through doughnut shop, and a place that sold lard-cooked breakfast tacos on the cheap to hungover punks and construction workers.

A special local type, commonly known as the Hyde Park Mom, frequented Shipe most often. A complex, impenetrable aura of self-righteous privilege and integrity, mixed with a little sacrifice, surrounded them. These were the ones who'd given up their careers, at least partially, to care for their little Evans or Tylers or Britneys, the obsessive overschedulers who wore brand-new Adidas sweatsuits or designer sundresses that they'd picked up on a shopping weekend in Houston. But they hadn't sullied their souls by making money in bad ways. These were academics, environmental engineers, or, at worst, marketing consultants. They listened to *Fresh Air* and subscribed to *The New Yorker*. Well, so did I, but unlike me, they actually liked those things. It was very hard to have a conversation.

Still, we went, because Elijah needed the air and exercise. But while the wonderkids of the supermoms barreled across the play set into oblivion, Elijah, almost two years old, stood at the top of the slide, looking down the entrance, prematurely all too aware of his mortality. When he did go down, it was backward, on his stomach, very slowly, whining the entire way. He wasn't interested in climbing, and couldn't get his feet off the ground to jump. All he wanted to do was swing.

I often pushed Elijah in the swing for a half hour or more. The whole time, he sang "Old McDonald Had a Farm," or at least a modified toddler version. It went:

"Had a Fa! Yi-yo! MOOOOOOOOO! BAAAAAAAA! Duck! Pwat! Pwat! Piggy! Snorrrrrrrrrrt! Ruff ruff! Had a Fa! Yi-yo!"

One day Elijah climbed off the play set quicker than usual and barged toward the swings. I was sitting on a particularly cozy patch of rubber safety play surface, sorting pebbles. It got pretty boring at the playground. By the time I got up, I was a couple of steps behind. He ran behind the swings, both of which were occupied by Hyde Park Kids getting pushed by Hyde Park Moms.

"Look out!" I said. "NOOOOOOOOOO!"

A pair of little feet connected with Elijah's little head. He sprawled into the smooth rocks. Immediately, he began to bawl. I ran and scooped him up.

"That was really scary," I said to one of the moms.

"Yeah? Well, that's what happens when you neglect your kid."

She was joking, right? I looked around at the other moms. They all stared at me with prim, self-righteous mouths, Puritans in *Morning Edition* baseball caps.

"I don't neglect my kid. It was an accident."

She gave me a little "hmph," and turned away without introducing herself.

After a new neighbor family moved into the rental two doors down from us, Elijah seemed even more frail and vulnerable to me than he had on the playground. They had a three-year-old boy named Gavin. Sometimes in the late afternoon, I would take Elijah over there to play, and drink a beer with Gavin's mother, Astrid.

One day at Gavin's house, Elijah found himself at the top of a play set, whimpering.

"Daddy," he said. "Down!"

"You can do it, buddy! Just slide!"

"Scared!"

"Elijah, come on. It's like three feet off the ground."

"Noooooooo!" he said.

"He needs his daddy," I said to Astrid.

"Sure," she said.

I went over to the swing set, picked up my son, and put him on the ground. Gavin ran past us and up the stairs. He turned around and, instead of sliding, pitched himself face-first into his mother's flowerbeds.

"Oh my God!" I said.

The kid got up. He was laughing. He went over to Elijah and bopped him on the head, with a closed fist.

"OW!" Elijah said.

"You two play nice, now."

I went back to my beer.

"He sure is coordinated," I said to Astrid, not considering the fact that her son was more than a year older than mine.

"A lot of that is because of his gymnastics classes."

"*Gymnastics?*" I said, as though I'd never heard the word before.

"Yeah. He just loves it! They've got him doing handstands and swinging from parallel bars."

"Daddy!" I heard Elijah say. I looked over. He was straddling a kiddie pool, one leg out, one leg in. He may have occasionally thought that he was an animal, but I now saw that he wouldn't survive long in the jungle.

"What?"

"Help!"

"Help you what?"

"Get out!"

I walked over and pulled him out.

"No! In!"

"What's it going to be, Elijah? Out or in?"

"In."

I put him in.

"No! Out!"

I pulled him out.

"In!"

"Oh, come on!"

Gavin roared past us and dove into the pool headfirst.

Gymnastics, I thought.

After Elijah went to bed that night, I presented to Regina the idea of sending him to gymnastics class once a week.

"When I was a kid," I said, "my grade-school P.E. teacher told me I was so bad at kickball that he wanted to throw up. I didn't learn to ride a bike until I was sixteen years old. I still can't climb a rope ladder. My son will not be like that."

"It's because you were a breech birth. You came out butt first and you have brain damage."

"That's what my mother says."

"I just don't think it's necessary."

"Gavin does it. He's good at it!"

"Gavin's father was a starting wide receiver for the University of Texas."

"Are you trying to tell me something?"

"Elijah might not be genetically predisposed toward coordination."

But I could push this initiative through, because I knew Regina's weak spots.

"I'll take him to class every week."

"Really?"

"Of course."

"Meaning I'll have time to myself?"

"Right."

Gymnastics was on, but I hadn't considered that our neighbors, while perfectly nice, didn't share our aversion to corporate parenting culture. You don't have to steer the ship differently when you're pretty sure that your kid will average two sacks a game in high school. My little miscalculation meant that, for one morning a week all summer, I found myself trapped in a world I hadn't made. It was the world of the Little Gym.

In 1976, a former grade-school gym teacher named Robin Wes started the Little Gym in Bellingham, Washington, because he saw that, at the dawn of the video-game age, kids were starting to get fat and lazy. Thirty years later, kids are fatter and lazier than he could possibly have imagined, but the Little Gym, once a community center with late-hippie-era values, has now become an international youth fitness super-chain. Every Little Gym comes with a full complement of parallel bars, balance beams, and springboards, and lots of mats, stairs, ramps, and balls. It provides a "professionally developed, non-competitive curriculum . . . designed to build motor skills while having fun, and simultaneously fostering enhanced emotional, intellectual and social skills." This is according to its website.

I called our local Little Gym, still a little disbelieving. A woman answered the phone with a sorority-girl lilt. I thought: Why are *you* so goddamn cheery?

"Thank you for calling the Little Gym! This is Heather!"

"Hey. Um. My son is kind of timid, physically."

"We'd be glad to see him!"

"Are you sure? He's not even two."

"Definitely!"

"So you have them run around and sing songs and stuff?"

"They actually do gymnastics! It's amazing what kids can accomplish at this age!"

"Right."

I looked behind me. Elijah was coming into my office to say hello. There were two steps between my office and the rest of the house. He was on his knees, moving very slowly. He made a whimpering noise and reached his hands out, pleading for help. This would be the Little Gym's greatest challenge.

Elijah's journey to coordination began at nine a.m. on a Wednesday. We pulled into the parking lot of an exurban strip center fifteen miles north of our house that, ten years before, had been a pristine swath of Texas Hill Country. There, next to an H&R Block outlet, was the Little Gym.

We walked in. Elijah was nestled in my right arm, clinging to my shoulder. I had a red nylon diaper bag slung over my other arm and a thirty-two-ounce iced tea in my other hand. A perfectly shaped young woman bounced over to us. Her brown eyes were as wide as gumballs and seemed to be propped open with invisible toothpicks. Her legs flowed nicely from the floor into the openings in her very low-cut navy-blue shorts. She wore a light-blue top that carried a lovely pair of breasts that had obviously never known a day of nursing. Her hair was long and sandy-brown, and she had drawn it back in a ponytail. I might have found her hot if cheerleading experience hadn't drained her demeanor of any last shred of irony. She was happily unaware of her own ridiculousness. This was Miss Stephanie, Elijah's Little Gym instructor.

"Well, who are you?" she said, addressing the kid.

"Elijah," I said.

She breathed in quickly.

"HIIIIIIII, ELIJAH!"

Elijah recoiled into my shoulder in terror. Miss Stephanie told us to take off our shoes and sanitize our hands. Class was about to begin.

There were a dozen kids in the class, most of whom seemed to be named after L.L. Bean colors. We had Ainsley and Paisley and Sydney. Miss Stephanie had us all lie on our bellies on the big red floor mat. She informed us that in Little Gym terminology, students at this class level were called "Beasties." Next she taught us the welcome song, which went to the tune of "If You're Happy and You Know It."

"Sing along, Beasties!" she said.

Not one of the kids, as far as I could tell, sang the song during any week of the class. Instead, Miss Stephanie sang enthusiastically, though not particularly on key, and the rest of us adults mumbled through the lyrics with little enthusiasm. It went:

How do you do, big beasts, how do you do?

We slapped the mat twice with open palms.

How do you do, big beasts, how do you do?

Repeat double slap.

When that horror ended, Miss Stephanie forced us onto our feet for the "warm-up," which mostly involved running in a circle. This was the part of the class Elijah enjoyed most. Any beneficial effects for me were diminished by the music Miss Stephanie played. The recording quality was equivalent to that of the little vinyl insert records that humor magazines sometimes included when I was a kid. It had tinny instrumentation that sounded very distant, with vocals that sounded like a cartoon turtle on Vicodin had recorded them. Though I tried very hard not to listen, I did absorb *some* of the lyrics: "Run, run, run, run with your partner, run with your partner all day."

I moved forward blankly, like an extra in a George Romero movie. I felt alienated and alone. There was only one other dad in the class, wearing a T-shirt that read SOUL HARVEST.

"Is that a band?" I said.

"No," he said. "It's a church youth program."

There was one woman in the class who appeared to have avoided the Soul Harvest. She was prodding her little Ethan, repeatedly saying, *"Joue, Ethan, joue."* She seemed like more my type of parent.

"They never play when you want them to," I said.

"You speak French!"

"Un petit peu."

"Oh my God! I've been looking for another parent who speaks French for so long! What are you guys doing after class?"

"Um. We're busy this week." That's also what I said to her when I ran into her later that summer at the grocery store.

Much of the gym equipment had interchangeable parts, and Miss Stephanie rearranged it every week. But Elijah wasn't particularly into any of the activities. No permutation seemed to appeal to him. One morning Miss Stephanie set up the furniture so that kids could climb some foam stairs onto a high mat. Elijah chose instead to crawl up, and then to back carefully down. Alternately, he wouldn't hang from bars or use the vault. He also spent the entire hour crawling in and out of the same tunnel. If we had a jumping exercise, he'd stand there, not jumping, until Miss Stephanie lifted him up and landed him again on his feet. Even then, he'd buckle into a blob on the mat.

"GREAT JOB, ELIJAH!" she said.

I thought the same thing, though I was mostly proud of him for not doing what she'd wanted.

One morning, after another useless warm-up, Miss Stephanie went to a corner of the room by the plate-glass windows that overlooked the parking lot.

"OK, Beasties!" she said. "Today we're going to work on a special piece of equipment. It's called the balance beam!"

Fabulous, I thought.

"Parents," she said. "Grab your Beasties!"

I did as I was instructed.

"Now I want you to lift your Beasties up!" she said.

Again, I obeyed. Elijah's knees immediately turned to seaweed.

"Today we're going to practice walking on the balance beam!" she said. "And to do that, we're going to sing a very special song!"

No.

"And the name of that song is 'Ride the Brown Pony.'"

NO!

"I want you to hold on to your Beasties' hands while they walk!" she said. "Here we go!"

She sang:

"Clippity clippity clop, ride the brown pony . . ."

I turned to the mother next to me.

"I guess it's better than riding the *white* pony," I said.

"Eh-heh," she said.

She looked at me like I was a guy who'd just cut her off in traffic. Admittedly, I hadn't shaved in a week and was wearing a dirty Cubs hat and a T-shirt depicting the Thing from *The Fantastic Four.* But I was still at the Little Gym, and I was still a dad. For pity's sake, couldn't a guy make a cocaine joke in mixed company anymore? Was there no other parent in this place who thought it was ridiculous that a dozen grown people were guiding kids who could barely walk across a balance beam while singing a song called "Ride the Brown Pony"?

"Now, Beasties," said Miss Stephanie, "I want you to *straddle* the Brown Pony."

It would be many years before Elijah would find that comment deeply ironic. I found myself longing for that time to arrive. But despite his daddy's aesthetic differences with the place, Elijah would occasionally enjoy himself at the Little Gym. This usually happened when he performed an activity of his own devising. His favorite was to run around flapping his arms, singing "Had a Fa! Had a Fa!" over and over again.

I thought about what Miss Stephanie had told us one day: "Parents. Make sure to give your children positive feedback!"

I absorbed this. One morning, as the rest of the class did something curriculum-based, Elijah went to Elijah-land.

"Had a Fa! Had a Fa!"

"That's great, Elijah! Now watch me!"

I ran in a circle and flapped my arms. He joined me, though none of the other parents or kids did. They were too busy building motor skills while having fun, and simultaneously fostering enhanced emotional, intellectual, and social skills.

Together my son and I chanted:

"Had a Fa! Had a Fa! Had a Fa!"

That was also the summer of Elijah's first haircut. Regina and I resisted cutting Elijah's hair for a while because he had beautiful blond curls. But at a certain point, it became a bit of a thicket. As Regina puts it, "Whenever he woke up from his nap, he looked like one of those things whose hair you twirl around. You know, a troll. His hair was a damn mess." We would have cut it ourselves, or at least Regina would have. But based on the screaming battles we faced whenever we tried to cut Elijah's nails, we figured that he'd probably end up in the emergency room if we tried for the hair.

The coming event made me nostalgic for *my* first haircut, though I could only remember the details thanks to my mother. She says it occurred in the fall of 1971 at a neighborhood barbershop in Memphis, Tennessee. The barber stood me on the counter, gave me a spray bottle full of water, and let me loose. I spent those magic fifteen minutes squirting the mirror, and I never knew that scissors had touched my head.

Elijah's inaugural shearing took place on a Tuesday morning in an entirely different America. We probably should have gone to a neighborhood barber, a species that did, after all, still exist. Instead, we went to Toys "Я" Us, which sat fifteen minutes up I-35 from our house, comprising a third of a generic supercenter. Yes, Toys "Я" Us does haircuts now. There's nothing less "alternative" about parenting than going to Toys "Я" Us, but Regina clipped a coupon. Also, Elijah liked it there. He didn't care whether Toys "Я" Us was cool or not.

I'm sorry. I meant to call it *Geoffrey's* Toys "Я" Us. Apparently, the cartoon giraffe that represents this mind-numbing behemoth has become so popular that he now owns the company. When I called Toys "Я" Us to get directions, the first thing I heard was "Hi! It's me, Geoffrey! Thanks for calling my store!"

If you want to strangle a giraffe, press "1."

On Haircut Day, Elijah and I walked in the door and heard a recording of Geoffrey say, like he does every time, "Thanks so much for coming to my store. Have a great time! Uh-huh-huh-huh-huh-huh." Inside Geoffrey's Toys "Я" Us, on the same side of the store as the Interactive Sports Game that Consumes Your Dollar Bills and Gives You Nothing in Return, the Really Tall Play Structure with Lots of Foam Balls That You Can Shoot Out of a Cannon, the Slurpee Bar, and Way Too Much Candy Land, is Cool Cuts 4 Kids. At some point in the last fifteen years, while I was off getting drunk somewhere, Toys "Я" Us got into the hair-cutting business. Maybe they'll add a dentist's office next.

Before the main event, I took Elijah to the playscape. As usual, he was mono-minded.

"Boo ba! Boo ba! Boo ba!" Elijah said.

"Yes, Elijah. That's a blue ball. Put it back in the cannon. And let's get our hair cut."

"Bye-bye, boo ba!"

There was to be a short wait. Both "stylists" were busy, one with a blond boy who sat, near lobotomized, with a finger up his nose as he received a scalp-whacking of which the Great Santini would have been proud. The other employee worked on a girl who was watching a *Dora the Explorer* video and apparently wanted to emulate Dora's hairstyle. The wait gave me a chance to examine my surroundings. I hesitate to say that Cool Cuts 4 Kids has bright lighting. It's something beyond light, something extra-dimensional. My sockets began to ache. Also, it was loud in there; not even an Interstate sound barrier could have blocked out the Jennifer Lopez songs roaring in from the store. Cool Cuts 4 Kids also allows its clients to play video games while they wait. Elijah sat at a terminal that featured a *Finding Nemo* game. Nemo helpfully summed up the objective for us: "Where are my friends? Help me swim around and find them."

"Fff-fff!" Elijah said. "Fff-fff!"

"That's right. A fish. Watch daddy make him swim."

After about a minute, I got Nemo stuck behind some rocks, and I couldn't figure out how the hell to get him out. Elijah seemed to want the controller. I vaguely considered putting on my sunglasses, because my eyes were really starting to hurt. Elijah played his first video game. This consisted of him pressing the pause button.

"Bloop bloop bloop!" the game said.

"Ah hah hah! Fff-fff!"

He then unpaused the game.

"Ah-hah-hah-hah!"

It was time to pause again.

"Bloop bloop bloop!"

"Fff-fff!"

"Elijah Pollack?" his stylist said.

Elijah looked up, surprised to hear his name.

"Huh?" he said.

"Are you ready?"

"Dah!"

He stood, and, without prompting, ran to the chair that looked like a New York City yellow cab. I put him in. He turned the wheel.

"Vroom! Vrooom! Vroooom!"

Cool Cuts 4 Kids has anticipated any distressing possibilities that might arise in the course of cutting a toddler's hair, and has sought to prevent them by placing a television in front of every chair. The kids have a choice between video games and actual videos. Elijah's "stylist" seemed patient enough, but she was totally impassive. I couldn't discern her personality. Perhaps, I thought, she was a hair-cutting android.

"You want a video?" she said.

"We'd better go with *Elmo in Grouchland.*"

She ejected the previous video, *The Wiggles Present Get Ready to Wiggle.*

"Actually, just leave that one in. It'll make our lives much easier."

I turned to Elijah, who was vroom-vrooming away.

"Who wants to watch the Wiggles?"

Hot lightning bolts of excitement shot from my son's eyes.

"Yi!"

This was Elijah-ese for "Wiggles."

The video played. The Wiggles began to wiggle.

"Ah-hah-hah! Yi!"

At no point did I have to put down my digital camera to prevent disaster. If Elijah posed any difficulty, it was only because he was performing all the hand gestures that the Wiggles commanded. During "Uncle Noah's Ark," Elijah stuck up his right arm, flapped his hand, and said, "Ah ah ah ah woo!" every time the Wiggles mentioned the rooster. He made the appropriate claw-hands and growly noises during "Here Comes a Bear," and he neighed during that creepy song where the Wiggles dance with a bunch of eight-year-old girls wearing horse costumes. Ride the brown pony indeed. I looked at the girl next to Elijah, who was playing the latest version of Zelda like a sullen automaton. My son was a tad more lively, and I felt proud.

"Ah ah ah woo!"

Elijah was shorn. I looked at the price board with my now permanently damaged eyes. For $16.95, I saw that an *adult* could get a haircut at Cool Cuts 4 Kids. I couldn't imagine going to Cool Cuts 4 Kids. Would they let me watch *Airplane!*? Could I play Halo II or Grand Theft Auto: Vice City? Was there a fire-truck chair big enough to hold a man of my stature? Could I maybe sit in a vintage Camaro?

The stylist interrupted my self-amusing reverie by handing me an envelope containing remnants of Elijah's first haircut.

"He was *such* a good boy."

"Thank you."

"Bye-bye, yi!" Elijah said. "Bye-bye!"

It was a busy summer, full of Daddy Time. Elijah and I took outdoor swimming lessons at a city park. There were six kids in the class. Half of them were Elijah's age and the other half were still infants. The pool was closer to downtown, not as far north as the Little Gym, so the parents were a little more laid-back. In fact, none of us really gave a shit at all. It's fun to take your kid to the pool, but I think we all realized that you're more likely to teach a loaf of unbaked bread than an eighteen-month-old how to swim.

By the city's arbitrary classification scheme, Elijah was a "Starfish." Our teacher was a super-tan, ultra-fit woman with several tattoos; she was one of Austin's vast army of professionally responsible hippies. She looked to be in her late forties. I imagined that she'd been partying at the Armadillo World Headquarters when I was still in short pants and watching *The Electric Company* every day. Because she was so cool, it added to the fun of standing in the shallow end of an Olympic-sized pool, holding Elijah by his armpits, and turning in a circle with the other parents, swishing the kid back and forth while I sang "The Wheels on the Bus." Still, I wondered if I really needed to spend $75 so I could throw Elijah up in the air, get him to stretch his arms in pursuit of a six-inch-long rubber dolphin, and participate in a group performance of "Motorboat, Motorboat." It really stretched the definition of "lesson."

Nonetheless, we re-upped for a second session with the same teacher. This time, she wasn't there as often. Her son came home unexpectedly on leave from Iraq, and she took a couple of weeks off to be with him.

"It's been really hard for us," she said. "Because we don't support this war."

"Me either!"

She looked at me scornfully, as if to say, "That doesn't mean we have anything in common."

One week her substitute was a nice young woman who knew all the same songs and even added "London Bridge Is Falling Down" to the repertoire. The next week, it was a nice young man who didn't exactly know what he was doing, but he tried hard and we all liked him. When Elijah and I checked in at the reception desk the following week, our official teacher had returned. I could see the previous week's substitute stacking foam noodle-floaties behind her.

"How are y'all?"

"Pretty good," I said, looking straight at the former substitute. "But thank God you're back. That guy last week was a *real loser.*"

I could see, from his expression, that he hadn't realized I was joking. He looked deeply pained, nearly suicidal. Oh, yeah, I remembered. I don't *know* him.

"Heh. I was kidding."

"Sometimes we say things we don't mean," our teacher said.

"No, really, I was kidding."

But I could see she didn't believe me. In the pool, she wasn't interested in helping Elijah out. Great. I'd told a stupid joke and now my son was never going to learn how to swim. Why did my actions always have consequences? I wanted to say, hey, it wasn't Elijah who accidentally insulted the sensitive substitute. He's a baby. Give him a break. Don't punish him for the petty sins of the father. After class, I asked about her visit with her army son. She turned to the woman next to me and told her all about it.

After that, I was a little better at keeping my mouth shut, particularly at the Little Gym. Ten weeks went by. Elijah learned to sort of jump, walk backward, and do an assisted handstand. He started walking down the stairs without grabbing a rail, going down slides without help, and throwing a ball through a hoop. I had to give the Little Gym credit, though the activity he still enjoyed the most was slapping the big red mat and saying "Floor!" over and over again.

Regina came with me for the last week of class and Elijah's "graduation," which featured no ceremony other than a plea from Miss Stephanie to re-up for the fall semester. That week was my last chance to get Elijah to achieve a goal that I'd set, unbeknownst to him. For the entire session, I'd been trying to get him to hang from a bar unassisted. He preferred to chant "up down, up down," while I supported his hips and did most of the work.

On that day, we hung him from the bar. He grabbed on. I let go. He hung, and he kept hanging for almost thirty seconds. You've never seen happier parents. We laid Elijah on the mat and tickled him aggressively.

"You're such a good boy!" I said.

"So brave," Regina said. "We're so proud of you."

"Up down," he said. "Up down."

"Watch this, son."

I lifted myself up onto the bottom bar until I was standing. Then I grabbed the top bar, swung, flipped over, and landed perfectly again on the bottom bar. I heard the sound of many childhood demons being vanquished and the spirit of my hopefully now-dead former P.E. teacher moaning in hell.

"How'd you do that?" said Regina.

"I don't know. I just did."

"Wow."

I raised my eyebrows suggestively.

"Really makes you want to have sex with me, doesn't it?"

"I did until you said that."

It had recently come to my attention that I hadn't had sex very often in the last year and a half. One morning, after waking up at 9:30, I went into the living room determined to change the situation. Elijah was asking Regina to draw pictures of sharks for him, and Regina was complying.

"Look who decided to join us," Regina said.

"Thanks for letting me sleep in."

"You're welcome."

"I feel terrific!"

"That's great for you. I've been up for three hours with a shrieking two-year-old."

"Honey? Do you think we could fuck sometime soon?"

"I had to wipe peanut butter off the television this morning. I'm not exactly in the mood."

"Please?"

"You have your Internet."

On the one hand, I was very grateful to be married to a woman who encouraged the use, even overuse, of web porn. On the other hand, I wanted ejaculation to at least *remotely* resemble something other than a purely biological imperative. I probed.

"Aren't you attracted to me anymore?"

"*Of course I am, honey.* It's just that I feel so . . . gross."

"You're not gross. I think you're *very* sexy."

I looked at her. She hadn't showered in two days and was wearing only brown sandals and a long nightshirt. On the shirt were pictures of middle-aged women doing yoga and shopping, though not at the same time. Above them, in cursive script, were the words DISCOVER THE DIVA WITHIN. This had been a gift from my mother, along with another nightshirt that read CAT NAP, featuring drawings of many lazy cats. Regina may have had body issues, but she hadn't given up to *that* extent.

"For instance. You look very hot in that shirt."

"That's because it brings out my diva within."

"Ah."

"You're looking pretty hot yourself."

I was wearing red paisley boxer shorts and a gray T-shirt with the words CLASSIC DADDY written on it in red script. I'd purchased the shirt for $2.50 in a fit of ironic pique during a Target diaper run. But at a certain age, what was meant to be ironic in a kitschy way ends up being ironic in the true sense of the word.

"Don't change the subject. I want to have sex with you."

"Look at me," she replied. "My breasts feel like they're hanging down to my knees. I'm like a cow. My body is horrible. My hair is thin. And I'm dry as the desert *down there.*"

"These are the natural consequences of early motherhood."

"That's easy for you to say."

"I am a man. And you have to satisfy me."

"We'll see."

"Please?"

I sounded like Elijah asking for a popsicle.

"I said, *We'll see!*"

Elijah was running around with a plastic sheep in his mouth, further dampening the erotic mood.

"You want to know what I've done so far today?" she said.

"What?"

"I made him cheese toast, which he promptly dumped all over the floor. Then I made him strawberries, which he threw at the dog. While I was cleaning cat puke off the washing machine, I heard him screaming because the dog was eating his strawberries that he didn't want anyway. I've watched *The Wiggles, Connie the Cow,* and *Baby Galileo* twice. He had the most disgusting shit in his diaper I've ever seen. And then thirty minutes later he shit in his pants again. Can you blame me if sex is the furthest thing from my mind?"

"I . . ."

"Please, *please,* don't put pressure on me."

"OK."

Here was a woman who made her living, or at least wanted to make her living, by creating fine art with erotic themes. On our first date, she told me that she slept naked. She had a hatbox full of dildos. She wasn't afraid of sexuality, so I didn't buy into our post-baby discussions about how certain things were more important to a marriage than sexual passion. This was my partner in life's great love-voyage, the person I had chosen to help me navigate the rocky waters of the rest of my life's great fuck-map. I didn't care that she was wearing an oversized nightie. She was still the woman who'd worn those cute boots on our first date and had taken her banjo for a hike. I still wanted to do it with her.

That night, I sat in my blue leather recliner while Regina was on the couch. We were eating big bowls of sweet-and-sour-chicken stir-fry. I contemplated going out to get some doughnuts, the eating of which often compensated for my lack of sex these days. We were watching the second season of *Six Feet Under* on DVD.

"These people have sex all the time," I said.

"But they're so unhappy," she said. "Sex isn't everything."

When we got into bed, I started kissing her.

"Don't."

I kissed her neck and ran my hand down her arms. With the other hand, I caressed her breast. My other hand strayed down her body to her thighs, brushing the Forbidden Zone.

"I have to wake up *so early.*"

I thought for a second. Then I realized that only one thing was going to get me laid that night.

"I'll get up with the boy tomorrow."

"*Really?*"

"Sure."

"Come here, stud."

When we were done, she looked so satisfied that I briefly considered letting her sleep in for a week.

"I'm gonna go watch *SportsCenter* now."

"You go right ahead, baby," she said. "Just remember that you have to get up with the boy. I love you."

"I love you, too. Maybe the boy will sleep late."

"Right."

At six a.m., Elijah began to shriek.

"That's to you," Regina said, and put a pillow over her head.

I rose and trudged toward Elijah's room. He was standing in the crib, holding a stuffed dolphin.

"I pee on dolfee!" he said.

FOURTEEN

Play That Monkey Music Wiper

August–September 2004

We got a call from a Montessori school. This was the place that we'd liked before, the one that was having the science fair on the day we toured. A spot had opened up for Elijah, the director said.

"Oh, *really?*" I said.

Regina overheard.

"What?"

"It's that school. Elijah's in."

"Ask them what time we have to drop him off."

For months, she'd been begging for a few hours a day so she could do her work, and suddenly now she was being difficult?

"Why do I have to be your bagman? You ask them."

"Come on! You know I hate to do stuff like that."

"Hello?" the director said.

"We'll take it. Just out of curiosity: By what time do we have to get Elijah there?"

She told me.

"Eight a.m.," I said to Regina.

"That's too early," she said.

"My wife says that's too early."

"I did not!"

We were the very model of parental responsibility.

"Can we take him in any time we want?" I said.

Every other preschool with whom I've ever talked has answered something along the lines of "Of course. He's your child." This director said, "He needs to be there by eight-fifteen at the latest."

We hated mornings and we didn't care who knew it. But he was in, and we could, if pressed, act. It was a Monday morning. Elijah could start Thursday, the director said. He'd go five mornings a week, until about one p.m.

"What exactly is a Montessori school, anyway?" I asked Regina later.

It was a better question than you might think, especially because there's no clear answer. Maria Montessori, the school-type's namesake, had a certain method, involving child self-direction within a fairly narrow frame of activities, which emphasized geometric shapes, household manners, and geography, with minors in other disciplines. But by the time Regina and I arrived as parents of a school-age kid, the Montessori Method had scattered to the winds. Schools in the United States could be certified under a national Montessori association, or they could be certified under an international one with different standards. Then it really got tricky, because any school could call itself "Montessori" without any certification at all. While there were many legitimate schools out there, calling something "Montessori" was about as legitimate as calling supermarket food "farm-fresh." It meant nothing. Unfortunately, we chose a farm-fresh Montessori school.

Before we dropped the check off at the director's office, Regina went online to see if she could find information on the school. As usual, there was a paucity of resources. In a country where educational institutions are constantly being ranked and assessed, there are no national standards of nursery-school evaluation. Really, there's no way at all to find out about good preschools, except by word of mouth, and those words often aren't worth the server space that carries them. On a bulletin board, Regina found someone complaining about the "accent" of our school director, who was Sri Lankan. "I've been warned," the post read, "not to send my children to schools run by International People." This sent me on a self-righteous liberal rant:

"God forbid our kids should be educated by people from different countries! You know, because Americans are *so much smarter* than other people. Just when you think bigotry is dead . . ."

"Neal, it was just one stupid woman on the Internet."

"One stupid ignorant bitch woman!"

"OK, dear. Still, we don't know for sure whether this school is any good or not."

"It's good. Don't you think?"

"I think so. But it's just so hard to tell."

Regina and Elijah went to Target to buy a lunchbox. Elijah chose a hideous plastic thing shaped like a sort-of dinosaur creature that was orange with purple spots. Regina worried that it looked too much like Barney. I assured her that it didn't. At that point, our child had no knowledge of Barney, and we intended to keep it that way. Barney, to us, represented everything that was infantilizing and reductive about kid's culture. The songs were bad, the skits were worse, the idolization and creature-worship were creepy. He was to be utterly avoided. Fortunately, we'd become parents after Barney's heyday, so this was now possible.

Later, while Elijah napped, we began to realize the emotional consequences of sending a child to school before his second birthday.

"I feel like a bad mother."

"You're the best mother ever."

"I'm not. But I know I'm pretty good."

"There you go."

"I feel guilty."

"Don't feel guilty."

"But I do!"

Regina isn't normally a guilt-ridden person, but motherhood ratchets up the guilt stakes. This time, she had apparently flashed her guilt to everyone she knew, because that night she forwarded me an e-mail my younger sister Margot had sent her. It was hard for me to imagine Margot expressing herself like an adult; in my mind she was still the little allergy-ridden girl whom I was always cruelly telling to "stop coughing," or maybe the teenager whose high-school football-player boyfriend once told me a joke with the punch line "Here nigger, nigger, nigger." But then I remembered that Margot was thirty-two, professionally successful, solidly married to a man whom I liked a lot, and had a daughter of her own.

The letter was quite lovely:

I guarantee you that it will be wonderful for him. I've often felt guilty about leaving Allison at daycare but one of the ladies said to me a while back, "she's happy here—so why aren't you?" I know Elijah has benefited from being home with both of you but I really do think that he will be so happy to have his space and learn from other children. As long as you feel that the place he is going is safe and clean I think it will be wonderful for him. You are such a GREAT Mommy and have devoted yourself completely to him. You and Neal once said that a child should enhance your life not hinder you from living it. I really admire how you've spent so much time with him, breastfed him as long as you did etc; my personality didn't let me do that. Although I love Ali more each day I couldn't have done what you did. You are an amazing woman and are making the right decision for your son and yourself. It really is true that if you aren't happy he won't be happy. Enjoy the hours you are with him and enjoy when you're not. He is in good hands and loves his Mommy more than anything else.

Now that we'd accepted the fact that Elijah was going to school, we figured it was time to tell him. Sometimes we ate dinner with him, and sometimes, if he was hungry at five p.m., we fed him early and then ate after he went to bed. On this night, we ate together, and I gave him a talk.

"Now, son, in a few days, we're going to take you to a school in the morning. There are going to be lots of other kids there for you to play with."

"And a nice big playground," Regina said.

"Right. And puzzles, and games, and songs to sing, and you're going to have so much fun and learn so much. Mommy and I just wanted you to know that we love you very much and that when you're done with school every day, we'll be there and then we can all have a good time together."

He stared at me soulfully, as though he were soaking in my wisdom.

"So what are we doing on Thursday?"

"Ummmmm . . . Paaaaaaa?"

"No, Elijah. Not the park. School."

"Ummmmm . . . Duck?"

He was twenty-one months old. I realized that he had no idea what school was. The fact that they called it "school" should have been our first sign that we'd chosen wrong.

Two nights later, Regina made Elijah's first school lunch. It was like something from an Alice Waters cookbook. There would be no peanut-butter-and-jelly for him, no mini-can of Pringles. She roasted an orange pepper and a yellow pepper, chopped them up, and tossed them with some basmati rice, kalamata olives, and cherry tomatoes. There was a fruit salad of fresh cantaloupe and pear, and a couple slices of nitrate-free turkey meat. For dessert, Elijah got six whole-wheat crackers. Within a few days, he was getting peanut-butter sandwiches and some grapes like all the other kids. But that first lunch was special, and to Regina's delight, he ate it all.

We dropped him off at 8:15. Three separate women said, "Elijah! We've been waiting for you!" though the director who'd enrolled us was absent. We put his lunchbox in its space, and his spare clothes and diapers in his cubbyhole. While we were doing that, Elijah went over the Montessori materials, found himself attracted to a shapes thingy, picked up a blue object, and said, "Ci!"

"That's right, Elijah," I said, like all the other type-A competitive parents who need to learn to relax around their kids, "cylinder!"

Then it was time for them to go to the playground. Elijah turned from us and booked toward the nearest slide. He didn't look behind him. We slinked away.

I'd expected tears from Regina, but she was pretty cool in the car. Maybe it was just shock. Neither of us had slept much the night before in anticipation of the loneliness we'd feel. We were home in about five minutes and immediately noticed how quiet it was. Since Elijah's birth, Regina and I hadn't been home together for a minute without him around.

"We sent him to school so we could work," I said. "So let's work."

Regina sat down at her easel behind me. I sat at my computer. I typed for a little while. She painted for a little while. We looked at each other. It was too quiet. Then we realized that we were alone. There was only one thing to do.

"Let's take a shower," I said.

The shower was, for lack of a better term, awesome. Oh yes, we realized. *This* is why we got married: Because we enjoyed each other, in just about every way. Afterward, I said, "I'm hungry."

"So am I."

We needed a loaf of bread, so we went to the grocery store, which conveniently also had a restaurant. There were lots of kids Elijah's age there, with their parents.

"Are you sure he doesn't hate us?" Regina said.

"I'm pretty sure."

A little boy walked by holding his mother's hand. A balloon slipped its moorings. He looked up at the sky.

"Bye-bye, balloon," he said.

"Awwwww," I said.

"I miss my little mookie bear," said Regina.

Two hours later, we went to pick up Elijah. He was sitting in the sandbox. He saw us and scrunched up his face. But he didn't cry. He walked over to us sullenly and attached himself to Regina's leg. The teacher said he'd had a good day: A few tears, but he hadn't been overwhelmed.

Elijah grumped his way out to the parking lot. He climbed into his safety seat. We drove for a couple of minutes.

"So what'd you do at school today?"

"Ummmmmm . . . PAAAAAA?"

"Well, there's a playground. That's kind of a park," Regina said.

"Ummmmm, boo ba?"

"There were balls on the playground?"

"Recta!"

"You played with rectangles? What else did you see at school today?"

"Ba Ma!"

"Elijah, did you really see Batman at school today?"

"Ba Ma Ba Ma Ba Ma! Ba Ma!"

Elijah's school days had begun. He took to running around in a circle and saying "Dahk, dahk, dahk, all fa down!" combining two popular childhood games in a sort of preschool version of a mash-up. One afternoon we distinctly heard the familiarly banal notes of the "Alphabet Song." When he was done, I held up a stuffed felt letter D.

"Elijah," I said. "What letter is this?"

"D!"

Regina and I exchanged an our-son-is-a-goddamn-genius look.

I held up a G.

"What letter is this?"

"D!" he said.

I held up a P.

"D!"

The best and most surprising improvement was in his eating manners. Within five days of starting school, he'd abandoned his booster seat to sit in a regular chair like Mommy and Daddy, which we called a "big-boy chair," a phrase that I've promised myself I'll never use unless it's framed by quote marks. He stopped throwing food and started eating nearly everything without our help. He was saying please and asking for a napkin. He must have picked this stuff up at school, I thought. He sure as hell didn't get it from me.

At home, where he wasn't in the hands of the Montessori Method, I had an extracurricular program for Elijah. I'd been preparing the curriculum for a while. After two years of living in Austin, I'd seen a band called Peelander-Z several times. These are three Japanese guys who dress in superhero costumes, sing about how much they like to eat steak, and play "human bowling" with their audience. I'd also seen the Aquabats, a seven-man ska ensemble from Southern California who also dress like superheroes, fight monsters like Dr. Space Mummy and Powdered Milk Man on stage, and sing songs with titles like "The Cat with Two Heads" and "Captain Hampton vs. the Midget Pirates." They're actually pretty annoying, but they're fun enough, and perfect for my purposes.

One night I went to an Aquabats show at a low-rent shithole called the Back Room, a metal bar that occasionally had all-ages shows. The audience was mostly under sixteen, with a few *alte cockers* like me dotted about. The Aquabats put a call out for the youngest member of the audience. A dad, who looked to be about my age, carried a kid up to the stage.

"What's your name, kid?" said the Bat Commander, the Aquabats' lead singer.

"Casey," said the little girl.

"Casey, how old are you?"

"Eight."

"Have you ever crowd-surfed before?"

"No."

"Would you like to?"

"Yeah!"

"Is your dad gonna sue us if someone drops you?"

"No!"

And they launched into a number. I believe it was "Martian Girl." Casey flopped into the crowd, which gingerly passed her around over their heads. She waved her arms and opened her mouth in a wide, joyous grin. I've never seen a kid look so happy; that was the kind of rock 'n' roll education I wanted to give my son. I went home, woke Regina up, and said, "I want Elijah to dive into a mosh pit when he's eight years old."

"That's too young."

"No it's not."

"Yes it is."

"What about ten? Your mom took you to see Oingo Boingo when you were ten."

"We'll see."

Obviously, Elijah was too young for a real rock show, but from Peelander-Z and the Aquabats, it's no odyssey to four sexually ambiguous Australians who wear primary-colored caveman outfits, drive around in a "big red car," and dance underwater with a top-hat-wearing octopus. That's why, when it comes to the Wiggles, the favorite band of every English-speaking person in the world under five, I place myself in the camp of tolerance, even admiration. At least the Wiggles actually play instruments. At least their songs don't have morals any more saccharine than "It's fun to eat vegetables with Anthony." Upon first encountering "Fruit Salad" and "Hot Potato," the "Please Please Me" and "All Shook Up" of children's music, I decided the Wiggles would be more than just something I endured. They would launch Elijah's rock 'n' roll education, and then we would discard them, because all rock must be destroyed by what comes next.

The Wiggles sell out basketball arenas full of screaming kids. They appeal to parents as well. That's the dirty secret of children's entertainment. It allows parents to have crushes when their own pop idols have begun to wither. Regina is an "Anthony girl," by her own admission, and kind of likes the second guy on *Blue's Clues,* not the creepy, skinny guy. I had the hots for the blond Wiggles backup dancer who gets a suspicious number of close-ups. The other Wiggles must serve as imaginary boyfriends to some people as well, though Jeff is a real specialty item. But if the Wiggles are the Beatles of contemporary children's music (without the psychedelic period), I'm still waiting for the Rolling Stones.

I became a parent during a boom time in kid's music. Noggin had just started to build up steam when Elijah was born. During Elijah's second year, they started showing music videos from performers like Dan Zanes and Laurie Berkner. This music was pleasant, both for kids and adults. Zanes is cute in a guitar-playing-guy-in-your-poetry-seminar kind of way, a frosty-haired, drippy-voiced Woody Guthrie for kids of parents who want to think they still know something about music but would secretly be happy listening to nothing but Norah Jones for the rest of their lives, and Berkner is a nice Upper West Side girl who wears tight red shirts. Obviously, Elijah wasn't in it for her boobies, but parents had to watch these videos, too.

As I write this, though, the industry has hit boom times. Noggin has begun airing its own music-video program, *Jack's Big Music Show,* in which a trio of cartoon puppets play songs with special guests and introduce videos by Berkner and several other bands, all of which seem to be made up of earnest young men with Jew-fros, goatees, or both. Dan Zanes is no longer on Noggin, as he has his own video development deal with the Disney Channel, which also exclusively airs the children's videos of They Might Be Giants, the only band in the world whose audience gets younger every year. Noggin is also sponsoring a tour, called Jamapalooza, with Berkner as the headliner and an annoying band called Milkshake as the number-two on the bill. I saw Zanes quoted in the *New York Times* as saying "It's like 1982 all over again."

Now, I understand what he's saying. This is the time when kids' videos are taking off, just like MTV did in the early '80s. But the hosts of *Jack's Big Music Show* are no Dr. Dre and Ed Lover. In fact, they're not even Kukla, Fran, and Ollie. Most of the music that Noggin puts forth is incredibly mediocre. Admittedly, they do play the real songs of real bands. It's a far, far better fate than having to watch Barney. But kids' music is still needlessly bland and wishy-washy. Kids don't only want to hear "under a shady tree, you and me," as Berkner sings. Kids are wild. They want anarchy, in the best way. This is where I came in.

No aspect of modern parenting annoyed me more than the "music class." Regina wanted the boy to learn piano, which was perfectly fine, and I would gladly pay for Elijah's guitar lessons if he asked for them down the line. But I was not about to entrust my son's music appreciation to some stranger in a strip mall who last bought an album when Edie Brickell was lingua franca, or to some video program that seemed to be appealing to the children of people who think Sheryl Crow is awesome.

So I searched. I bought. I downloaded. I gathered albums that had been sitting dusty on our shelves for a while. It was my intention to do a music class of my own, a rock 'n' roll home school. I called it Music Hour, and it went a little something like this.

We began each Music Hour with a mid-1990s album called *For the Kids,* a VH1 "Save the Music" fund-raising project that was one of the earliest musical examples of hipsters trying to hang on to a shred of their dignity after waking up and discovering that they were parents. The opening song is the band Cake doing a cover of "Mahna Mahna." Upon hearing the first notes, Elijah would run into his room and bring back a small basket of musical instruments. These included a twin pair of monkey rattles, a giraffe rattle, several other rattles, the ubiquitous shaky eggs, and various toys that made some noise vaguely resembling rhythm.

He danced around to this for a while. Then I ejected the record. The only other songs on it that were even remotely worth considering are the Barenaked Ladies singing "La La La La La Lemon," but Elijah explicitly disdained that cut, as well as a lovely Sarah McLachlan cover of "The Rainbow Connection." I generally used that one as a tender cool-down song. Otherwise, we were staring down the likes of Darius Rucker from Hootie and the Blowfish singing "It's All Right to Cry" (hell, no!). There was also a number from the ubiquitous Dan Zanes. He couldn't fool me, though. My kid was not going to grow up listening to his lame-o cover of "The Sidewalks of New York."

"What's next, Elijah?" I said.

"Huh?"

"Pay attention. What song comes second in Music Hour?"

"Elfant Song!"

"That's right."

He meant "SOS Elephants," a supremely silly number from Les Sans Culottes, one of my favorite bands, who pretend to be *chouette* musicians from Saint-Tropez circa 1967 but actually live in Brooklyn. "SOS Elephants" is a catchy, peppy tale of elephants that are liberated from the Paris zoo. The song started off slowly. Upon my first listening, I told Elijah that he had to lie down on the floor when it began. Now he was lying down automatically. As the song picked up steam toward the first chorus, he got up with a crap-eating grin. And as it kicked in, he began to jump around loonily, making sure that I joined him. At various points, I lifted him over my head, swung him around by his armpits, and ordered him to aggressively mime-play an electric keyboard by saying, "Elijah! Keyboard! Now!" There was a quiet bridge section in "SOS Elephants" where we dropped to the floor and pretended to sleep again. Then we rose up and bounced anew for about a minute. After that ended, I staggered over to the CD player, heaving for breath, and said, "Elijah, now is a very special time in Music Hour."

"Huh?"

"Pay attention."

I fingered a CD.

"This is an amazing kind of music that you love."

"What is it?"

"At this time, we leave the world of rock behind us, and suddenly, Music Hour becomes the exclusive domain of . . ."

I pushed PLAY.

"POLKA!"

I had a brief early-'90s fixation with a band called Brave Combo, from Denton, Texas, that specializes in psycho-polka and klezmer. Elijah enjoyed the Italian Medley from the *Night on Earth* album, but his Music Hour favorite, far and away, was their cover of the "Happy Wanderer" song. This is probably because, from the first note, I scooped him up and twirled him around the room madly and sweatily, as though this were 1950s rural Wisconsin and he was my girl. Apparently, though, he absorbed the lyrics. One afternoon, I took him hiking in a state park. Unbidden, he sang the following, and I was proud:

> *Val ree*
> *Val ra*
> *Val ree*
> *Val Raaaaaaaaaaaa*
> *Val ree*
> *Val ra*
> *I ride on Daddy's back!*

By that point in the lesson, Daddy was very tired, so he had to go into the kitchen for a drink of water. This was a dangerous point in Music Hour, because if I put on the wrong thing, Elijah would lose focus and wander off. A fairly reliable choice was usually Kelly Hogan doing a fancy "Rubber Duckie" cover from Bloodshot Records' excellent alt-country kid's album *The Bottle Let Me Down.* If Regina was in the room during Music Hour, I often initiated a slow "Mommy Dance" to Patsy Cline's "Walkin' After Midnight." Another decent choice was the Flaming Lips' *Yoshimi Battles the Pink Robots,* almost any track, or "Birdhouse in Your Soul" from They Might Be Giants' *Flood* album, or a selection or two from John Lithgow's surprisingly fun *Singin' in the Bathtub* album, which is mostly comprised of covers of nonsense songs from the 1930s, '40s, and '50s. After one or two transitional songs, I was ready to return to the fray for the most important part of Music Hour: The rock lesson.

We did a few Music Hours before Elijah was truly ready to rock. After reviewing my collection carefully, I decided that the Hives' *Veni Vidi Vicious* album would be the best. The songs are short, loud, silly, melodic, and not particularly complicated. My thesis proved instantly correct from the first notes of "Hate to Say I Told You So." When Howlin' Pelle Almquist opened the song with a guttural scream, Elijah recognized the sound from direct experience, and howled back. He began to flap his arms and run in a circle.

"That's good, Elijah. You're rocking out!"

"Ah ah ah!"

"Rock out, boy!"

"Rock out! Rock out! Thunder Music, Daddy! This is thunder!"

Yes! He got it! It *was* thunder.

I bounced along with him. He looked at me and, flapping his arms madly, left the ground and launched himself at my midsection. I caught him and threw him back. He landed on his feet. Then, gently, I launched myself into him.

My son and I were moshing!

Awesome!

"We're moshing, Elijah! Let's mosh!"

"Mosh! Mosh!"

From there, I branched out, quickly discovering that my son likes his "thunder music" fast and loud. The Ramones are a popular choice when people are trying to teach their kids the essence of rock, but after fifteen seconds of "I Wanna Be Sedated" Elijah turned his attention toward his Fisher-Price Little People farm. The next week, he surprised me when he said, "I wanna hear the Ramones, Daddy." I nearly wept.

He didn't really seem to dig Creedence, so I stopped trying with the classic rock immediately. But if I put on *Never Mind the Bollocks— Here's the Sex Pistols,* he could keep himself entertained by moshing for ten minutes or more. Sometimes I couldn't understand his choices at all. He found the White Stripes ponderous, but happily thrashed his head around to the original Black Sabbath version of "Iron Man."

Music Hour often continued in the car. There, my fallback album was one put out by WFMU, an independent radio station in New Jersey that produces a great kids' music program called *Greasy Kid Stuff.* There were two CD compilations, though we owned only one. It was a garage-rock primer for kids, mostly surf guitar and absurd lyrics. There's very little difference, I decided, between "Wild Thing," a supposedly grown-up song, and "Ants in My Pants," whose lyrics consist of "I've got ants in my pants!" and "I've got ants in my pants, too!"

Other favorites included a classic cavestomp ditty called "Abba Dabba Doo," a song about a monkey that escapes from a research lab and plays hockey at the local pond (Elijah called this "The Monkey Song"), and a song about how monkeys are tired of entertaining their human masters (the "Other Monkey Song"). The absolute highlight, however, was "Snik-Snack Skiduliak," by a band called the Go-Nuts, a paean to snack time and greed that is, undoubtedly, the greatest children's song I've ever heard, and one of my favorite rock songs—fast, loud, dumb, and hellishly catchy. My favorite verse, sung by the lead singer, Captain Corn Nut, goes:

> *I am Captain Corn Nut*
> *(He is Captain Corn Nut)*
> *I bought a candy bar*
> *(He bought a candy bar)*
> *I didn't share my candy*
> *(He didn't share his candy)*
> *No, I ate it all!*
> *(No, he ate it all!)*

The somewhat dubious message is rescued by the fact that the song rocks very hard. In the car, Elijah asked for a snack.

"Che buns!"

"OK. I'll give you cheddar bunnies. But first, since it's snack time, you know what we have to do, don't you?"

"Snack song! Snack song!"

"That's right."

I turned on the snack song. Elijah thrashed his arms and legs in the seat and whipped his head back and forth.

"Don't forget to stick out your tongue!" I said.

He did.

"One two three rock out!" he said. "Daddy too!"

"Daddy can't rock out right now," I said. "He's driving."

In those early days of Driving Music Hour, as opposed to Living Room Music Hour, I played Elijah jazz. He particularly liked the Max Roach drum solo on a Dinah Washington album. I also had an early-'90s *History of Funk* compilation put out by Rhino Records. One morning, I brought it into the car. It opened with "Jungle Boogie," which later became known, in our house, as "Jungle Song." Elijah certainly enjoyed singing "get down, get down" over and over again. Then on a hunch, I turned it to Track 12, "Play That Funky Music."

When the song was over, Elijah said, "Again."

When it was over again, Elijah said, "Again."

Soon, I was regretting ever having introduced him to "Play That Funky Music," which these days is, at best, a barely acceptable wedding standard. There was no stopping this passion, though. Elijah screeched, "Monkey music, Daddy! Monkey music!"

So I turned it on. Again. He sang along, or at least he sang the last syllable of every word. I don't think his comprehension was very high, judging by the way he interpreted the chorus. Actually, I like his lyrics better.

> *Play that monkey music, wiper*
> *Play that monkey music right*
> *Play that monkey music wiper*
> *Play down that booger, die, die, die!*

Occasionally, I would descend into the depths of children's music, bobbing for tasty apples among the rotten. Elijah liked an album from Jason Ringenberg, who used to be the lead singer of Jason and the Scorchers. Apparently, he's now "Farmer Jason," and he sings songs about barnyard animals. I also tried an album from the *Ralph's World* series, because I'd read somewhere that it was good. One day, while we were driving somewhere, I put it on. Two songs in, Elijah said, "Daddy, this music is bad."

I thought about it for a second.

"You know what, Elijah? You're right. This music *is* bad."

"Snack song!" he said. "Snack song!"

So I put on the snack song. He thrashed wildly and said "ARRRRRRGH! ARRRRRRRGH!"

"That's it, son!" I said. "Yes! That's rock 'n' roll!"

Elijah instinctively knew how to be loud. Now I had to teach him, as part of his rock 'n' roll education, about loudness' first cousin, supreme silliness. It's an important weapon to have in your life's arsenal. A comedy-punk attitude isn't necessarily going to keep you from getting your ass kicked, but at least it will allow you to feel morally superior to those who are doing the kicking. I began somewhere near Elijah's second birthday, by going after his own name.

"What's your name?"

"Li-jah!"

"Elijah what?"

"Li-jah Allen Pollack."

"Poolick," I said.

"No! Li-jah Allen Pollack!"

"Elijah Poolick."

A glint appeared in his eye.

"Poolick?" he said.

"Yes. Poolick."

"Poolick! Pooooooooooolick!"

Later that day, I was in my office pretending to work. Regina entered.

"Neal, did you teach Elijah that his last name is Poolick?"

"I cannot tell a lie."

"Dammit, Neal, you can't be telling him stuff like that!"

"Why not? It's funny."

Elijah came into the room, lips puckered.

"Pooooooooooooo-liiiiiiiiiick!"

"See what you did? You explain that to his grandparents."

This from a woman who, years ago, had put in her personal ad that she was seeking a man with a "penchant for scatological humor."

"Fine. Elijah. Don't say 'Poolick' anymore."

"Poolick," he said.

Later that evening, I was passing through the hall. I heard voices from the bathroom.

"He's peeing! Oops! Now he's pooping!"

Elijah giggled manically.

"Uh-oh. He has diarrhea!"

I peeked. Regina held a plastic Cookie Monster bath toy, and she was squeezing it to make water come out of the air hole in its bottom.

"His diarrhea is really bad! Elijah, what are we going to do?"

"What kind of a thing is that to be teaching our son?"

"You caught me."

"Ah-ha, Daddy. Cookie Monster has diarrhea!"

"OK, Elijah Poolick.

"Pooooooooooooolick."

"Look!" said Regina. "He's peeing again!"

Allow me to briefly subvert narrative order. Follow me to a year later, when Elijah was nearly three, to show how our efforts bore scatological fruit. One summer evening, after we'd been to a neighborhood swimming pool and had eaten dinner on a restaurant patio, Elijah sat in the backseat, singing a song of his own devising about our pets.

"Gabby like to eat boogers with her paw. Gabby like to eat poo. Herky also like to eat poo and boogers sometimes too . . ."

"Look at that," Regina said. "You are giving him a filthy potty mouth."

"You're one to talk. Besides, it's not all potty stuff in these songs."

As if to back me up, Elijah sang, "Herky like to eat stop lights, Herky like to eat lampposts . . ."

"See. That's good, Elijah!"

"My mother is going to be appalled."

"Then he mixes them with boogers in his mouth," sang Elijah, "and they're yummy in his tummy . . ."

And we all screamed with laughter.

In September of 2004, as a key part of his rock education, I decided to take Elijah on a field trip to the Austin City Limits Music Festival. Regina begged me to reconsider. We'd gone two years earlier, when she'd been eight months pregnant. It had been hot and crowded, and full of a toxically obnoxious mix of college-aged hippies, college-aged Pat Green fans, middle-aged hippies, and middle-aged Pat Green fans. You had to bring in your own water and there weren't many trees for shade. Ryan Adams and Wilco were headlining. Reading those previous sentences now, I don't know why I'd ever wanted to go in the first place. I managed to avoid ACL Fest temptation the next year.

But starting with the 2004 Festival, Austin City Limits got kind of hip. In addition to the jam bands, the alt-country washouts, the token Spanish-speaking acts, and several "safe" black performers, they decided to go after the skinny-tie-wearing kids. Their choice of bands spoke specifically to my growing insecurity that I was too old to stay current. I looked at the roster. Franz Ferdinand! The Killers! The Soundtrack of Our Lives! Modest Mouse! I imagined myself saying to my son, "Elijah, we took you to see Modest Mouse before you were even two." Not Mickey Mouse! Modest Mouse! I was going to be the coolest dad ever! Regina was skeptical that it would work with a kid. "It's gonna be a pain in the ass," she said.

"Don't be so damn negative. He loves music!"

Our neighbors across the street were going; as I've mentioned, their son's favorite band was Devo. We had to keep up with the indie Joneses. We could all head over there together and some of us would watch the boys while the others went to the music. It would be a rock 'n' roll co-op. We'd take turns! It would be easy! I told Regina that I'd set this up.

"I'm telling you. It'll be fun."

"And I'm telling *you,* that it won't."

"Don't be lame."

"I hate it when you accuse me of being lame. You make me feel like a party-pooper."

"Then don't be one."

"Don't tell me what to be!"

An occasional tension in our marriage had surfaced. I didn't think

Regina was adventurous enough. She thought that I was always pressuring her to be "cooler" than she wanted. We were both right some of the time. But this weekend, I wasn't going to let her point of view prevail. This time, I was determined not to let having a kid stop my pre-kid life from occasionally returning, even though, as I said before, I actually didn't like the Austin City Limits Festival. I went online and bought tickets.

The first day started breezily enough. I enjoyed a breakfast of cheese toast sprinkled with marijuana shake, the cheese would activate the essential qualities of the THC. Elijah went to school in the morning, which gave Regina and me time to fool around. We were glowing modestly at eleven a.m. when she dropped me at the bus that would take me to Zilker Park. Elijah would nap after school, and then they'd join me. I got to go ahead of them because I'd thrown a snit about not wanting to waste my investment. I was like Elijah with a credit card.

A few minutes later, cooler strapped over my shoulder, I made my way across a sweltering fairground of dried brown grass and tie-dyed memorabilia. Those of us who got to the festival early sought shade around the edges, which is where the trees were. As the day lurched on, shade became much more important than hearing music. I found a nice spot under a big tree over by the west wall of Port-A-Pottys. It was noon, so I got a beer.

The Killers were playing on a small stage. This was just before they got super-famous. I'd never heard them before, but I'd heard of people who'd heard of them. Regina had been a big Duran Duran fan back when. I was sure she'd enjoy them, and I thought about what I'd say to the kid: "Elijah! Your thirty-five-year-old daddy saw the Killers! A band from Las Vegas where the lead singer wears a sleeveless argyle sweater!"

I went back to my tree and was suddenly seized by inspiration for a screenplay. The THC from my breakfast had obviously kicked in. I pulled a receipt out of my pocket and a pen from my backpack and took notes. Goddamn, it was hot! But I was so happy! So alive! As of now, the screenplay hasn't gone anywhere. But I'm still developing it, as they say.

At 2:30, Regina called me to say that Elijah had woken up from his nap and they were leaving for the bus.

"Great!" I said. "I'll see you guys soon!"

At 3:10, when she hadn't shown up yet, I called her. She answered with this:

"I can't find a fucking place to park anywhere!"

"You haven't even *gotten on* the bus yet?"

"All the garages are closed off, and I can see the state troopers. They're ticketing everyone! We're gonna get a ticket if I park on the street! What a disaster!"

"Just park on the street. You won't get a ticket."

Twenty minutes later, I called her again.

"I am in the longest line you've ever seen," she said. "Elijah is screaming his head off. I'm going to go crazy!"

Part of me thought, you know, she's being miserable on purpose to spite me. She could always sense when I was trying to enjoy myself. That wouldn't do. The other part of me, however, wasn't a selfish asshole, so I sympathized.

"I'm so sorry."

"Oh. Oh. We're moving. I gotta go. Elijah, don't put that in your mouth!"

I hung up the phone, feeling numb and desperate. Were they really suffering? Was it my fault? Why is it so hard to have fun when you have a family? I'm sure Regina was thinking the same thing. I resented the cloud of mutual resentment that hung over our marriage. Twenty minutes later, I called her again.

"I'm on the bus! The air conditioning is broken and we're stuck in the worst traffic I've ever seen. We haven't moved! The sweat is pouring down Elijah's face! I have to hang up now! Elijah! Stop that!"

Around 4:30, a twenty-passenger bus pulled up to the entrance.

A guy got off holding the back end of Elijah's stroller. Regina was at the other end. The front of her shirt was nothing but sweat, like she'd just run a 5K, and her hair was a matted mess. Elijah's shirt was off. His body was slick to the touch. They both looked stunned, like they'd just survived a terrible accident. I felt horrible, and I was overwhelmed with a desire to take care of both of them forever. My wife, in particular, had suffered once again for my sins. I'm sure at that moment she wanted to take care of me as well, permanently.

"I'm never doing this again," Regina said.

"I love you," I said.

"I love you, too. Now find me some shade."

I walked them through the crowd, which must have been 50,000 people at that point, to our little shady spot. Elijah wanted out of his stroller.

"Da-deeeeee!" he screamed.

In the cooler was a treat waiting for Regina. I'd gone to the concession stand to buy her a "Death by Chocolate" brownie.

"You have fun," I said. "I'm taking the boy."

"Are you sure?"

"Get out of here! Have a beer and go see Patty Griffin."

"Come with me."

"I would rather eat my own arm than attend a Patty Griffin show."

I pushed Elijah over huge sunken tree roots and a menacing area of mysterious wood chips. I had his water bottle and I had a squirt bottle full of water that I would use to mist him. I had snacks. I had water for myself. I had extra water for both of us. It was five p.m. on the hottest day of the year, and I was strolling my son through a hellhole advertised as fun.

We went to the "Austin Kiddie Limits" tent. Whoever came up with that name should be court-martialed. We just missed the puppet show. I parked the stroller under the tent, took Elijah out, and said, "Watch my stuff" to some people I'd never seen before and would never see again.

Next to the tent was something that the ACL Fest organizers had decided to call "The Beach." They'd placed umbrellas and deck chairs inside a basketball-court-sized sand pit and provided buckets and shovels. Elijah didn't seem to mind how hot it was.

"Sand!" he said. "Sand sand sand!"

I stuck him in a patch of shade about the width of a barbecue pit, sat in a chair with a spritzer, and squirted him while he loaded sand into a bucket and dumped it over his head. Yeah. This was worth the money.

That activity went on for a while, but I soon began to think, god-damn it. This is a music festival. I'm going to take my son to hear some music. It would require trickery.

"Elijah, do you want to go to the park?"

"Pak pak pak pak!"

"It's a special kind of park. A jazz park!"

"Ja pak!"

"That's right."

"Bye-bye sand!"

I went to the stroller and looked at the map. The stage I wanted was so far south of me, it was almost in San Antonio. No way I was going to be able to push Elijah that distance. I knew he'd never stay in the stroller that long. So I made an executive decision. The stroller would stay where it was; I trusted that drunken rock fans wouldn't steal our stuff. I took his water, my water, and the squirt bottle in one arm, loaded him in the other arm, and headed for the SBC Communications stage.

Elijah wanted down from my arm. He preferred to run and skip the whole time. I just loved that kid. He was a really good boy some-times. I kept spritzing him. We landed in another grove of trees. Solomon Burke was about to start.

"Here you go, son. This is the music you were asking for."

The music started. I hopped up and down. Elijah flapped his arms. He'd really wanted to see Solomon Burke.

Elijah enjoyed himself for fifteen minutes, but only as long as I put him on my shoulders and flung him around like a rag doll in time to the music. I guess we were having some fun because two young women of Girls Gone Wild vintage came up to us.

"You are so *cute!*" said one of them.

They wouldn't have been talking about me even in my youthful prime. But I'm not afraid to exploit my son for an ego boost. I'm certainly not the first dad to imagine his kid as a wingman.

"That's my boy."

"You guys are quite a pair," said one of them.

Before they asked Elijah for his phone number, I maneuvered him closer to the stage. Suddenly, I remembered that I'd seen Solomon Burke already, in Philadelphia, at a similar outdoor festival with a much smaller audience that had been at least half black. This audience was 99.9 percent white, either aging "blues fans" or gawking hipsters who'd heard that Solomon Burke was real fat, wore flashy suits, and sat on a throne on stage. All that was true, and I kind of qualified in both categories. But it seemed that in the last three years, King Solomon had begun phoning it in a bit. His set was all medleys of other people's tunes, and there was no intersong chatter. Then again, if I weighed 350 pounds and I was performing outdoors in Central Texas in mid-September, I wouldn't want to chat with my audience, either. My internal rock-critic monologue broke when my son began to scream for food.

"Chow time!" I said.

"Chow ti!"

It was another Bataan-like trudge across a steaming field to the concession area. We stopped at a misting tent. I put Elijah's face directly in front of a fan. It blew water all over him.

"Raiiiiiin!" he said. "Ah ha ha! Raiiiiiin!"

"That's right, son. Rain."

And then he kissed me on the cheek.

We were at the food court soon after. I made a quick scan, and I saw that one of the booths offered hummus with chips. Regina would approve if I fed that to him. I got the order pretty quickly and then sat down at a picnic table. I put the paper container in front of him.

"Ah! Chee!"

"Um, sure. It's cheese."

He started eating. My cell phone rang.

"Are you guys doing OK?"

"We're great! How was your show?"

"It was really hot and crowded and I couldn't hear anything."

"Right. Well, we're eating right now."

I told her to come and meet us and to pick up the stroller on the way.

A few minutes later, she called again.

"Where are you! I'm looking for you everywhere!"

"I told you that I'm at the far end of the food court."

"What end? I'm at the end!"

Some nice guy sitting across from me saw Regina about ten yards away, screaming into her cell phone. He brought her over. She was wearing a big floppy hat and her shirt was still drenched.

"He's eating hummus," she said.

"He thinks it's cheese."

"That's adorable."

"Chee!" said Elijah.

"We flirted with some college girls."

"That's nice for you, dear. Was it fun?"

"Pretty fun."

"And is it out of your system now?"

"Oh, for a while."

"Good."

She looked miserably hot. So did the boy, and so, I imagine, did I.

"Let's get the hell out of here."

We went home, gave Elijah a bath, and watched *All About Eve* on Turner Classic Movies. It was far and away the most enjoyable thing we'd done all day.

On Saturday morning, our neighbor called. Our rock 'n' roll co-op had never materialized. We told her what a lousy time we'd had.

"We didn't get there until almost six," she said. "Right in the middle of Broken Social Scene."

I wanted to say: "Did your three-year-old *really* enjoy Broken Social Scene?" But I resisted.

We still had our wristbands. We were supposed to drop Elijah off at his friend Mia's so we could go back to the festival. In the morning, I said to Regina, "There's no way I'm going back into that shit pit."

"But we already spent the money!"

"That's right. So it doesn't really matter if we go or not. We can either go and be miserable that we spent the money or not go, be comfortable, and be a little anxious that we spent the money."

We dropped Elijah off at his friend's, drove to a movie theater, and spent four hours luxuriating in a blissfully cool double feature. The fact that the two movies were *Sky Captain and the World of Tomorrow* and *Wimbledon* didn't matter to us. We were at peace, taking solace in the fact that the same thing was currently happening to hundreds of parents in Austin who'd thought it would be cool to take a toddler to a jam-band festival.

The next morning, Regina was supposed to go to the festival by herself so she could see Wilco. It was pretty obvious early on that she wasn't going anywhere. By noon, our wristbands were in the garbage. Instead, we went to Target to buy Elijah a potty-training seat, and then to this Japanese pearl-drink place we like. I never once thought, "Gee, I'd rather be at the Austin City Limits Festival." I'm sure Elijah didn't, either.

FIFTEEN

Wild Pig Bite?

October–December 2004

Regina forced me to go to Coo de Tot from time to time. I hated it, but she needed something to do on Sunday mornings with the kid. This particular one was at Ruta Maya, a place that served fair-trade coffee and hosted Howard Dean rallies, though it was redeemed somewhat by the fact that there was a cigar store in the back. When we entered, the weekly kiddie yoga class was under way. I slapped Elijah onto a mat while Regina waited in line for coffee.

The instructor was trying to get the kids to arch their backs and meow from their diaphragms. She then asked the kids to find their "inner dog," pointing to different spots on her tummy and saying "Sometimes I find my inner dog here, or here."

Elijah lay on his back on the yoga mat, looked up at the red-and-blue gel stage lighting and shrieked "Li! Li! Li!" This was his yoga experience pretty much until the class's conclusion, when the instructor said, "We're gonna end today by becoming sponges, like SpongeBob, except without eyes, or legs, or arms, and we don't make jokes." That didn't sound like much fun to me at all.

After yoga ended, we looked at kids' T-shirts and pants made of recycled fabric, including an orange-and-green number complete with an illustration of Mao wearing black-and-white spiral sunglasses. That shirt was $20. It was a little much, I thought. Who needed rave wear for toddlers?

Regina fell into conversation with the mother of Noah, a little boy from Elijah's swim class. Elijah was comporting himself nicely in a nearby playhouse. Suddenly, a plastic spear flew through the air and smacked little Noah square in the temple.

"Morrison!" I heard a woman shout. "Don't throw things."

I looked around. There was Morrison. Sure enough, he had hair that looked like Jim Morrison's, or at least like Val Kilmer's when he played Jim Morrison. I thought: Can I meet your brother Hendrix? Goddamn stupid hippie parents.

"Thank God it wasn't our kid," I said to Regina.

"Nope," she said, knocking on a nearby wooden post. "We haven't had any discipline problems. Yet."

Not long after that, the problems began. One late afternoon, Regina walked through the back door with Elijah, who, by now, had been in school for two months and would soon celebrate his second birthday. I immediately sought cover under the large cardboard box that we kept handy for just such emergencies. They entered the living room.

"Where's Daddy?" Regina said. "Where is he? I don't know where Daddy is! Oh. Oh. Is that Daddy under there?"

I threw off the box, emitted a mighty "RAWRRRR," and cranked the tickle monster up to ten. Elijah was delighted, as always.

"We had a little problem at school today," Regina said.

"What?"

"He bit someone."

Regina had borne witness to the victimized boy's arm. Elijah left "big old teeth marks," she said. The teachers had sat Elijah on a bench and told him that biting was bad, that you used your teeth for eating only. On the car ride home, Regina told him the same thing.

I'd been a dad long enough now to recognize a crisis, and I knew that it couldn't be neglected.

"Elijah," I said in my most stentorian voice. "Look at me."

He did, his eyes big, sheepish, and serious.

"Biting is very, very bad."

"It makes other kids sad," Regina said. "And they cry."

"It's wrong, and you can't do it anymore. Now, what did you do at school today that was wrong?"

Elijah glanced at Regina.

"Don't look at me. Talk to your daddy."

"All fa down!"

"I'm not talking about Ring Around the Rosie. What did you do that was *bad*?"

"Um. BI! BI BA!"

"That's right. Biting is bad. Are you going to bite someone again?"

"Nuuuuuuuu."

"Good boy. Now go get *Green Eggs and Ham* so Mommy can read it to you."

My son was a biter. Where it had come from, I didn't care; I just knew that it would have to stop. Fortunately, I'd established what I thought was a very effective discipline strategy. It was basically a "time out" system, but a little stricter. I just decided that "time out" needed a cooler name. Apparently, it had eluded me that punishment, by its nature, shouldn't be cool.

The strategy evolved gradually, beginning with a period when Elijah decided that he enjoyed jumping on the sofa. Though nothing when compared with the later problem of handling a biter, this was still our first real discipline challenge. Every time he jumped on the sofa, we told him to stop. He looked at us, smiled, and kept jumping. I came up with the brilliant idea of taking him off the sofa, putting him in his room, and closing the door. After I did that, he came out of his room, resumed jumping on the sofa, got down, went into his room, and closed the door himself.

"He thinks it's a game," Regina said.

"It is a game. And it's hilarious. But we have to stop him anyway."

We thought about his weak spots. He hated being held down or restrained. So when he jumped on the sofa, we pinned his arms and legs, and then he stopped jumping. This method also got him to stop putting his feet on the dining-room table. But soon, we realized, there would have to be a more comprehensive strategy, because I didn't feel like wrestling with my son every time he did something wrong.

So I came up with the Penalty Box. This, I decided, would be an actual box, large enough to contain a small child. Regina would paint the words "Penalty Box" on it, and then, in smaller letters, "For Bad Boys." The Penalty Box would face a blank wall, or a door, and Elijah would have to sit in the box for the duration of the penalty, without the company of toys, stuffed animals, or music. The penalty would be doubled every time he attempted to leave the box.

I wanted to structure the penalty system using cards, like in soccer. A minor infraction, such as jumping on the sofa, dumping green beans on the floor, or pulling Gabby's tail, would net Elijah a yellow card. Three yellow cards equaled a penalty. The card system reset every day, but it went right up until bedtime. A major offense, such as biting Mommy, would mean an automatic red card and an automatic penalty. In addition, I determined, after Elijah received a red card, each subsequent yellow card would be an automatic penalty, and every ten penalties would score him an extra penalty.

Regina immediately flagged this system as thoroughly retarded, and she muted my worst instincts. By the time we actually got around to it, the Penalty Box had become a Penalty Chair. There were no cards. Discipline was not a game, and it was becoming apparent that we had our hands full. Elijah was a gorgeous thing, all blond curls and blue eyes glinting with intelligence and humor. But he was also a difficult child.

For instance, there was the time when I caught Elijah attempting to swallow his mother's sunglasses.

"Take those out of your mouth," I said. "Please."

He bit on them harder.

"I mean it, Elijah. Remove the sunglasses from your mouth. Now."

He stared at me defiantly, and threw the glasses on the floor.

"That's it! Penalty Chair!"

I tucked him under my right arm and marched him off to the living room, where I sat him in the Penalty Chair. He wiggled and whined.

"Nooooo, Daddy! Nooooo!"

"Why am I doing this to you?"

He moved to bite me on the hand.

"Don't you dare!"

He tried it again.

"I mean it, Elijah. You can't throw stuff when you're mad. Now why are you in the Penalty Chair?"

"No throw glasses!"

"Are you going to do it again?"

"No."

"Good boy."

The Penalty Chair had worked, at least until the next time he threw something.

But even as we tried to work in tandem with the school to control Elijah's behavior, our relations with them deteriorated into a low-simmering conflict. Regina spent a considerable amount of time vigilantly monitoring the Internet for potentially disastrous health news. One government study set off particularly loud bells. Even one sugared drink a day, it said, greatly increased a child's risk of getting diabetes, and maybe even cancer. Regina seemed frightfully concerned.

"Why? We don't give him sugared drinks."

"I saw them giving kids this pink stuff to drink at the school. I'm a little disappointed."

"What kind of pink stuff?"

"I don't know. Something bad."

The next day, I went to pick up Elijah armed with a highlighted *Washington Post* article that said high-fructose corn syrup increases your child's risk of contracting diabetes, complete with quotes from health experts who said no responsible parent or caregiver should ever give sugared drinks to their kids. I came upon Elijah's teacher in the kitchen.

"While I've got you here. I just wanted to ask?"

"Uh-huh," she said, warily.

"When you give the kids juice, what kinds of juice are they drinking?"

She opened up the cabinet and showed me two huge purple plastic jugs of a horrible looking grape drink that promised 100 percent of the daily requirement of vitamin C.

"But they don't make this anymore. So . . ."

She showed me a carton of powdered Country Time pink lemonade.

"That's not juice," I said.

"The health department only requires that the kids get vitamin C. Besides, juice is too expensive."

I thought, What *are* you spending my $500 a month on, then?

"Do you want me to put him on the water-only list?" the teacher said. "I have five kids on it already."

"Sure! I just wish you had told us about this before."

"I totally understand your concern. I have a fourteen-year-old son, and we don't have any sugared drinks in the house. We never have."

She then went on to explain, convincingly, that the government pushed sugared drinks for political reasons because they were trying to diminish our corn surplus. Still, I wondered, if she doesn't give her own kid sugared drinks, why would she give them to my kid?

What kind of school made you put in a special request to not give your kid a sugared drink?

I went next door to give the article to the school's director. She wasn't in. The five-year-olds were gathered around a TV watching a video of *Goof Troop,* a cartoon featuring the work of Serbia-Montenegro's finest animators. I went back to Elijah's building to complain again. The teacher explained that the older kids beg for Disney on Fridays. She showed her toddlers only *Baby Einstein* or sing-along videos, and then only during diaper-changing time.

Later, at home, Regina and I couldn't remember them telling us anything about showing the kids TV when we'd signed up. We didn't think the Montessori Method approved of TV in the school. It was particularly depressing because he was watching crap there that we'd never show him at home.

The director never got back to us about the study. In fact, we never saw her again, not once. From there, things with the school just got messier. And Elijah kept biting.

Around that time, I went to a housewarming party. Our friends invited all of us, telling us there would be other parents with kids there, but the party started at dusk and we hadn't yet loosened up about Elijah's bedtime. Also, there would be smoke at the party, of various kinds, and I didn't want Elijah getting exposed. Regina was feeling tired that night. But I hadn't been out all week, except to see a matinee of *Napoleon Dynamite,* which had made me feel old. She and I still alternated going out without the other, to save money on sitters. I wanted to go to the party.

When I got there, I saw three different women carrying babies that were younger than Elijah. One of the moms was a bass player and another looked more or less like Betty Page, with extra tattoos. The third one offered me some weed, and we smoked together. I wouldn't let my kid into a room where people were smoking pot, but these weren't my kids and I wanted to get stoned. My smoking partner had an eight-year-old stepdaughter who was running around, acting very sassy and ironic, saying things like, "That's a groovy mirror ball on the ceiling! I'm a disco devil!"

Her mom and I got to talking about schools.

She'd sent her daughter to the Children's Discovery Center. We'd rejected that because we'd found it a little squalid. But we hadn't known that the school kept a private wooded estate in the Hill Country. When the kids turned four, they'd bus them ten miles a day to the estate so the kids could take their lessons amid nature. They frolicked together in sylvan bliss, just like little Truman Capote and Harper Lee back in the day. "They're so loving and nurturing," the mother said. "And they want the parents to be involved. We meet once a month at the Central Market Café. The kids love it. They're filthy when they come home, but one time I went up to the camp and my daughter was sitting in a tree. Just being a kid."

Her daughter had previously attended the school that Elijah was at now. The first year was wonderful, she said. Her daughter had a lovely teacher and developed a deep and abiding friendship with another girl. The next year, the school decided to split up the two friends, whom they nastily called "Thelma and Louise," and wouldn't even allow them to play together at recess.

"They were trying to touch each other through a chain-link fence," the mom said, "and the teachers kept tearing them apart. They told me the friendship was disrupting the educational process."

"Good lord," I said.

The mom had been suitably appalled. She also found it strange that late in the afternoon, every afternoon, the kids would spend two hours watching a Disney movie. There was no quality control over the movies. Apparently, they'd show whatever the kids brought in. When she complained, the director told her it was none of her business.

All the minor misgivings I'd been feeling about Elijah's school coalesced into a shining moment of clarity. The little plastic toys that looked like they'd come from Happy Meals! The sugared popsicle every Friday! The giving the kids pink Country Time lemonade and calling it juice! The zombie five-year-olds watching a low-rent Mickey Mouse cartoon that looked like it had been dubbed from the original Croatian! This school was a farce! A scam! And an evil one at that! It didn't reflect my values at all! Or maybe I was just stoned. I called Regina immediately.

"We have to pull him out of school immediately," I said. "I think we made a big mistake."

Over the next five minutes, I took Regina's perfectly calm Saturday evening of novel reading and bath-taking and tore it to shreds, eventually getting her to agree with me. On Monday morning, we decided, I would go into the school and present the director with a list of questions. If those questions weren't answered to my satisfaction, Regina and I would withdraw our son.

When I got off the phone, the stoner mom said to me, "Your son only has one life. You should do what you think is right."

Later, I played tag with her eight-year-old daughter and a very large, very drunk woman whom the girl obviously knew. I was dubbed "it," and I proceeded to dart around the backyard.

"I am a chameleon who melds into the night! Where do the shadows end and I begin? You will never tag me! Ha-ha!"

The girl seemed to like it. I ran around quite lithely for ten minutes until the girl threw a giggle fit and I was fairly out of breath. The large woman collapsed, heaving, to the ground. A friend picked her up. She put her hand to her mouth and they ran toward the bathroom. By comparison, I thought, I'm in pretty good shape.

I went inside. My new friend's baby was crawling around. He had an Altoids tin in his mouth. I'd used that tin earlier, and knew it didn't contain Altoids.

"Unless you want your baby to eat your weed," I said. "You'd better take that away from him."

"Dude!" said the baby's father.

I wanted to be a cool parent, but there was free and loose and open-minded, and then there was sordid. We may have made mistakes in Elijah's upbringing, but you'd never catch him crawling around a shag carpet at eleven p.m. on a Saturday night with a container of marijuana in his mouth. At least I could say that. My phone rang.

"Are you coming home?"

"Oh yeah. I forgot."

I pulled in fifteen minutes later with a half-dozen doughnuts. Regina was sitting up, waiting to talk. "Look," she said. "Elijah seems happy. We've both noticed that he's learning things. He's saying new words, he's much better with his puzzles, he counts, he knows his shapes and colors, and he's still interested in books. I don't want him drinking Country Time lemonade, but I think he'll survive."

"You're probably right."

The next Monday, I went to pick up Elijah from school at 12:45 p.m. He was sitting on the floor, with all the other kids, and they were watching a video. It was horrible. Clowns in cowboy costumes were singing "Home on the Range" with a dancing cactus.

"He ate his sandwich and fruit today, but not his vegetables," his teacher said.

"Can I talk to you for a minute?"

"Sure."

We went into the other room. I was holding Elijah.

"Listen, I'm a little worried about these videos."

"Well, you can talk to the director . . ."

"We both know that's not going to change anything."

She explained that they were watching the video because the kids had been outside and they needed to cool down. I said that wasn't very Montessori. She said that this was a "mixed" school. At a true Montessori school, the teachers don't pick the kids up and cuddle them. There's a lot less affection. It's almost all direct observation. But they did have some Montessori materials. And she assured me that they sang the Montessori song about the continents, whatever that meant.

"The older kids watch TV, too," I said.

"But you should see their work. They're five years old and writing in journals."

"Look. He seems very happy here. You all obviously give him a lot of attention and love and he's definitely learning. His manners are a whole lot better."

"He loves pouring things. He *really* loves it. And stacking."

"Great."

Elijah was getting yitchy, so she picked him up.

"We sing all kinds of songs."

"What did you sing today, Elijah?" I said.

"Had a Fa!"

"That's 'Old McDonald,'" I said to his teacher.

"We didn't do that one today."

"I'm sorry to be a noodge. But this is our first kid."

"You'll chill out with the second one."

Fuck you, lady, I thought, but said, "Education is really important to us."

"It's important to us, too," she said.

We didn't have anywhere else to send him, and we weren't happy about that. Still, within a month, Elijah was able to recognize all his colors, and even some words. He started singing the "Alphabet Song" and recognizing letters. We caught him counting up to twenty by himself in his room.

"Our son is smart," Regina said. "This parenting book says that kids might be able to recognize one color by thirty-three months. He's twenty-three months, and he recognizes all his colors."

"Wow! By the time he's thirty-three months, he might be inventing his *own* colors."

"Hush."

Elijah displayed new knowledge all the time, and we received each piece with stunned enthusiasm. We couldn't help ourselves; parental pride is genetic. The fact that he could now identify a donkey by sight was, to us, a miracle that qualified him for canonization, or at least recognition as a Nobel Prize finalist.

We attempted to supplement his knowledge at home as often as we could, whether we knew what we were talking about or not. One afternoon, a weather front moved in. I was in my office, happily reading about baseball on the Internet and thinking about maybe starting a screenplay. Regina flung open the door. Elijah was squalling in her arms.

"There was some lightning right in front of our house. It really scared him. He's asking for you."

"Aw. Come to Daddy."

I held Elijah, kissed his cheeks, and stroked his hair.

"It's OK, buddy," I said. "Sometimes when it rains, there are things called thunder and lightning."

"Rain! Uh! Rain!"

"That's right. And thunder makes a loud noise that sounds kind of like . . ."

I made my best thunder noise.

"And then there's lightning," I said, "which is like a quick shot of light that comes down from the sky."

"Rain! Rain!" Elijah said.

"And the reason there's thunder sounds is because the lightning makes noise. So first you hear the thunder, and then you see the lightning, and it's the same thing. But it's nothing to be afraid of."

"Actually," Regina said, "you see the lightning before you hear the thunder because the speed of light is faster than the speed of sound."

"That's right, Elijah. Listen to your mother."

I wanted to be able to answer every question that Elijah had. Unfortunately, having a kid also forces a person to realize that he really doesn't know shit. It occurred to me that I should be enjoying these days when I was an unqualified object of worship to my son. Because there would come a time when he'd realize that his dad is an idiot.

Fortunately, if you realize your mental deficiencies early enough, you can at least make plans to supplement your child's education in other ways. The morning after my weather-related brain fart, I stepped out of the shower and said to Regina, "We're keeping Elijah out of school tomorrow."

"For what?"

"You'll see."

I'd made it a habit of collecting notices of special places where I could take Elijah. On my desk was a postcard, which I'd picked up at the ice-cream store, for something called "Crowe's Nest Farm." I Googled.

There it was. Open to the public, just twenty miles outside of town. I e-mailed the link on their website. About an hour later, I got an e-mail back saying that I was welcome to bring Elijah as long as I didn't mind the "Food and Fiber" exhibition that was going on for grade-schoolers that day. I wrote back saying that I love food and I love fiber and I will see you tomorrow.

That evening, I said, "Elijah, guess where we're going tomorrow."

"Skew!"

"No. Not school. Where do the sheep and pigs live?"

"Um. Fa?"

"Yes. And tomorrow we're going to a farm."

"Ahhh! Fa! Fa! Fa!"

He stood up and ran into the other room.

"Mommy! Fa! Daddy fa! Jah Fa! Fa fa fa!"

Farm day featured perfect Texas fall weather, about 85 degrees and 95 percent humidity and some cloud cover. We took a highway out of town, turned right at the Texaco, followed a road past what used to be farmland but was now tract homes starting at $80,000, turned right again, and then we were at the Crowe's Nest Farm, nestled into a peaceful, sloping, tree-groved corner of the Hill Country. There were several school buses in the parking lot. We got out of the car. A guy scooted by on a golf cart.

"Are you the folks who e-mailed yesterday?"

"Yep."

"Well, if you don't mind, we don't have our usual hayride tour today. Once a year we have an expo for inner-city kids."

I wanted to say that Austin doesn't really have an inner city. But I didn't.

"That's not a problem."

"Welcome to our farm."

Crowe's Nest isn't a working farm per se. It's more of a "living farm," with exhibits showing how farm animals live when they're treated right. There are also small exhibits that show off small wild animals and exotic birds. It's a magical, beautiful place, the perfect mix of country and hippie values, an agricultural utopia in the middle of overdevelopment hell. Elijah was insane with joy. He ran from one exhibit to the next, shrieking.

"Don-tey! Don-tey!"

"Don't just yell at the donkey, son," I said. "Say hi."

"Hi, don-tey!"

Next it was on to the sheep, and the llamas and the emus.

"Yama! E-bu!"

We happily strolled through a bestiary that wouldn't have been out of place in Shangri-La, marveling at the gorgeous pheasant plumage and the sinister beauty of various hawks and owls. Then we arrived at the javelina pen, which contained a sign warning children not to stick their hands through the fence. This wasn't going to be a problem because there were two layers of fencing, and the javelinas were at least six feet back.

Regina and I got into a conversation, forgetting about Elijah for a second.

"They must have had problems with biting here," she said.

"I'm not surprised. Look at those crazy wild pigs!"

The javelinas, though technically not pigs, wild or otherwise, lifted their snouts and snorted, revealing hideous foot-long yellow fangs that could easily pierce human bone. They hissed and stuck out their vile tongues.

"Creepy," Regina said.

"Like horrible monsters."

We hadn't thought that Elijah might be listening to us. He stared at them, wide-eyed and shivering. He looked up at his daddy.

"Wild pig bite?"

Oh, dear.

"No, Elijah. They won't bite you."

"Wild pig bite Jah! Bite! Bite! Bite!"

We attempted to distract Elijah by taking him to see some tame domestic pigs. At the pen, a gruff-looking man in overalls was showing off a porker the size and shape of a Peugeot. Behind a gate, a smaller pig was trying to get into the pen, sticking his nose under and squealing horribly. The big pig was busy trying to push the small pig back in. Two medium-size pigs, both covered in filth, made an equal ruckus.

"Wild pig bite?"

"No, Elijah."

"Big pig bite?"

"No, the big pig just eats corn."

"E-bu bite?"

In a further attempt to soothe Elijah's now-troubled soul, we took him to the "Faerie Wood," which was a feeble imitation of the kind of miniature playlands one encounters in Holland, not that one goes to Holland with one's kids very often. Basically, it was a bunch of cheesy roadside fairy statues perched in trees. Various trees had faces drawn on them, and bits of bunting and sparkly glass abounded. The Faeries could probably afford better digs. Elijah was even less interested than we were. Fortunately, a big shaggy white puppy bounded out of the woods, sending the boy into peals of ecstasy.

After that, Elijah demanded that we visit the big pigs again. Then we went to see the bobcats. Finally, it was time to say hello to Mr. Cow, who was being shown off to a group of multiethnic third graders by a wide-eyed old man wearing overalls and no shirt.

"Now here is what we all call an udder. That's where the cow makes milk, but this cow dried up years ago. And to get the milk, we squeeze this, which is called a teat."

A couple of the more savvy children giggled.

"Now who all can tell me what pasteurization is?"

We were off to see the roosters. Elijah held his hand over his head like it was a coxcomb and shouted, "Doo doo doo do doo!" It was hard for all of us to leave the farm.

For the rest of that day, Elijah repeated, over and over again, "Wild pig bite? Wild pig bite? Big pig bite?"

The answer was always no.

The next day, Elijah was scooting around the house on his Rock, Roll, and Ride tricycle. He popped a wheelie, tipped over, and smacked his head on the floor. After a certain amount of agonized screaming on his part, I managed to soothe him with an animal cracker.

"Ja fa down!"

"Yes."

"Daddy fa down!"

"No, Daddy did not fall down."

"Mommy fa down!"

"No."

"Wild pig fa down!"

What was it with the damn wild pigs?

"Yes, Elijah. The wild pig fell down."

By the end of that day, Elijah had broken a wineglass, dumped his lunch on the floor, and run out into the street, cackling, disobeying Regina's direct orders. Also, we'd caught him on all fours in the bathtub, drinking from the faucet again.

"What are we going to do, Neal? He thinks he's an animal. Part of the reason I think he's biting is because he's obsessed with the wild pigs. He can't stop talking about them."

"Our son is a little strange."

"He is. I swear."

No one could come up with a strategy to stop our little Jaws. His teacher told us that he seemed to have trouble empathizing with the other kids, that he didn't understand that biting hurt. She said we should try some role-playing with stuffed animals. I didn't think that would work, because stuffed animals don't cry if you bite them. We tried an incentive program. If he bit, he didn't get ice cream, or he didn't get to watch a Wiggles video. Every discipline guide in the world says this is the worst possible way to correct any kind of behavior at any age; but naturally, our school had suggested it, and for some reason we tried.

Meanwhile, Regina's mother called to say that she'd been talking to the director of her church's preschool about Elijah's problems. The director said that you should never punish a child at home for something he does at school, particularly not at this age, when they have little conception of right and wrong, and almost no comprehension of emotions. So we were basically dealing with a behavioral black hole. No one ever brought up the subject of spanking. When it comes to contemporary kids' discipline, spanking is the 800-pound paddle in the middle of the room. Was it cruel, or just effective? Was it making a comeback, or should it be banished forever? We tried not to think about it at all.

Our school was incompetent, Regina and I were confused and a little selfish, and Elijah, let's face it, was naughty. It was a bad combination. And yet we pressed on.

Two months past his second birthday, Elijah was on waiting lists across the city. We didn't want him in the "best" preschool. We just wanted him in a preschool that didn't try to justify showing kids Barney videos and giving them Country Time lemonade. But the lists didn't budge, and there was little hope that they would. So holiday time rolled around, and Elijah was still in the "Montessori" school. Despite our growing doubts, we thought there'd been progress. It had been weeks since the last report of an Elijah-related behavior incident. With that in our hip pockets, we anticipated Elijah's school holiday program with great enthusiasm.

"It's going to be so cute," Regina said. "All those kids singing." I was in a good mood about the day, because the Phoenix Suns were having a great season and there was a game on ESPN that night.

The day of the holiday program, we put Elijah down for his nap. Instead of sleeping right away, he threw all his toys and blankets out of the crib. We couldn't take them away, because if they weren't in his crib, he'd never sleep. He knew he had us in a bind, so he threw them out again. And again. And again. I went in. Half his toys had landed in his laundry basket.

"Cut the crap, junior."

"Daddy, I did it!"

"Did what?"

"Elijah throw animals in basket!"

I sighed and repressed a smile.

"Yes, you did, son. Good job."

Finally, he fell asleep. We had to be at the school at four p.m. at the latest. At 3:25, Regina went into Elijah's room, where he'd been conked out for only half an hour.

"Elijah! Wake up! It's time to go to school!"

Elijah did what we all do when woken up suddenly from a deep afternoon nap. He stood, shook his head around, and said, "Whuuh? Whuhhh? Whuhhh?"

"Don't you want to go to school and sing?"

"Yeah," he said, softly.

But he was humoring us. As soon as he got into the car, he began to shriek. The vicious late-afternoon sun was nailing him. Elijah reacts to sun in his eyes as though it were holy water. He began smacking himself in the face.

"Nice," Regina said.

We drove and Elijah shrieked. I tried my usual sun-distraction methods.

"Elijah. Look the other way and tell me what animals you see."

"NOOOOOOO! Go away sun! Go away! AHHHHHHH!"

"OK, Nosferatu."

We eventually turned away from the sun and got to the school. Judging by the number of cars in the parking lot and in all adjacent parking lots, we were the last family to arrive. Regina got out of the car. Elijah's shrieking had left her a little frayed.

"Where's the video camera?"

"That was your job."

"Shit! Shit! Fuck! I can't believe we didn't bring the fucking video camera!"

Elijah was looking at her.

"Regina. Language."

"I'm just really upset, OK?"

The balance between Regina's life as a mother and the rest of her life was proving difficult. She felt so overwhelmed. Nothing was getting done, she told me. She had to finish a painting, and clean the house, and take care of the boy, and then there was this other big project that she was supposed to do but hadn't started on yet. She remembered things she had to do and then forgot them. I told her to make lists, and she did, but then she lost them. She'd accidentally left a school paycheck in her jeans, and had washed the jeans. Nothing was going right.

"I'm becoming one of those ladies who puts eggs in the pantry," she said.

It didn't matter that she'd forgotten the video camera. There was no way we could have videotaped anything. The room where they were holding the pageant was designed to hold twenty children, but it was swarming with the parents and grandparents of thirty children. We were stacked up on top of one another like refugees loaded into steerage. One of the teachers got up at a music stand with a guitar and said something about how it was the twentieth anniversary of the school, which was "pretty cool." She thanked the director for making this a nice place to work. Sorry, I thought. There's still no holiday bonus for you this year.

The program was comprised of several unreligious Christmas songs written by Jews, including "Deck the Halls," "Rudolph the Red-Nosed Reindeer," "Jingle Bells," and "We Wish You a Merry Christmas." The children were supposed to sing, but it was mostly the teachers who sang, while the parents said to their kids, "Come on, Evan. Sing! You know the words! Don't be shy!" You haven't lived until you've seen thirty sets of parents trying to enjoy themselves by tunelessly mouthing the words to "Jingle Bells."

We were also treated to the Pledge of Allegiance, and then we got to hear more songs. Most of the kids sang now, but Elijah stared blankly off into the distance like little Tommy Westphal from *St. Elsewhere,* probably wishing very much that he were still in bed. I wished I were in bed as well.

The second set was education-based. They sang the "days of the week" song, "Twinkle, Twinkle, Little Star," and the "Alphabet Song." Then came "The Continent Song," which I believe is standard throughout all Montessori schools. The lyrics almost defy belief. Australia, according to the song, "is the land of the kangaroo" and also the koala bear; Asia is the largest continent; Africa has the hippopotamus and the rhinoceros, and "Europe is the land of the poets and musicians, artists, and the scientists, sculptors and discoverers." Oh, I thought. Is that so?

This seemed pretty dated to me for a Montessori school, or for any school, really. While I realize that Europe doesn't boast very many interesting animals, is it really fair to give them poets, musicians, artists, scientists, sculptors, and discoverers, when Africa gets credit only for jungle beasts? I looked around the room. At least half the parents were from the Indian subcontinent. Their ancestors had been speaking hundreds of different languages, building cities of stones and brick, developing sewer systems and alphabets, making jewelry, and writing the *Kama Sutra* while most Europeans were still picking nits out of their body hair. I wondered what they thought about "The Continent Song." The director was a first-generation Sri Lankan immigrant. Did she even listen to the lyrics of the song? How did she live with herself?

Then we did a gift exchange. Elijah got a fish puzzle and some Play-Doh from Savannah, one of the school's standouts, an absolutely delightful elf-girl with just the slightest amount of fuzzy red hair. I thanked Savannah's parents on Elijah's behalf.

"Too bad your daughter's not more friendly."

"Aw," said Savannah's mother. "Don't say that."

"I meant that she is actually very friendly and adorable."

"Oh."

I made a note to self: Don't use irony with Texans you don't know.

Then it was on to another room, where we had a potluck buffet. I was thankful for the Indian parents, because they rescued the buffet from being another pasta-salad-and-brownie-mix nightmare. Mmmm. Homemade samosas. And those deep-fried dough balls in thick syrup: God, they're so delicious! We all sat on the ground with about two inches between families. Either the school was too small to accommodate all these adults, or they had too many students enrolled, or both. I huddled around my plate so no one would step on it.

Before we left, we had a brief conversation with Elijah's teacher. The problems with Elijah hadn't stopped, apparently. They'd just stopped telling us about them.

"Is he being a good boy?" I said.

"He's being a boy."

"Oh."

"We have to work on impulse control."

"What's impulse control?"

"Pushing. Hitting. Putting rocks down other kids' shirts. That sort of thing. He's been bothering the kids in the older class because we told him to stop picking on the babies."

"Ugh."

"Impulse control."

4

FORWARD

SIXTEEN

The Jew Who Cooked a Ham for Christmas

December 2004

Then it was Christmas, a holiday that, until Regina came along, I'd celebrated in the American Jewish manner by going to the movies and seeing *Tootsie* or whatever movie that year most resembled *Tootsie*. But, also in the American Jewish manner, I intermarried, and therefore found myself every late December in Nashville, Tennessee, a Christian place where you can't go five minutes in December without hearing that damn "Christmas Shoes" song on the radio. I concentrated my secular attentions on food.

In December 2004, as Regina and I lurched through her mother's neighborhood store, I felt my seasonal joy, never high to begin with, draining away under the gray-dim fluorescent lighting and because I couldn't find any organic peanut butter. Why, I wondered, don't the stores here have better food at Christmastime? In reality, it was a perfectly ordinary American supermarket, but I walked the aisles as though it were a crematorium.

Living in Austin had spoiled me. The grocery stores are so good that people from Europe visit to study them. On its worst day, my neighborhood store has sixty different varieties of citrus. I've purchased three kinds of blue cheese made by the Amish in Iowa. Elijah asks to snack on peanut-butter yogurt pretzels. His favorite food, other than ice cream, is capers. And, because we're careful, we don't spend any more money than we would at a regular store.

My nose crinkled in disdain. My mouth curled into a sneer usually reserved for people who wear baseball caps backward.

"This is horrible."

"It's not that bad."

"How many different kinds of cereal can people actually eat?"

"Yes, dear."

"Why do they call this a grocery store?"

"Because this *is* a grocery store."

When we arrived at protein alley, the fish looked like it had been in the deep freeze since June. I chose some tilapia for that night, December 23; I could render it inoffensive with tomatoes, garlic, and parsley. The beef, however, looked slimy, with a slight greenish tint beneath the wrapping. I nearly gagged at the sense-memory of the sour-sweet smell that red meat gives off just as it's going bad.

"Look at this chicken," I said. "It's all . . . *muscle.*"

Then I saw my dream food, enveloped in a golden glow. A sweet chorus of angels drowned out the tinny Christmas-carol Muzak. It sat there alone on the shelf, the last survivor of its kind, in a light-brown burlap bag tied with a little metal ring.

A Smithfield ham.

I'd been dying to eat a Smithfield for years, ever since I'd read an essay somewhere by Southern culinary historian John Egerton in which he called country ham "an ancient and inimitable treasure, the highest form of the Southern gastronomic art." The only thing I coveted more than a Smithfield was a ham from Trigg County, Kentucky, which was supposed to be even better. I'd even briefly considered buying a Trigg off the Internet for dinner. After all, the mail-order turducken had been a big success two years before. But it was obvious that this Smithfield ham and I were destiny.

"That's our dinner. Glory be!"

"Are you sure you want to spend forty dollars? It's awfully big."

I looked at her indignantly.

"Woman. Don't you understand? I've longed to prepare a Smithfield ham my entire adult life."

I picked up my ham and cradled it. The bony back end poked me in the ribs. I bent down and gave it a kiss.

"I love this ham!"

"You're frightening me."

"Do you see anyone else volunteering to make dinner this year?"

My joy at having found my dream ham buoyed me all the way through an interminable checkout line. The grumbly clerk ran my items through the scanner without enthusiasm. My enthusiasm, on the other hand, couldn't be checked.

"Gosh, I got a really big ham!"

"Uh-huh."

"When I saw that Smithfield ham, I just had to have it!"

"Uh-huh."

"Happy Holidays to you!"

"I hate it when people say Happy Holidays. It's anti-Christian. You say Merry Christmas."

I looked back at the other people in line. Surely they would mock the provincial attitudes of this foolish woman. No one would put up with this kind of crap where I lived. But then I remembered where I was. They all stood there, dour and disapproving.

Here's what I thought: You people belong to a majority religion in a right-wing theocracy, yet loudmouthed jackasses have somehow persuaded you that you're some kind of oppressed class! Meanwhile, the government you love is collapsing the economy on purpose. You're all idiots!

Here's what I said: "Heh."

Here's what I should have said: "Yeah? Well, screw you, bitch! This year, Christmas belongs to me! I'm a Jew! *And I'm gonna cook a ham!*"

Child-related problems threatened the integrity of my perfect meal. Elijah had caught a stomach virus and a head cold. He was reduced to a simpering, tantrum-throwing mess. The day after we got to Nashville, Regina went off to see some friends, and my mother-in-law embarked on a mysterious five-hour errand. This left Elijah and me all alone.

At two p.m., he woke up from his nap.

"Daddy, pick up!" he screamed.

For twenty minutes, he sobbed relentlessly. Unable to console him, I put him down. Maybe he wanted to play with his toys.

"Noooooo! Daddy pick up! Walk! Pick up walk, Daaaa-deeeee!"

"Do you want something to eat?"

"No, Daddy. Pick up! Walk!"

"How about we play with some of your toys!"

"Daddy pick up! Walk!"

A great ice storm had hit Nashville that week, more or less hemming us all into my mother-in-law's townhouse, into which she'd just moved. Elijah remained sick and restless. Television was the only answer. But the cable had yet to be installed. I turned on PBS until *Between the Lions* ended. Regina came home to find the TV off and Elijah wailing.

"Can't you show him regular TV?"

"Babe, it's six p.m."

"So? Put on PBS again."

"Do you think Elijah likes the *News Hour with Jim Lehrer*? Just asking."

Our only fallback was the *Baby Foucault* video, or Baby Something, anyway, that we'd brought from home. But Elijah didn't seem to be interested in that anymore, either. Regina was mostly comatose. The stomach virus had struck her as well. There was no way out.

"I feel like throwing up every second," she said. "Maybe I'm gonna die."

From the other room I heard it.

"Dad-deeeeee! WahhhHH! Daaa-deeeeee! Pick up!"

I wouldn't let this stop me. Regina and I had been married four and a half years. I was the father of a toddler. By degrees, I'd become a man, and I was part of this family now. And on Christmas, a man cooks his ham.

I took my ham out of its bag as soon as I got it back to the house. It was majestic, but also kind of disturbing. I'd expected something bright pink that was ready for immediate consumption. This thing looked like it had just been unearthed in an archeological dig.

"There's a lot of fat," I said.

Regina, who'd been dealing with hams her whole life, just shook her head. I was on my own with the ham.

Smithfields are very salty, or so I'd read. I filled the kitchen sink with water. Gingerly, I lowered my prize and went upstairs to hide from my mother-in-law. A few minutes later, she knocked.

"Excuse me."

"Yes?"

"Why is that ham sitting in my sink?"

"It's soaking."

"Don't you need water for something to soak?"

No! The sink couldn't have drained! Stupid cheap sink! I needed every minute until that ham went into the oven. It had to be the perfect ham.

I roared down the stairs and into the kitchen. This time, I slammed the stopper down hard. I rubbed the ham. A little chunk of slimy fat lodged between my fingers. Eww, I thought. No, I corrected myself. Not eww. This is how hams are supposed to behave.

"It's going to be OK, baby," I said.

Regina entered the kitchen.

"Are you giving that ham a massage?"

"It needs me."

As the ice storm continued its assault on Nashville, the ham became a growing point of contention.

"That's too big for my oven," my mother-in-law said.

"No it's not."

"Yes. It is. I don't have a pot big enough to cook it in."

"We'll figure something out."

"I'm worried that it'll be too salty."

"I'm still soaking it. Don't worry."

"I really don't see how you're going to cook it."

"Listen here. I bought this ham and I *am* going to cook it!"

"Don't get mad at my mom," Regina said. "She's just trying to help."

Later, under my breath, I said to Regina, "She's not trying to help. She's trying to ruin my ham. I know she doesn't want to eat it. I know that none of you do. But I'm making this ham and no one is going to stop me. DO YOU UNDERSTAND?"

"Mommy, Daddy," Elijah said. "Pick me up!"

"Just a second, honey. Daddy has to soak his ham."

After a couple of days, the health situation improved, and we went over to my brother-in-law's house. Elijah's cousin Westlund was five years old. He owned a gecko named Charlie Cheddar and a parrot named Jambo. He was a polite young man with an interest in karate, exactly the kind of boy that Elijah should idolize. My brother-in-law Brett had been a fullback at Auburn, before his knee blew out. This was a very different kind of father-son combination.

There was an aesthetic difference between the cousins, which didn't matter at all. But there was also an age difference, which proved more difficult to traverse. Westlund liked to follow the rules of Christmas. Elijah had no idea what those rules were.

"Elijah open presents!"

"Elijah! No!" Westlund said. "You're ruining Christmas! Daaaaaaad! Elijah is ruining Christmas!"

"No he's not, Westlund," said my brother-in-law.

"Westlund," I said. "He's two. He doesn't understand."

"Elijah open presents! Elijah want presents!"

"They're not your presents!"

I managed to distract the two of them from their conflict by engaging them in a spirited round of karate. Westlund took lessons, and he wanted to show off his moves to me. Elijah seemed to enjoy butting his head into my groin. We went upstairs and got on top of the queen-size guest bed. They entered my dojo.

"I am the master of the ancient arts of the I Ching. If you follow my seven precepts, I will teach you to move objects with your mind, and minds with your object."

I found that last bit hilarious, and howled at my own joke.

"I'm going to kick you in the face!" Westlund said.

I grabbed his foot, mid-air, and sent him flopping on the bed.

"You are young and foolish."

"You're good at karate, Uncle Neal."

"No. I'm just bigger than you. In less than ten years' time, it has been prophesized, you will kick my butt."

"Elijah kick Daddy face," Elijah said.

"No, Elijah. You never kick anyone in the face."

Later, I found myself distracted by a brownie in the kitchen. The kids were on their own for a minute. I heard a horrified wail from around the corner.

"Aiiiieeeeeeeee! Da-deeeeeee!"

That wasn't my child's scream, but I knew what had happened.

"Elijah bit me!"

Westlund began to shriek, in pain and shock.

"Elijah Allen Pollack!" I said. "You're going to the Penalty Chair!"

Elijah hadn't eaten in three days because of the illness. He'd entered insane mode. He shrieked and thrashed and wouldn't respond to me at all. Westlund came into the room, looking deeply hurt.

"Apologize to Westlund, Elijah."

"Noooooooooooooooo!"

"I apologize, Westlund," I said.

"I don't accept," Westlund said.

He ran into the closet and stayed there until we left. Brett stayed out of the situation entirely. It's not as though he didn't care about Elijah's tantrum, but he had his own problems. He looked like he hadn't slept in a month. In addition to Westlund, he had a newborn baby girl on his hands. It was all he could do to keep from falling down the stairs.

Frighteningly, that left me as the family's only fully active Christmastime adult male that year. Later that evening, as I continued to massage my ham in its cold-water bath, I accidentally got into another conversation with my mother-in-law about faith. She'd continued to gently press her line over the years.

"You don't really practice, do you?"

"Well, um, uh, well, uh, not really, but I still observe the holidays for Elijah, because I think it's, uh, good for him to, um, know traditions and all. We light Chanukah candles and have Passover dinner."

"Eventually y'all are going to have to make a decision."

"I think that if we raise him knowing about a lot of different faiths, it'll be fine. I kind of think of it as an education in comparative religion."

By the look on her face, I might as well have told her that I will raise my son to believe that Satan is King.

That night, my son sensed that the golden day was drawing near. I desperately tried to be a good dad on Christmas.

"Santa outside!"

"Soon."

"Elijah see Santa!"

"Santa will come while you're sleeping."

Regina had found a forty-year-old Little Golden Book edition of *The Night Before Christmas*. It had been hers when she was a kid. I read it to Elijah as a bedtime story, taking time between verses to stop him from drinking a bottle of Nana's Wite-Out. He went to sleep at seven, but at eight, we heard him rumbling. I went in.

"Elijah miss Santa Claus."

"No you didn't. He's not here yet."

"Elijah want open presents from Santa!"

"Elijah, you have to go to sleep, or Santa won't bring you any presents. He'll bring them while you're sleeping."

"Waaaaah! Santa!"

Regina had taken to bed again with a return of the evil stomach virus. I was baking her yearly batch of oatmeal–chocolate chip cookies. I'd decided I could do anything in the kitchen.

"Daddy's making cookies for Santa."

"Santa eat Daddy cookies!" said Elijah.

"That's right. Now can you go to sleep like a good boy?"

"Yeah."

So I went downstairs and lovingly mixed up the batter and put it in the oven while my mother-in-law watched *Law & Order* in the next room, petting her ancient, bitter, long-haired black cat. The cookies got done and they were delicious. I put half a cookie and some crumbs on a plate, and put a little milk in a plastic cup, then covered it with foil so the cat wouldn't spill it overnight. I put the plate and cup by the fireplace.

"So Elijah can see it when he wakes up," I said.

"Isn't that sweet?" my mother-in-law said.

I've never believed in Santa. He wasn't a presence in my child-hood. But why shouldn't Elijah? The kid was two, for God's sake. What kind of dad doesn't let his kid believe in Santa Claus?

Meanwhile, in the sink, my ham soaked in its seventh change of water.

"Tomorrow," I said to it, "you're gonna shine."

Cooking day, that glorious day, arrived. The recipe called for the ham to bake in the oven for three-hours-plus in a roasting pan, wrapped in foil with four cups of water. Regina did the wrapping and the water-pouring.

"Shit!" she said.

"What?" I said.

"The water keeps coming out onto the pan. Why didn't you get heavy-duty foil?"

I gritted my teeth.

"Because. No one told me to."

"Everyone knows you cook ham in heavy-duty foil."

"I don't even know what heavy-duty foil is."

We'd all been stuck in the house, with very little break, for four days. The pressure built. We were like a bunch of snakes in a gag jar of peanut brittle. Something was going to pop.

Regina and I fought the first battle. I was in the kitchen, boiling water for potatoes. The water boiled over. I took it off the stove. Regina came rushing in.

"You're ruining my mother's stove!"

"No, I'm not. It was an accident."

"You were doing it all wrong."

At that point, I became my *own* mother.

"I can't do anything right! If I'm so worthless, why don't you just marry someone else?"

"Calm down."

"I will not calm down! You finish making dinner! I don't care!"

"That's the Christmas spirit," said my mother-in-law.

I stormed upstairs to steam.

Five minutes passed. Elijah came into the room. He'd seen me throw a temper tantrum, just like he usually did. This was not the kind of thing I should have been teaching him by example. But he surprised me. Rather than imitate, he did the grown-up thing.

"Daddy-doo!"

"What?"

"Elijah miss Daddy-doo!"

My son had become a peacemaker, and I was glad. Wasn't that one of the reasons you had kids? Sometimes a marriage needs a referee, and no one would ever know us as well as he did. Maybe he'd continue to step in on the occasions when Regina and I were arguing. That fantasy quickly dissolved.

Regina and I went back to cooking. Five minutes after saving the day, our referee utterly lost his mind. Two-year-olds are nothing if not inconsistent.

"Daddy, pick up!"

"I can't right now."

"Mommy, pick up!"

"Mommy's cooking!"

"Noooooooooooooooo! Daddy pick up Mommy pick up!"

He was on the floor, grasping at my legs, screaming.

"Mom!" Regina shouted. "Get him out of here!"

"Come on, Elijah," said my mother-in-law.

She moved to pick him up. He slapped at her, shrieking horribly, as she dragged him out of the kitchen. Regina and I heard them stomp up the stairs and we heard her voice rise, and then we heard a door slam, and more shrieking, and I said, "I'd better do something."

I walked into Elijah's room to see my mother-in-law desperately trying to read him a story. He sat in her lap, shrieking and twisting. She was trying to contain him peacefully, but he'd obviously driven her close to madness. I knew the feeling.

"Let me take him!"

She left, probably grateful.

"I scared."

"What are you scared of?"

"I just a little scared."

"There's nothing to be scared of. Now, when we go downstairs, I want you to give Nana a hug and tell her you're sorry. OK?"

"OK."

He did what I'd asked him to.

"I'm sorry, Nana."

"That's OK, sweetie," she said. "We're all family."

Dinner arrived soon enough. The audience for my ham included: My mother- and sister-in-law, both of whom eat like rabbits that can't wait to get to the gym; my wife, who had the aforementioned nasty stomach virus; Westlund; my newborn niece Mackensie (also not Jewish); Elijah; my brother-in-law; and me. The ham came out of the oven. Expecting something magnificent, I unfolded the heavy-duty foil that we'd picked up from Walgreens at the eleventh hour. The ham looked slimy and unappealing, like something on a veterinarian's autopsy table. I spent forty-five minutes trimming off just enough fat to make it edible. And then I tried to make red-eye gravy, which just tasted like smoky water. My sister-in-law added extra coffee, and then it tasted like smoky, watery coffee.

The ham was very salty. I might as well have rubbed a lick in bacon fat and set it on the table.

"This is delicious," said my sister-in-law, as she ate other things.

Regina and I cook all the time, and often with great success. But the ham tasted vile. After dinner, we had thirty pounds of it left. We tried to pawn some off on my relatives, but they weren't about to tango with the death ham.

"We don't really eat stuff that's already been cured," Brett said. "So it would be wasted on us."

There are moments when a man sees himself clearly. That was, for me, one of those moments. I'd failed.

It wouldn't do for me to throw 90 percent of my prize ham into the trash, so I started carving off the bone. I carved and carved. My wrists ached worse than after my typical four-hour workday.

"I'm done."

My mother-in-law turned the ham over.

"You've still got half a ham to go."

"Stupid ham," I said.

Regina and I took almost the entire ham home with us on the airplane. For two days, it sat in the refrigerator. Then we froze it. One morning a month later I said, "Let's do ham and eggs."

We got a serving of ham out of the freezer. The fat had coagulated into thick yellow globules. We looked at it, and looked at each other. And I threw the bag into the trash.

"Next year," I said, "We're making lasagne."

SEVENTEEN

Fear and Loathing in the Harmon Triangle

January 2005

So this is adulthood, I thought. It wasn't so bad. I was a father, a husband, a man of limited property, and a taxpayer. And I guess I was still pretty cool. At least I still listened to music and played video games sometimes. No one seemed to be stopping me. No one even seemed interested enough to pay attention. This gave me confidence that I could, at will, shape my world's parameters while no one else was looking. The logical next step, along my highway to responsible citizenship, was to enter politics.

The anti-immigrant guy had moved. The only remnant of the Harmon Triangle's previous neighborhood association was $500 in a checking account. But there were surrounding neighborhoods, so I, along with the woman across the street, lobbied a larger, more organized group just to the north of us, asking for the Triangle to be included. We met with these people. They were smart, dedicated, and anywhere on the political spectrum from far left to dogmatic libertarian. At their next meeting, they voted us in unanimously. Our problems were theirs now. This time, someone with a crypto-racist cable-access show wasn't leading. The liberals were in charge now. And thus I became the co–vice president, Harmon Triangle sector, of the Ridgetop/Morningside Neighborhood Association.

I vigorously went about my duties. With the closing of Al's house, our neighborhood turned its activist attentions toward the three run-down apartment complexes a few blocks away from my house on Harmon Avenue. Some anonymous investors purchased one of the buildings. At our urging, they installed a new property manager and a new philosophy: They would cater only to immigrant families. The Austin Police Department helped this building, throwing a job fair for the residents and raising money for school supplies. This was all part of something they called "Operation Cooperation."

The other buildings were less cooperative. They lapsed into decay. One of them, after much harassment by the cops and by various code-enforcement types, was shut down. Its apartments became home to night creatures. Gaunt, dangerous figures roamed its edges, living in dark, waterless apartments, selling drugs, squatting, whoring themselves on soiled mattresses pulled from Dumpsters. It was a relief when someone bought it, renamed it "The Montecito," put up a security gate, and started whitewashing the exterior walls. That left a third building, "The Highland," as the last fortress of constant illegal activity in the neighborhood. We would, I figured, contain it in due time. I declared public safety as the neighborhood's number-one priority, followed by traffic control and local business development. These weren't particularly original goals, I realized, but they were what we needed.

Once I'd squared away my new role as community leader, I decided it was time for me to reform my marijuana-smoking habits. One of my best friends from high school, who'd become a successful family-practice physician with a specialty in infectious disease, spurred the change. He had a son a few months younger than Elijah.

"Dude. You're gonna be thirty-five soon. You can't be inhaling all that shit into your lungs."

"You're probably right," I said. He had a degree from Harvard. I sighed as I imagined what the next four and a half decades would be like without pot.

"You need to get a vaporizer. It doesn't combust the weed. It cooks. You're sucking down like one hundred percent THC vapor."

"And it works?"

"It works so well that you barely have to use any weed at all. A quarter can last you for *months*. It is awesome."

I was faced with a purchasing decision that could get me very high and save me money at the same time; I didn't need to think on this for long.

"Where can I get one?"

An hour later, I'd found my quarry on the Internet. An hour and five minutes later, I'd placed the order. My vaporizer was on its way. I went into the living room to tell Regina of my lifestyle upgrade.

"How much did you spend on this thing?" she said.

I told her.

"Neal Ross Pollack! You're the one who's been saying we need to cut back on our expenses. And you spend that on something to help you smoke marijuana?"

"No, no. It's not about smoking. It's about vaporizing."

"Whatever."

"Besides. It's almost my thirty-fifth birthday. And I'm going to treat myself."

It arrived a week later. I waited for Elijah to go down for his nap before I opened the package. A shiny metal cylinder emerged from a red plastic base at about a 45-degree angle. On the downward slope, a half-moon three inches in diameter had been welding-torched out of the cylinder. Inside was the "heat source," a six-inch piece of glass tubing that curved out for the final two inches, culminating in a soothing blue-and-green blown-glass pattern of the type that you see at a gift shop in Eugene, Oregon. Inside the tubing was a white heat wand that looked like a Tootsie-Pop stick without its candy. On the other side of the cylinder was a glass knob done in the same blue-green pattern. A thick black electrical cord emerged from the base of the cylinder. The other component of my vaporizer was a two-foot-long piece of soft plastic tubing. On one end of that was a six-inch piece of glass, topped with a two-inch-deep oval container with a screen at the bottom. On the other end was a little glass circle with a blowhole. The manufacturer had also thrown in a weed grinder and a pick for tamping down the weed and for scooping it out when it was cashed. It was beautiful; I'd invested in the top of the line.

"That's some contraption," Regina said.

"They call it the Silver Surfer."

That night, the Silver Surfer made its inaugural voyage. I waited until at least an hour after Elijah had fallen asleep. It came into the living room with me.

"Wanna surf?" I said.

"Oh, all right."

This was a once-a-year venture for her, at best, so I felt honored. I pulled a nugget of homegrown out of a film canister. It went into the grinder, which I twisted a few times. A smattering of tasty shake remained when I was done. It poured easily into the wand, and then I patted it down with the pick. After about thirty seconds, the heat source glowed a deep orange. I turned the heat down a little and placed the contained end of the wand on it. After about fifteen seconds, I sucked on the tube.

"I don't think I'm getting anything."

"Let me try."

She had about the same result. I placed it on again, and sucked in, breathing from the bottom of my lungs. I tasted something sweet on my tongue as I blew out. A cool, fragrant mist dispersed out of my mouth. A few minutes later, we were watching *Giant* on Turner.

"Oh my God," I said. "This is such a good movie."

Regina appeared to be receding back into the couch. It threatened to swallow her entirely.

"You need to go get some doughnuts now," she said. "Don't you think?"

Though Regina returned to civilian life after that night, I've always tended to attack new enthusiasms obsessively. The Silver Surfer was a transformative technology. For the first time in my life, I found myself waking and baking. On days when I didn't have to drive anywhere, I stayed high all the time. I bled every drop of THC out of every tiny little pinchful of weed I had. Suddenly, pot had become an inexpensive habit. It was like going to the store and buying a six-pack, only to open it up and find that there were twenty beers inside.

One afternoon around two p.m., after some particularly vigorous surfing, I headed out into the neighborhood. My first stop was the Shamrock station. I walked in whistling and bought a Diet Cherry Coke. Then I bounced across the street, where a new business appeared to be opening up in the vacant lot on the corner of Airport Boulevard and 49th Street. I went into the trailer at the back of the lot. A young guy was sitting at a desk in an undecorated fly-by-night office. I extended my hand.

"Howdy! I'm from the neighborhood association!"

He shook my hand reluctantly.

"We just like to get to know our neighbors around here!"

"Sure," he said, probably thinking that he should have set up shop in another neighborhood. I intended to make him feel that way as often as possible.

"So what kind of a business are you going to be running?"

"Selling cars."

"Oh! To whom?"

Very matter-of-factly, he said, "Mostly shitty cars to immigrants who don't know any better."

"I see. And how long . . ."

"We have a five-year lease."

My thought was: Great. Coffeehouses and little boutiques are springing up around the city like mushrooms after a rain. And I have to live in this neighborhood. I wanted to tell him that businesses like his weren't welcome in the Triangle, but that obviously wasn't true, since a sleazy property owner had just given him a five-year lease. I vowed to keep a constant watch on this guy and his dealings. Then I walked into the afternoon, still baked out of my wits.

Regina and Elijah were out talking to our neighbor Astrid (Gavin's mom), who was rocking her newborn daughter. Mikki (Eamon's mom) came across the street with Eamon. By that summer, she'd also have a new baby.

"Oh, look," I said. "Desperate Housewives."

They all looked at me scornfully.

"Do I look desperate?" Regina said.

"No."

"Hey," Mikki said. "I thought you should know about something."

"OK."

"I went to pick Eamon up at school. And on the way home, I tried to drive down Harmon. There were all kinds of police cars. They'd blocked off the street with yellow tape."

"That sounds like a murder scene. I worked as a reporter for years, so I know."

Regina looked at me with more scorn.

"Plus, I watch a lot of TV."

The previous two weeks had been menacing ones. Groups of shirtless drunks paced in the dirt in front of the apartments, glowering. Late in the afternoon, they started standing in the middle of the road, playing a perverse game of chicken with passing cars. I worried that one of them might throw a forty-ouncer through a windshield at any moment. It was only a matter of time before someone got killed.

I took a two-block stroll toward the yellow CAUTION plastic. There must have been a dozen police cars. Thank God I'd arrived. I was a vice president of the neighborhood association. A few people were milling around.

Here's what I learned: The dead guy had been twenty-two. He'd come out of the building to defend his father, who was in the street fighting over a woman. A guy brained him with a shovel. The woman ran into her apartment, came out with an unraveled coathanger, and stabbed the guy in the heart until he died.

"Holy fucking shit," I said.

I walked around, looking to heal the situation. The poor guy at the rental house across the street was trembling, saying that he was going to break his lease and bail on the neighborhood for sure. The rest of the people milling were apartment residents, all of whom were saying that they had to get out now. There were TV reporters about. Residents were telling them that this neighborhood was a crime-infested rathole. I knew that something had to be done immediately to save our neighborhood's reputation. I presented myself in front of the cameras, speaking for the people. Stoned to the gills or not, I was still an elected representative.

The neighborhood association responded quickly, and with outrage. I was at the hot center of this one. My co-VP for the area had gone out of town. First, I wrote a letter that I copied at OfficeMax and distributed, with some help, the following Saturday morning. It went:

Dear Neighbors:

My name is Neal Pollack. I'm a Vice President, representing the Harmon Triangle area, of the Ridgetop Neighborhood Association. And I'm writing to let you know that we're all stunned and saddened by the tragic murder that occurred on the 4700 block of Harmon Avenue on Wednesday.

But I'm also writing to let you know that we understand, from discussions with the Austin Police Department, that this was an isolated incident, a personal argument gone terribly wrong. Over the last several months, the Austin Police Department, in conjunction with neighbors, has been working very hard to improve the crime situation and living conditions in this neighborhood, with great efficiency and great success. The crime that happened on Wednesday was extremely unfortunate, but it was also the kind of crime that could have happened anywhere in the city.

This neighborhood has had problems in the past. But we are working to change this and have made significant progress. With the redevelopment of the old airport across the street, new home construction everywhere, and new businesses opening up on Airport Boulevard, the possibilities and realities of change have never been brighter in the Harmon Triangle. Recently, our area became a part of the larger Ridgetop Neighborhood Association, an established, well-organized group that will work hard to represent our interests to the city. We will be isolated and forgotten no more.

But we still have more work to do, and we need your help. We must use this sad incident as an opportunity to build a stronger, safer neighborhood. We'll hold a community meeting within the next ten days or so, with the neighborhood association and with representatives from the APD, where we can discuss the situation in greater detail. I encourage you to come, and to help make this a better neighborhood for all of us.

I held a small meeting at my house the night after the murder with four other guys from the neighborhood. We decided to take a three-pronged approach. One, we'd work with the police to get the bad apartments shut down. I felt confident we'd accomplish this goal in a month. Two, we had to build a broad organization of people who could form a real neighborhood association—homeowners and renters, store owners and retail property owners, school officials, apartment managers, and so on. Everyone had an interest in making this a nice place to live. Three, we had to start doing long-term political work, hooking up with state and local officials and big-time developers, so we could use this incident as a catalyst to remake the neighborhood. Most important of all, we needed to bring the families from the apartment buildings into the fold. We'd received an e-mail from the principal at the neighborhood school. It went, in part:

As we've met with parents we've found out that there are prostitutes that frequent (and some may even live in) the apartments because there are a lot of single men that live there. Our students that live there say that the police come by frequently because of brawls that break out due to the drinking. Some of the Moms have expressed concerns at our Parent breakfasts saying that they have been threatened when they try to seek help from the authorities. The Managers and the owners are trying to remodel the complexes and this is good. However, the children that do live there are in harm's way daily when they go home. School is their safe haven and many treasure the days when we have after school programs for them because they don't have to go home right away. Some of the parents say that drugs have been offered to their children and it's difficult for them to let their children go outside to play after 5 pm on most days because of what might be going on outside. One of the parents is having to move because the harassment she puts up with from drunk men who may not even live in the apartment complex. She's a single parent with 4 small children. There's a good group of parents that wants to help find a solution to this problem because it's in their best interest to make the apartments safer for the children.

Any problems Regina and I had as parents were birthday cake compared with what the parents in the apartment buildings, many of whom wouldn't call the police because they were afraid they'd be deported, faced every day. At the same time, I started to think that maybe I didn't want to raise my kid in a neighborhood where someone gets stabbed to death with a coat hanger in broad daylight. I believed in fighting for my community, but did I really want this crime-plagued sliver of land between two major urban thoroughfares to *be* my community? I enjoyed drinking beer with my neighbors, but I sometimes wished we could do it elsewhere. My handling of the situation should have exhilarated me. Instead, I found myself depressed. About everything.

That night, Regina rubbed my shoulders.

"You're a good man," she said.

"I don't feel like a good man. I feel totally lost. How in the world did we end up here?"

"Are you still stoned?"

"Not at all. I've made so many terrible mistakes. Every project I try is a failure, and every decision I make is disastrous. I couldn't even pick the right neighborhood in which to raise my son."

"Neal, you say and do a lot of dumb things."

"Not a lot."

"Yes, a lot. And sometimes that gets you in trouble. But you're not a failure at all. Look at you. You own a house. You have a wife and a son and a dog that love you. You support your family doing work that you love on your own terms. You're on the board of the neighborhood association. For some people, that's the very definition of success."

"But I want more."

"We all want more."

This was why we'd gotten married, to boost each other in hours of darkness. But now in addition to being the agents of each other's fondest artistic dreams, we also had to prevent our son from getting hit by a stray bullet on his way to school. Adult responsibility had deepened our relationship. This made us very horny. We needed to get it on immediately.

"Last night I had a dream we were doing it doggy-style," she said.

"Is that so?"

"Oh yeah."

"Then consider me the man who'll make your dreams come true."

"God, it makes me so hot that you're our neighborhood police liaison."

"That's right, baby. And I've got the nine-one-one on you."

We copulated blissfully that night. Ironic sex talk is still sex talk, after all. But sex was one thing and drugs were another. At that crossroads, our passions divided. One day about a week before my thirty-fifth birthday, Regina came into the back of the house, where I was at my computer. She sniffed. It was around noon.

"Have you been smoking pot?"

"Not smoking. Vaporizing."

She stood there, austere, her face sallow with pity.

"What?"

"It just makes me sad."

"Why's that?"

"It's like you can't function without marijuana anymore."

"That's ridiculous. I can quit any time I want to."

I realized what I'd just said. That was the standard justification of the addict. But I wasn't one of those. Pot was maybe a little mentally addictive, sure, I thought, but . . . and there was another standard justification of the addict.

"Maybe I am doing too much."

"I'm just worried that you're not going to be able to quit without help."

"Give me a break. It's not heroin. Or even whiskey. What are you going to do? Have an intervention?"

Her stare indicated that she would, if necessary. Who, I wondered, would come to a marijuana intervention, precisely? But when you hear that marriage is about compromise, this is the kind of situation they're talking about.

"Fine," I said. I reached into the place where I kept my stash and handed her most of what was left. "Hide this from me."

We were throwing me a big thirty-fifth-birthday party over the weekend, cosponsored by Regina's hedonist book group. I had ordered an array of decadent chocolate desserts from the ladies. We would provide tasty pizza, a keg of Shiner, and a sound system set up so that people could bring their iPods to "MP3J." Regina thought this was pretentious, but I didn't care.

"You should make brownies."

"Are you serious?"

"Totally. Then the weed would be gone. Except for the little bit I'm going to save for my actual birthday."

"I don't know how to make pot brownies."

Oh, but I did.

"Just cook it in the butter."

My actual thirty-fifth birthday fell on a Tuesday. The party, which had been hazy fun, was already forty-eight hours in the past. Regina woke me at eight a.m. Elijah was with her and had been since 5:30. She didn't feel like celebrating.

"The bar in my closet collapsed again," she said. "My clothes are all over the floor."

"Hiyo, Daddy!"

"Hiyo, Elijah."

"I eat tomato for breakfast!"

"That's great!"

"And egg!"

"Yeah," Regina said, bitterly. "He 'ate' egg."

After this chipper birthday greeting, and a bowl of oatmeal with dried cherries, I went down to City Hall, along with other people from the neighborhood association, to discuss continued code violations at the apartment buildings. As I attempted to lobby representatives from the city's solid-waste division, I thought, this is how adults spend their birthdays.

Regina made a dinner of breaded pork loin, Tater Tots, and spinach salad. She had her book club that night. Ordinarily, I'd be cooking dinner on those nights. But it was my birthday and no one should cook for themselves on their birthday. The three of us sat down to dinner. Regina flipped open her laptop.

"If I did that at the dinner table, you'd divorce me."

"I'm sorry. I forgot you were there."

"Why are you mad at me?"

"I'm not mad. I'm just distracted."

"I eating ketchup!" Elijah said.

Then Regina was off to book group, to discuss *The Bastard in the House.* A group of women had chosen an anthology of essays by middle-class men who were trying to come to terms with their feelings about fatherhood and adult responsibility. Why? I thought. Who wants to read about that shit? Then I put Elijah into the tub with a new brand of bubble bath because the old one had been irritating his "peenie."

"Bubbles fuzzy!" Elijah said.

"They are fuzzy."

"Fuzzy in my mouf! Daddy-doo take a baf with Elijah?"

"No. Elijah take a bath himself."

He picked up a cup, filled it, and dumped water over his head.

"I give myself a baf! I do it!"

"Yes. That's good."

He put a bath toy to his lips.

"I kiss my purple dolphin!"

He held it out to me.

"Daddy kiss my dolphin?"

"That's OK."

He dropped the dolphin into the bubbles.

"Uh-oh. Where'd my dolphin go?"

This went on delightfully for a while. He got out of the water, and demanded that I dry off the dolphin as well. Then he urinated on my foot and cackled.

"I pee on the floor!"

"Ugh."

"I pee on Daddy!"

I'd been a dad for more than two years. Getting urinated on was, at best, a level-one crisis. I couldn't even get mad at Elijah. In fact, I was almost delighted at his enjoyment of this situation. Pissing on people was very punk rock.

Soon, it was bedtime. He demanded various snacks. Of late, his fancy had turned to frozen corn. I don't mean frozen corn that we then heated up for him in the microwave. He liked to eat it while it was still frozen, straight from the bag. I gave him a heaping bowl. He held up a spoonful.

"You like frozen corn, Daddy?"

"Not really."

"NO! You like it!"

So I ate some frozen corn with him. Afterward, we sat on the couch and I peeled a tangerine. He lifted his sippy cup to my lips.

"Daddy drink soy milk?"

"No. That's yours."

He drank. He picked up a tangerine wedge.

"Daddy eat?"

I looked at the wedge. It was an organic temptress.

"Sure."

We fed each other tangerine wedges until it was time for bed.

"Good night!" I said, as I closed the door.

I walked into the living room. The game began.

"Night!" he said.

"Good night!" I shouted through the door.

"Good night!"

"Good night!"

"Good night, Neal!"

He thought it was hilarious that I had a name besides "Daddy" or "Daddy-doo."

"Good night, Elijah!"

"Good night!"

He was down. I went into the back and opened up the cabinet over the refrigerator, moving the Scotch and tequila bottles to get what I really wanted. There she was, the Silver Surfer. I took her down and plugged her in. Within seconds, the heat source had sparked. I took my pick and pulled the cashed pot out of the wand, replacing it with the fresh stuff without grinding. I placed the glass end of the tube on the heat source, gave it about five seconds, and took a long suck. Nectar filled my nostrils. I breathed deeply and closed my eyes.

As I drained the juice from that nugget of pungent homegrown, the utter ordinariness of the day filled me with a deep satisfaction. This feeling had been building for a while. I now wore my family man–ness like a French-tailored suit. Just being with my family in a house that I owned satisfied me, primally. No amount of poop, vomit, and urine from three species could wash that feeling away.

I wasn't even particularly annoyed the next morning, at six a.m., when Elijah began to shriek in his crib. Regina went to sleep in the back, prearranged. I went to the boy.

"What's the matter, honey?"

"I no scared of monsters, Daddy."

"Of course not."

"I scared of lightning."

"Aww."

"And thunder little bit."

"Sure you are. But don't worry. Daddy will always protect you."

"Thanks, Daddy!"

"You're welcome, son."

"No more bad things, Daddy."

"Never. The bad things are all gone now."

EIGHTEEN

Queen for a Weekend

February 2005

I finally managed to persuade Regina to spend a night away from the boy. My parents, whom we were visiting in Arizona, had agreed to keep him. Relations with them had improved steadily since Peeniegate. In fact, they'd become model grandparents, lavishing Elijah with presents, visiting us every few months despite their utter loathing of Austin, praising us all the time for the "great job" we were doing, and actually caring about his life. They had no idea what to do about his biting, either.

"He'll do fine," I said.

"I know he'll do fine," said Regina. "It's me that I'm worried about."

I found an off-season rack-rate room at a high-end resort on the northern edge of Scottsdale. At the hotel, we had a swim and a sauna and a dinner and fell asleep with our clothes on at 8:30. After eleven hours of sleep and breakfast in bed, we watched television. Then we had another swim and another sauna. Too quickly, we were home. But Regina did, indeed, seem fine.

That night, I was sitting on my parents' sofa, watching baseball on television. Regina called me from the bathroom, where she was changing Elijah's diaper.

"Neal!"

"What?"

"There's this white oily stuff on his toothbrush!"

"Yes. It's called toothpaste."

"I don't think so."

She sniffed the brush.

"It smells like Desitin. I think your mother accidentally brushed his teeth with Desitin last night."

"Let me check."

My mom was in the kitchen.

"Mom? Did you accidentally brush Elijah's teeth with Desitin last night?"

"Please, Neal. I know the difference between Desitin and tooth-paste."

"Could you come to the bathroom with me?"

She did.

"What did you use to brush Elijah's teeth?"

She held up the tube.

"This."

"Mom. This is Boudreaux's Butt Paste."

To be fair, Boudreaux's Butt Paste is not a commonly identifiable brand. But while it may be an organic diaper-rash cream, it's still a diaper-rash cream. It contains boric acid and the tube bears a warning to call poison control if ingested.

"I thought it was toothpaste!" my mom said. "He was saying *mmmmmmm* the whole time I had it in his mouth."

As always in times of crisis, Regina shot toward the Internet. She quickly fired off a worried e-mail to the Boudreaux Butt Paste Company.

"Your mother brushed our son's teeth with diaper-rash cream."

"I know. Pretty funny, right?"

"No! You don't understand! He could die!"

Within an hour, Regina had received an e-mail from Dr.

Boudreaux himself. If ingested in small amounts, he said, his butt paste was completely harmless. He told her she could have called the number on the tube. That was his personal phone.

It was nice to know we could get in touch with Dr. Boudreaux whenever we wanted. I doubt the CEO of the company that makes Desitin would be so accommodating. But after that, it was hard to persuade Regina to leave Elijah for the night again.

I may have grown confident in fatherhood, but Regina remained in constant conflict with herself. In my opinion, she denied herself happiness, deliberately maneuvering into the regret and self-pity that can often attach itself to mothers as they grow older. I wanted to help her recapture the shared thrill and need for adventure that had characterized our life before we'd had a child. But she wouldn't meet me at that mental place. I tried to be sympathetic when we talked.

"Look at me. I wanted to be a world-famous painter by now. And I'm nowhere."

"Are you kidding? You're just now hitting the age where painters really start to get recognized."

"I'm never going to get there, though."

"What are you talking about? You're making the best art of your life."

"Do you really think so?"

"Of course I do. I'm proud of you."

"I just know that I'm going to have to give it all up."

At this point, I stopped being totally sympathetic. My mood inched closer to pissed.

"Don't be such a martyr!"

"I can't be a martyr. Because martyrs do things they don't want to do, but still don't complain."

"Oh, well, then I'm wrong. You're definitely not a martyr, because you fucking complain all the time! And I'm sick of it!"

Rather than berate her further, which would only breed more fights, I acted. Just after New Year's, I got a Fare Flash e-mail from

American Airlines. It would cost $98 round-trip from Austin to Chicago. That was in our price range. I booked a ticket for Regina. She'd be leaving at 7:56 on a Saturday morning and returning around one p.m. on Tuesday.

"Check your e-mail," I said to her.

She did.

"Why didn't you tell me about this?"

"Because I knew that if I brought it up, you'd start saying 'Should I do it?' or 'What if he misses me?' or 'Do you really think we can afford this, wait, let's think for a little bit,' and by the time you'd decided, the fare would already be gone. I wasn't going to deal with your bullshit this time."

"But who am I going to stay with?"

"You have more friends in Chicago than anywhere else in the world."

"What if they have plans?"

"You haven't been to Chicago in more than four years. Unless they're scheduled for surgery, they'll change their plans."

She began preparations for her trip a week ahead of time.

"I'm going to freeze my tits off in Chicago. It's fourteen degrees there. Fourteen degrees, Neal."

"Of course it is. It's Chicago. Don't be such a pussy. Just enjoy yourself."

"But I'm going to be cold."

"So wear a lot of socks and go buy yourself some long johns."

"No one sells long johns in Texas."

"Buy them online, then."

"I'm going to be cold."

"Suit yourself."

My job was to soothe Elijah, who Regina imagined would be completely destroyed by her absence. I doubted that, but in case it was true, I explained it to him tenderheartedly one day in the car on the way home from school.

"Elijah. Do you know where Mommy's going this weekend?"

"Sea World!"

"No. Not Sea World. Mommy's going on an airplane."

"Mommy go on airplane in the sky!"

"That's right."

"Daddy-doo go on airplane?"

"No. I'm going to stay here with you."

"Lijah Allen Pollack go on airplane with Mommy."

"You're staying here with me."

"And Gabby and Teacake and Herclees!"

"Yes, the pets are staying with us."

"Mommy go on airplane to Los Angeles!"

"No, that's where Daddy goes to try to sell his screenplay. Mommy's going to Chicago to see her friends."

"In the sky!"

"Yes."

"Lijah want to eat Cheddar Bunnies! And raisins!" he said, his mind now on other things.

Elijah rarely gets up later than we do, and then only on mornings when we have to get up anyway. The morning Regina left was, naturally, one of his lie-ins. She woke him anyway.

Elijah was in the living room watching the Wiggles, drinking orange juice, and eating dry cereal. Regina's taxi arrived. She gave me a nice little kiss, and then bent down to snuggle her true love.

"My wittle pookie wookie ookie. I'm gonna miss you so much."

"Bye-bye!" Elijah said, very loudly. He picked up his basketball, which he promptly dunked through his Little Tykes net.

"SHAZAM!" he said, as I'd taught him.

"Humph," Regina said.

"Have a good time," I said. "Pretend we don't exist. We'll be fine."

She left. The taxi pulled away. Elijah was simultaneously playing basketball and watching the Wiggles.

"Hey, man," I said. "Pass that ball to Daddy."

. . .

I considered my first weekend alone with Elijah to be an important one, but not because I was nervous about the responsibility. He'd been under my care before. I already knew how to feed, clothe, bathe, change, and regulate him. I would do a fine and efficient job. In fact, I wouldn't be the one tested at all this weekend. Elijah was going up against me. He didn't know it, but this was his audition to see if he could hang with the Nealster. He would learn how to live the Pollack way.

Around nine a.m., after all the tolerable shows had ended on Noggin and I'd drunk three cups of tea, I decided that it was time for me to have my daily squat. This lasted five seconds before Elijah walked in.

"Lijah in the bafroom."

"Yes," I sighed.

"Daddy going pee-pee potty!"

"Daddy is trying to do something else."

He walked over and flushed the toilet.

"Generally, you wait until someone is off the toilet before you flush."

He flushed it again.

Damn it, boy, I wanted to say. Can't you let your old man read *The Onion* for five minutes on the can in peace? But instead, I said, "Who wants to go to Yoga Storytime?"

Bookpeople, our local independent store, was hosting Yoga Story-time at eleven a.m. that day, as it did occasionally on Saturdays. There must have been forty kids present and at least an equal number of parents. This was something I'd run into time and again in Austin. There were lots of "family-friendly" activities, but that's because there were lots of families. Everything involving kids was crowded to the point of swarming. It was a good argument for staying home and doing nothing. Elijah was interested in a rack of remaindered books advertising some failed Disney cartoon feature or another.

"Elijah," I said. "Put that book down. It contains product place-ments. Here. Read *Walter the Farting Dog* instead."

"I fart. I have gas!"

"Yes," I said proudly. "Yes you do."

The Yoga Storytime person took her own sweet time getting there. Eleven-thirty came and went. I was close to complaining, but everyone else seemed to have caught a politeness virus. Finally, a bookstore employee came up and said, "Our yoga instructor is in traffic, but she should be here soon. Instead, we're going to read this ABC book."

I was wondering if the older kids in the crowd were happy to have come to Yoga Storytime only to find themselves being taught the alphabet. Before the story, one man had been reading a *My Little Pony* book to an eight-year-old.

"Look, there's Buttercup," he said.

I thought, why do we always treat kids like they're idiots? And then I remembered. Sometimes they *are* idiots.

"Elijah," I said. "Please pull your pants back up."

Finally, the yogi came. She was a nice-looking middle-aged Indian woman, and she spent what seemed like half an hour setting up her audio-visual display, which were slides projected on a piece of card-board that no one could see but her, because it was behind us. Then she informed us that she has regular classes twice a week and also teaches in the public schools. Finally, she asked, "Do you want a story first or yoga first? Let's see a show of hands."

The kids wanted yoga. Elijah did surprisingly well. He sat cross-legged when she asked him to. He particularly seemed to enjoy any-thing involving the hands. Otherwise he just lay on his back and kicked his feet in the air. The story, on the other hand, was com-prised of flash cards with pictures of animals on them. I knew that Elijah was capable of absorbing a narrative more complex than that. When he walked over to the window and pulled down his pants again, I also knew it was time for us to leave.

That evening, after Elijah and I had a nap and went to the ice-cream store and to the park with Elijah's friend Sam and his mommy, Regina called.

"I'm having a great time!"

"Good!"

She told me all about her great time.

"I don't think I'm gonna be calling you until the morning."

"That's fine."

"Or maybe tomorrow night."

"We'll live."

"I might get pretty drunk."

My plan had worked!

I considered this an important weekend in my child's life. I had limitless chances to expose him to what I considered the finer points of childhood culture. By that, I mean that I wanted him to enjoy the things I enjoyed as a kid. But there was no reason that he had to consider this stuff dated. He didn't need to know that this cultural material had been made twenty to thirty years before he was born. He didn't even know what time *was*.

Elijah learned, for instance, that the man on my "The Thing" T-shirt is named Ben Grimm, is made of orange rocks, and wears a big blue diaper. Later, I rented him some *Pee-wee's Playhouse* episodes, and was delighted when he started asking for the episode where "Kiwi" (which is what he called Pee-wee) "dances with the cowboy." Meanwhile, I continually asked Regina how old Elijah had to be before he could start watching *Ren and Stimpy*.

"I don't know," she said. "It's pretty violent. Seven?"

"What about *Airplane!* When's the first time he can see that?"

"Not for a while."

She was right. I shouldn't let Elijah grow up too fast. I just needed to continue to enjoy the benefits of having introduced him to *The Muppet Show* on his first birthday. At first, he could barely focus. But then a catchy song in the Harry Belafonte, Julie Andrews, or John

Denver episode would grab him. Eventually, Elijah was watching an entire episode all the way through, and then he could watch two in a row without his attention flagging. I was teaching my boy to consume television. The apogee came on the day when he came up to me, tugged on my shirt, and said, "Daddy, I want to see John Cleese."

I nearly sobbed with pride, particularly because his other favorite episode was the Peter Sellers one. My two-year-old son could identify John Cleese by sight. What else did I need as confirmation of my success as a father?

"What does John Cleese do?"

"John Cleese is a funny pirate."

This was based on one of the episode's skits in which John Cleese appears.

"He has a hat on his head and a parrot on his shoulder."

"That's right. What else happens on *The Muppet Show*?"

"Gonzo sits on top of a pole and a beaver chews it and he falls down."

"Yes!"

"And Gonzo catches a cannonball. With his arm!"

"That's right, son!"

Elijah ran off, shouting, "Piiiiiiiiiigs iiiiiiiiiin Spaaaaaaaaaaaace!"

Fully confident now, I ordered more *Muppet Show* episodes for Elijah. But there's only so much I can do to control his tastes. As I write this, Elijah's favorite episodes now feature Connie Stevens and Jim Nabors, instead of John Cleese and Peter Sellers, though, as a consolation, he also likes the Vincent Price episode and he refers to Jim Nabors as "Mr. Dead Neighbors."

Kids' culture today isn't necessarily a precipitous drop down from the heyday of the Muppets. For instance, the weekend of Regina's Chicago vacation was also the weekend of Elijah's first trip to the cinema. I took him to a rough contemporary Muppet equivalent: *The SpongeBob SquarePants Movie*. I'd been telling him about it all weekend.

"Elijah go movie show!" he said, constantly.

"That's right. And who's in the movie?"

"Spun Ba!"

"That's right. SpongeBob!"

"Yaaaaaaay! Spun Ba! And dolphin!"

"There may or may not be dolphins in the movie, Elijah."

"Dolphin! Yaaaaaaay!"

I loaded the diaper bag with a cup of apple slices, an organic Rice Krispies peanut-butter bar, water, and soy milk. We left at 4:10 and were at the movies by 4:20.

"Heh," I said to myself. "Four-twenty."

No one was around to hear my wry recognition of 4:20 as the universally recognized daily time for smoking pot. For some reason, I chose this moment to think about what I'll do when it comes to talking to Elijah about drugs. I will, I decided, take the approach that my parents did, which worked well enough, keeping me mostly drug-free until I turned about twenty-five, at which point I went over to the stoner dark side. They didn't vilify the weedly arts, nor did they glorify them. Moralism rarely came into play as long as I did my homework and stayed out of trouble, which I almost always did. This still seems eminently sensible to me. Once he's of consenting age, Elijah is free to make his own choices, or mistakes, if you want to look at it that way. As for whether or not I'm going to get stoned with him someday, I can only say, probably not, though maybe if I'm still alive when he's a grown-up. Actually, who cares, and it's none of your business.

"Spun Ba!" Elijah said.

This was one of the theaters that features "The Twenty" before the movie. The Twenty, for those of you who've been fortunate enough to avoid it, is essentially loud commercials punctuated by promotional material for shows on NBC and bad TNT original movies. Elijah wasn't impressed. He didn't wanna Fanta.

"Spun Ba on soon, Daddy?"

"Soon. Eat your apples."

"Uh-oh. Where'd Spun Ba go?"

I lifted Elijah into a seat, which immediately collapsed inward on him. His feet nearly touched his head.

"Help, Daddy!"

"Maybe you should sit on the edge of the seat."

"No! Elijah stand!"

Then there were the previews. Elijah seemed to have no interest in the Lemony Snicket movie. Thank God he also showed no interest in the *Winnie-the-Pooh Heffalump Adventure*. I thought to myself that it's about time for the Pooh to hang up his jersey.

"Spun Ba on soon?"

"Soon."

The movie began. I attempted to involve Elijah through subtle verbal cues like "Who's that, Elijah? Who's that on the screen? Is that SpongeBob?"

"Spun Ba," he whispered.

For about twenty minutes, Elijah stood, looking up at the screen, transfixed but probably not taking in the narrative, which was pretty complicated for a two-year-old. For him, *Clifford the Big Red Dog* might as well have been *The Brothers Karamazov* in terms of literary complexity. I enjoyed the movie immensely, especially the Bubble Party scene. I imagined what it would be like if Scarlett Johansson really were a mermaid. From time to time, Elijah would turn to me and request another food item. Occasionally, he would recognize a character.

"Mr. Bab."

"That *is* Mr. Krabs."

He began running up and down the row. I had to stop this when he went up to an eight-year-old boy and deliberately slapped him on the knee. This being a movie theater full of toddlers, many of whom were behaving the same way, or worse, the kid's mother didn't even acknowledge Elijah's act. At another point, he lay down on the floor, which explained the mysterious black gunk that I later found on his pants. He started to whimper.

"What?"

"Stuck, Daddy!"

His feet had gotten trapped under the seat. He squirmed. I pulled him out.

"Just watch the damn movie."

During one particularly harrowing chase scene, he came to life. He whispered to me.

"Daddy."

"Yes."

"Spun Ba scared of red monster!"

"That's right. But remember that the monster is only a cartoon. It's not real."

"Monster real?"

"No."

"I scared."

Now what? I thought. Grasping, I said,

"Monsters are our friends. Who else is a monster?"

"Cookie Monster!"

"Right. And . . ."

"Tell-yee!"

"Yes, and Telly. And also Elmo."

"Elmo eat Spun Ba?"

"No," I said. "Elmo wants to give SpongeBob a kiss."

That was the moment that I officially stopped pretending to be cool.

Before I put Elijah down that night, Turner Classic Movies aired its *Cartoon Alley* show. I thought it would be a nice introduction to the forefathers of modern animation. Unfortunately, the first cartoon they showed was an anti-Hitler Tex Avery propaganda short from 1940 that was as didactic as it was violent. Hitler was portrayed as a wolf, and the allies were the three little pigs. There were lots of bombs dropping in people's pants, and guns, and fire, and bleak land-scapes. Elijah wasn't familiar with the language or setting of war.

"Uh-oh. Wolf fall down in fire!"

"Um, that's right."

"Where'd piggies go?"

"They're hiding."

"Piggies hiding! Uh-oh! Wolf fall down again!"

We watched the next cartoon together, which featured an archival Sylvester chasing around a proto-Tweety. But Elijah had endured enough of my cultural instruction for one day. He was really much more interested in jumping on my stomach and having me give him airplane rides. We also put on the Aquabats video and wrestled each other while the Aquabats fought a monster. He listed off all the things we'd done that weekend: "Elijah go to ice-cream store with Sam, and other ice-cream store with Daddy-doo, and hiking with Ben and Herclees, and do yoga at Bookpeople and go to restaurant and grocery store and Spun Ba movie! I had fun, Daddy!"

I read three books to him, gave him some milk, took him outside, showed him the moon, and put him to bed. He'd enjoyed himself. At that moment, I loved being a daddy. Of course, at other moments, I kind of hated being a daddy. But that, as I was learning, comes with the daddy territory.

NINETEEN

The Posterboard Jungle

March–April 2005

E
ven as I self-indulgently congratulated myself for Elijah's sharp vocabulary, fun taste in popular culture, and adorable love of nature, he continued to be the scourge of the playground. Two or three days would go by with no behavior reports, but then we'd have two or three days in a row of biting. On days when he was a "good boy," he got to go out for ice cream. And then he went back to school the next day and bit anyway. By now, he was drawing blood. Before we'd had a kid, we'd read that parents shouldn't delay punishment, and if they did, they definitely shouldn't offer rewards in lieu of punishment. But when faced with an actual crisis, we'd choked and ignored all normal advice. The school's failed incentive system combined with our confused naïveté as first-time parents had helped create a kid who was causing more problems than before.

Elijah mostly bit girls and kids who were younger than he was. In particular, he seemed obsessed with an olive-skinned, dark-haired, sad-eyed little girl named Sophie. We suspected he was in love, but love has a nasty way of turning into obsession, even in two-year-olds. In the evenings, he'd say:

"I saw Sophie at school today!"

"Is that right?" I'd say.

"Uh-huh," he'd say. "She was there!"

"Do you like Sophie?"

"I do! I like Sophie!"

"That's great!"

"I bite Sophie too!"

"You can't bite, Elijah. It hurts kids."

"I won't bite Sophie anymore."

"That's great!"

The next day, he'd bite Sophie.

He'd gone up a level, into a toddler class. His new teacher wasn't as patient as the old one; she'd been at the preschool game for at least two decades, and she was as burned out as you'd expect of anyone who'd had the same job for that amount of time. She was always saying "I love you" to the kids. The way she said it, it sounded insincere, even though she probably did mean it in her heart. Still, she was grumpy, and occasionally mean. There were definitely days when she seemed close to snapping.

Her disciplinary methods were also a bit strange. She suggested that we have Elijah carry a family picture in his pocket. If he were bad, she said, she'd take the picture away from him. According to her reasoning, the mere thought of losing a photograph of Mommy and Daddy would deter Elijah from something he'd been doing at least once a week for almost a year. We'd grown so frustrated by the situation that we didn't criticize this obviously wrong idea.

This new teacher also gave up much more quickly then the other one had, or was at least worse at admitting that the end was near. We went in one day to pick up Elijah. His teacher was sitting at a table, looking exhausted. I knew then that something was going to go down.

"I'm at my wits' end," the teacher said.

The next day, Regina came home to tell me that we'd have a conference with Elijah's teachers at 1:30 on Monday.

"Great."

"We're probably going to talk about solutions. We need to be on the same page."

"Sure, we do."

Elijah's teacher acted like he was a problem child the likes of whom she'd never seen before. While I didn't discount that his biting had made her life exceedingly difficult, this seemed absurd to me. Like all two-year-olds, Elijah was determined to drive everyone around him insane. He threw shrieking fits if we wanted him to take a bath, and also if we tried to take him out of the bath. If I wasn't interested in eating a popsicle with him, he'd have a fit, and if I did eat a popsicle, he'd have a fit if it was the wrong color. He didn't want dinner. He wanted dinner. He didn't want what we'd made him for dinner. He wanted milk and didn't want milk. For some reason, he wanted to go to The Home Depot. When we said we didn't need to go to The Home Depot, he threw a fit. In the timeline of life, we'd arrived at the desperate hours of our child's toddlerhood. This must happen to other parents, we thought.

No moment in my life was safe from the spectre of toddler mayhem. One weekend in May, I was out mooching happy hour drinks off friends, something I only got to do twice a week, maybe three times. Regina called.

"Your *son*," she said, "stuck a noodle in his nose. He won't let me get it out and he thinks it's funny."

Like everything else related to fatherhood, this wasn't a situation for which I had any training.

"Do you want me to come home?"

"Of course I want you to come home! I'm trying to get this noodle out of his nose. What are we going to do? I looked it up online. He could get an *infection*. Thank God at least that it's a cooked noodle."

"Could you get him to blow it out?"

"I tried that. He doesn't get it. He just keeps sucking the noodle farther in."

"Call me if anything changes."

"Neal! Don't . . ."

As I went back to my margarita, deep-seated, permanent, selfish feelings bubbled up from the depths of my mind. I felt like Regina resented that I sometimes set aside time to enjoy myself. She, on the other hand, felt that I made her feel lame because she wasn't cool enough. So then she created overblown situations to make me feel guilty and to assuage her own insecurities. But sometimes she didn't do that; I just thought that she did. Goddamn it, we were so neurotic. But we also realized that such *meshugass* must be put aside in times of family crisis. A few minutes later, she called again.

"He still has the noodle in his nose."

I sighed.

"I'll be right home."

When I got there, Elijah was running around in his pajamas, grinning like the cat who'd eaten the rat who'd eaten the cheese. His voice made him sound like he had sinus problems.

"Daddy! I got a noodle in my nose."

"I know, son. We really should see about getting that out."

"I don't want to get it out!"

"Ah, but you have to. Or you might die."

"Don't say that, Neal!" Regina said.

"He doesn't know what death is," I said.

I sat Elijah on the couch and tried to get him to blow into a tissue. He sucked the noodle in farther. Regina stood by, marveling at my stupidity.

"Noodle noodle noodle," Elijah said. "Nooooooooodle."

By the time his eight p.m. bedtime came along, we were starting to get worried. The pressure built. Regina was worried about Elijah's health, but I was more worried about how much a trip to the emergency room would cost. She called Elijah's pediatrician. The office had an emergency hotline that cost $12 a call. Money had been scarce recently.

"We can't afford twelve bucks for a phone call," I said.

Regina, ever practical, said, "It's a lot cheaper than going to the ER."

The hotline told us that we needed nose drops, which we had, and an air bulb, which we also had. They were already on the coffee table.

"Yeah, that was worth twelve bucks."

"Be quiet."

"Come over here," I said to Elijah.

He did.

"You're not going to like this."

Quickly, before he could realize what was happening, I held his arms. Regina shoved the dropper up his nose.

"NOOOOOOOOOOOOOOO!"

She stuck the bulb in his other nostril. He really began to howl then, shrieking like an animal for us to stop. He probably felt a lot less pain than I did at that moment, though also probably a lot more fear.

"Daddy Mommy! Stop it, please! I no have noodle in my nose!"

"Don't let him open his mouth!" Regina said.

"What?"

"The nurse says that if we want to get the noodle out, he can only breathe through his nose!"

With one hand, I tried to hold Elijah's hands still, and with the other, I clamped his jaw shut. "Don't breathe through your mouth!" I shouted. He writhed as though we were disemboweling him.

"I can see it!" Regina said.

"You can?"

A piece of cooked pasta squirted out of Elijah's nose. It was about the size of a ladybug. For *this* I'd given up Happy Hour?

"That was it?"

"I guess so."

Elijah snuffled.

"I no have noodle in my nose anymore."

After he went to bed, Regina and I popped open some whiskey and each had a double. We sipped our drinks and stared at the walls for a while. The next morning, on the way to school, Elijah sneezed out the rest of the noodle.

But that incident was just The Phantom Menace of Orifice Wars. The situation hadn't ended badly enough to dissuade Elijah from such behavior. Unfortunately, this also meant that the habit bled into his school life, thereby sending us hurtling into another crisis of near-violent proportions.

The medevac began one afternoon, when I was sitting at my desk in my underwear, peacefully doing something semi-constructive. Regina burst through the door. She was on her cell phone.

"Elijah put a rock up his nose at school! They can't get it out."

I shot up and ran into the other room, because that's where my pants were.

"Call his doctor!"

On the way to school, I talked to the physician's assistant at his pediatrician's office. She was very sympathetic. She made us an emergency appointment. We got to school, and there was Elijah, looking normal.

"I put a rock up my nose, Daddy."

"That's what I heard."

"We have to go to the doctor," Regina said.

"No! I don't want to go doctor with rock up my nose! I want popsicle!"

"Well, we have to."

We sat in an examining room for thirty minutes. I read *Green Eggs and Ham* to Elijah twice, until he figured out how to open the door. Then it was a battle with him to get him not to run into the hallway.

He shrieked. I figured out that the best way to keep him distracted was to hold him upside down by his feet. I didn't really consider what that would do to the rock.

The PA came in. She could see the rock, but couldn't get it out. Instead, she made us an appointment with an ear, nose, and throat specialist up north. We had to travel to Round Rock, an overdeveloped suburb that we snobbishly, but justifiably, avoided as though it were full of flesh-eating zombies.

She gave us directions. We followed them, but at the turnoff, we looped around and found ourselves at a crossroads. I called the doctor's office. The person who answered the phone told us to turn left. Elijah began to scream. In our hurry to get the rock out, we'd forgotten to bring him any snacks or water.

"I don't want to go to another doctor! I no have rock in my nose! Please, Mommy, Daddy! Please!"

Imagine that in the background for twenty minutes, which was the amount of time that we drove in the wrong direction. We called the doctor's office again. They told us to turn around.

"I can't believe this!" Regina said. "This is a nightmare!"

"You need to calm down."

"I am calm! Stop calling me hysterical! You're the one who's getting me all worked up!"

"No. I'm not."

"You are! You are! You are!"

"Nooooooo!" Elijah said.

And, then, the dam broke. I rocked back and forth and slammed my hands on the dashboard hard enough that we were lucky that the airbag didn't pop out. It must have set a fine example for my son.

"Goddamn it all to hell! No! No! No!" and so on.

Of course, once we got to the doctor's office, Elijah was immediately fine, as though someone had simply taken a dark room and brightened it by throwing a switch. Regina found a small stuffed lobster in her bag. I hid it in various places in the office. Elijah tried to hide it from me as well, but when I opened my eyes, he was usually still holding it, and then he'd throw it under a chair.

"Lobsters live at the grocery store!" he said.

"The ones you see do. They're being held prisoner against their wishes. But they're also really delicious."

"Yummy in my tummy!"

"Yep!"

The receptionist, who called us into the office, interrupted this important father-son conversation. This was no Northwest Pediatrics, with its Disney videos and Beanie Baby collection. They'd chosen a design scheme that featured photos of punctured eardrums. Elijah's face took on a thin film of fear.

The doctor came in. He was a tall, goofy guy who was wearing one of those metal headbands with the big circle on it. I couldn't tell if he was trying to be funny.

"Is this our Rocky?" he said.

I concluded that he was probably trying to be funny. He asked me to sit in his examination chair and to put Elijah in my lap. My chair was for a kid and his chair wasn't, so when he leaned in, our thighs were touching. This was quite awkward for me, as I'm sure it was for him, but I tried to focus on keeping Elijah still.

The doctor put drops up Elijah's nose. Elijah flinched, but he didn't lose his mind. This was reserved for when the doctor inserted an inch-thick suction tube up Elijah's left nostril. Elijah screamed like he was dying. The other sound in the room was that of my heart breaking. The rock popped out.

The doctor showed it to me. It was no more than an inch in diameter, reddish brown with little white flecks, basically circular, with some irregularities. Upon a closer look, it resembled a tiny hamburger patty.

He gave Elijah a sticker. Elijah left happy. We left happy. There was a great place nearby, owned by a guy from New Jersey, that had the only decent pizza within 100 miles. It was Elijah's dinnertime, and we were hungry, too.

"Who wants to have a pizza party?" Regina said.

Elijah hopped up and down.

"Pizza party pizza party! Pizza party song!"

"Pizza party!" I said.

"Can we wear hats?"

"Sure. We can wear hats. We've got a lot to celebrate. For instance, you're never going to put a rock up your nose again, are you?"

"No, Daddy."

"Are you going to put anything up your nose again?"

"Hercules!"

"OK. Besides Hercules."

"Hercules sits on my butt!"

"Elijah, I'm serious . . ."

"Let it go," Regina said. "I think he gets it."

That ended up being an expensive little lesson. Our health insurance, which cost us nearly 600 dollars a month, had a "surgery deductible." If any of us required surgery, we had to pay the first 1,000 dollars—each. We knew about the deductible, which is pretty much standard in most of the crappy health plans Americans have these days. But we weren't aware that, according to Blue Cross, sticking a tube up a child's nose to extract a rock is "surgery." Elijah's little escapade brought us a 600-dollar bill. We didn't have that money. Instead, we had to go on an eight-month payment plan. The health-care system, that anonymous beast, that lurking purveyor of bureaucratic greed, had once again nibbled at my nuts.

We had a whole weekend to recover from Rock Day. Then it was time to face Grendel's Mother. Regina took Elijah into school on Monday, the day of our conference.

"Did you hear about the rock?" she said to Elijah's teacher.

The teacher sighed.

"I got a call at *home* about the rock. Last week, I pulled a different rock out of his nose. Two weeks ago, Laura pulled spaghetti out of his nose."

So sorry to inconvenience you, I thought. Next time, just leave the spaghetti in his nose and see what happens.

"So we'll see you at one-thirty?" Regina said.

"Yep," said the teacher, merrily. "One-thirty."

Regina suddenly realized what was about to happen. She came home and said this to me:

"If they do boot him out, screw them. I'm tired of feeling like I have a child who's especially difficult. Every kid has his issues. It's not like he's seven years old and doing this."

Acceptance is followed by denial, followed by anger and then a little groveling. One-thirty arrived. Elijah was sitting alone in a room with three teachers. His main teacher came up to us with two chairs designed for toddlers. The school didn't have a conference room, and the director's office was off-limits for some reason. Regina and I sat in the little chairs while the scary teacher sat in a big person's chair. It felt like she was about to punish us.

She presented us with a half-dozen injury reports of damage Elijah had done to other kids.

"These are just for this month," she said. "And they're just the ones where he drew blood. It also doesn't include the dozens of times we've caught him just *before* he attacked another kid. We have to pull him off kids three or four times a day. Even on days when he doesn't bite or scratch, he throws toys at their faces."

She sighed.

"I have *seven* new kids coming into my class next month. And they're *little*."

Wait for it . . . I thought.

"I just think it'll be better for everyone. And that Elijah might be happier, if he went somewhere else."

There is no cataloging the twin feelings of helplessness and shame that washed over Regina and me then. Our child was being expelled from preschool. How had we failed him? Had we been selfish in wanting a few hours a day to work without a kid around? Had we coddled him, or not coddled him enough? Should we have chosen another school for him? Or did he just suffer from intrinsically bad behavior? Were we doomed to a lifetime of Elijah-related conferences?

"I guess we knew there was a problem," Regina said. "But . . ."

"I feel just sick about this," said the teacher. "Finally, I had to go to my director. She came in and saw him. And said, 'That boy? He looks like a little Botticelli cherub . . .' "

She went on.

"He's smart as a whip. I can see it in his eyes when I talk to him. He understands *everything*. He just has problems with *impulse control*. Maybe you should get him some clay. Something he can pound his aggression into. Or find him a nanny who can give him individual attention."

I was angry, and I wanted to say: He already *has* clay, dumbass. And do we look like we can afford a nanny? That's why we're sending him to your crappy school in the first place! Besides, what's that nanny gonna do? Swoop down with her magical umbrella and teach him to fly a kite? Instead, I said . . .

"Can we just have until June first?"

On the drive home, Regina and I could barely keep from weeping. Elijah liked to draw and tell stories and play make-believe games, and to play on his own schedule. This school had no imagination, and everything was scheduled rigidly, which would have been fine if it had been a dental academy. But this was preschool. Kids, or at least our kid, needed to be in a place that would let him run free. Schools like that did exist, and we knew it, so we felt doubly bad. We were largely to blame for keeping Elijah so long in a place where he was so obviously unhappy. Of course, just because you're unhappy doesn't mean you can go around inflicting pain on little girls.

At eight a.m. the next day, going out the door, Elijah said to me, "I be a nice boy at school today, Daddy!" When Regina brought him back five hours later, she had the news that he hadn't bitten today. But he had scratched Sophie above the eye. And there was blood. The next morning, Regina took Elijah back to school, where the teacher was waiting. Next to the teacher stood a little droopy-eyed girl.

"This is Sophie."

She pulled up Sophie's shirt. On Sophie's back was an enormous bite mark that the school hadn't caught yesterday. Sophie's father had called the school. From here on, Elijah was no longer allowed to play outside with the other kids.

Regina came home and told me the story. Elijah was done. He couldn't go back tomorrow. And now that Regina had seen Elijah's victim, she felt horrible shame. We could only imagine what Sophie's parents, whose daughter was being stalked by a relentless predator, felt. He couldn't go back.

I spent the next hour researching stuff for Elijah to do over the summer. Regina was outside watering the plants. I went to her to tell her what I'd found. She started to sob.

"I feel like a bad mother! I don't want to spend all summer with him! He's difficult! He's a difficult child! He wants too much from me. And you're going to go crazy if he's around all the time. Our marriage always suffers when he's home!"

Sometimes I don't understand my wife. She is a wonderful mother and a great support to me. But she didn't want to take care of the kid full-time, which would have been fine if she hadn't also seemed allergic to making money. She worked a lot, but with almost no financial return. And she hated doing housework. I felt like I was carrying a lot of the childcare and housework load, but that I also had to support the family in toto. Then again, I slept until ten several mornings a week and got to go out any night I wanted.

"I love you," I said. "Sorry I'm such a failure."

"You're not the failure. I'm the failure."

"Don't be ridiculous. I'm way more of a failure than you are."

The pity party lasted until I went to pick Elijah up at school that afternoon. His teacher was leading him around by the hand. They were watering flowers out front. He'd been her "little helper" all day, she said. This was shorthand for "We're not letting him within fifty feet of the other kids."

"He's great one-on-one," the teacher said.

Everything was an insult with this teacher. Or maybe he really was a nightmare around other kids. All I knew is that I felt horrible, in every way.

That evening, Regina had some paintings on display at a local gallery. My job was to make sure Elijah didn't completely destroy her good time. He and I had a "picnic" on the lawn in front. I couldn't keep him out for two hours, though, and he eventually ran into the gallery, threw a bunch of grapes on the ground, and got hold of a plastic doorstop, running around and laughing gleefully until the gallery owner caught up with him.

When we got home, I was assigned to carry stuff in from the car. This is what I heard.

"Elijah, close that refrigerator. Now!"

"NOOOOOOOO!"

"AHHHH! He bit me!"

I dropped my armload and picked Elijah up by the armpits. The Penalty Chair was a few feet away.

"I've had it with the goddamn biting!"

Our family's darkest hour had arrived. But it got a lot darker when I wrote about my family's problems on the Internet.

On the very day that Elijah got kicked out of preschool, a study came out that said American preschoolers were being expelled at a greater rate than American grade-school students. In other words, this was a genuine social problem, or at least a policy issue, and I'd just experienced it firsthand. I saw this as an opportunity to illuminate the problem, and also to cash in on our small-scale misery. Salon.com bought my pitch.

I wrote the article quickly, trying to summarize in 2,000 words a situation that I've explicated here over hundreds of pages. What resulted was, because the expulsion was fresh and the wounds raw, a little histrionic. I didn't have enough time and distance from the situation. The piece lacked the subtlety and graceful wisdom that generally characterizes my writing. The Internet, or at least a small corner of it, went insane.

I got a foretaste of the coming onslaught in an e-mail from Tokyo, from someone who'd read the article while American busybodies were still sleeping. It went:

> I just read your Salon article, and I am going to bet that even in a publication like Salon, the mail is going to run at least 3 to 1 against you. So I figured that instead of writing a Letter to the Editor which would probably just disappear into the void, I should email you directly and say, WOW your life SUCKS—you have my full sympathies. Make that empathies—two of ours were biters, too, but that wasn't grounds for expulsion in public daycare in Tokyo. Kids outgrow it. Really, they do. But that's cold comfort to you now. Hang in there. . . .

The tone was so kind and sympathetic that it lulled me. But by the next afternoon, blogs were aspark with headlines like "Some People Just REALLY, Really Shouldn't Breed. Really," "If You Don't Want Kids, Don't Have Them," and "A Putz Writes for Salon." The tone was set by one blogger in particular, who decided to become the one-stop shopping source for "The Neal Pollack Debacle of 2005." Considering that her previous post had been a Flickr photo tour of her spring garden, it was probably her shot at the big time.

The assault commenced with a posting called "People Who Shouldn't Have Children." She wrote: "These people—Neal Pollack and his wife, Regina—are just horrible!" And later continued, regarding Elijah: "They think he isn't aware on some level that he's not particularly wanted?" The kicker was this:

> I've got a news flash for Regina: babe, you ARE a bad mother. And your husband is a bad father. You people should never have reproduced. You're irresponsible. You're stupid. You're selfish.
>
> Here's my advice: Give that poor little kid away to someone who's actually capable of taking care of him and, both of you, get sterilized right away so you won't produce any more unwanted children.
>
> Sadly, the Pollacks will probably not heed my advice. Little Elijah will mature into a screwed-up teenager and then into a completely fucked-up adult and the elder Pollacks will spend their golden years wringing their hands and whining about what victims they are and why should all of this bad stuff have happened to them and why couldn't Elijah just have behaved when he was small.
>
> God, I hate people like Neal and Regina Pollack.

In the comments section, the part of all websites where civility goes to die, we were referred to as "clueless, artsy types," "self-indulgent artiste nitwits," and "fucking self-absorbed fuckwads." One person concluded that Elijah is a "victim of inherited biochemical imbalances and tremendously unskilled parenting." Another said that we "wouldn't know responsibility if it bit [us] in the ass." Someone else suggested that I get trained as an EMT so we'd have a regular income, which was absurd *prima facie,* because I'm the last person you'd want helping you in an emergency. Still another person wrote, "Why can't white people understand that sometimes a child needs to get spanked?" The following comment was particularly pungent:

> This poor child isn't going to get any better unless his stupid selfish parents get parenting lessons. Christ, do they have any sympathy

for the poor little girl being terrorized? I feel very sorry for Elijah, his life with those morons is going to suck. But they'll probably buy him a lot of stuff to make themselves feel better, because that's all they seem to be concerned with—how they feel.

The letters to Salon were more thoughtful and varied in their response. One person wrote, "Elijah needs a spanking, and quite frankly so do his parents." In fact, spanking came up often. This line of critique intrigued me. My parents had applied spanking judiciously, without malice, and so had Regina's. Many parents had. But now people considered a spank to be anathema, needlessly violent, something that taught kids how to be aggressive. I didn't necessarily think that was true. But I also wondered where one drew the line, and once that line's been drawn, is it easier to cross? I didn't see myself as a spanker, but then again, neither do most people before they have children.

As my initial correspondent had warned, the letters ran against Regina and me three-to-one, though there was also a second wave that supported us three-to-one. There were hundreds of letters and blog posts, and thousands of comments. We'd touched some sort of cultural nerve, though to this day I'm not entirely sure what that nerve was. And some of the comments were accurate. Perhaps we had been overly dependent on the school. Perhaps we were sometimes overabsorbed in our artistic careers. And maybe we were a little confused about how to discipline the boy. But never, for one moment, had Elijah been anything less than Priority One.

I was used to getting attacked unfairly on the Internet. I'd made a career of it, in fact. But Regina wasn't quite as ready for the onslaught. For a few days, she seemed to sort of enjoy it. Then one night, after putting Elijah to bed, she broke down in my arms:

"How DARE they say that about me! I gave my body over to him for eighteen months—so he could have a good start! No! Almost three years. I gave up everything! And it was all for him! All that reading I did! All the sleep schedules and the food planning and the books—and I gave up my painting! I gave up my life for that kid, and I was glad to do it! Because I wanted him to have a good start! And I don't want anything in return. I don't resent him for anything! I don't regret anything at all! I love him more than anything! And now they're saying, they're saying . . ."

I knew it was partly my fault, and I felt terrible. I'd written a hurried, hysterical parenting article and had opened Regina, a decidedly private person, up to criticism. Of course we hadn't done everything perfectly. But all parents make ludicrous mistakes, and all parents have selfish thoughts. Show me a perfect parent and I'll show you a liar. Suddenly, I knew what my parents, and all parents, meant when they said, "We did the best we could."

Just as we thought the "debate" over our parenting skills had died, Regina signed on to her community-college e-mail server, which she checked about once a month during the summer. Her address there uses her real last name; she never officially took my name, anyway. Also, she never gives the address out. So it was a bit of a surprise when she received a note from someone who called himself "Sophie's Dad," who had this to say about how she was raising our son: "I find it especially hypocritical that your work seems to concentrate on images of abused and victimized women, but you and your husband seem to think it's a joking matter that your son terrorizes a girl because he's in love with her. Hello—that's what all spouse abusers say." He encouraged her to become a "real parent" to Elijah, before he fell into the claws of the juvenile justice system.

"Take a look at this," Regina said.

I did.

"It's crazy," I said.

For God's sake, the kid was only two. Couldn't we have a little time to adjust to this behavior problem before declaring him a spouse abuser?

"You don't understand. This really creeps me out. He knows about my artwork. He knows where I *teach*. He knows my real last name. None of this was in the article."

She started typing.

"Don't write him back."

"I have to. I'm not going to take this."

"Seriously, Regina. This guy—if it really is a guy—has got problems. He, or she, might even be someone with a bone to pick with me. There are lots of those people out there."

"Wait a minute. Why would women have a bone to pick with you?"

"People of all types have a bone to pick with me, for all kinds of reasons. But that's my problem, not yours. Trust me, you don't want to get into an Internet war with someone like that."

"I'm going to write him back. Someone has to tell him the truth."

"I'm begging you. Please don't write him back."

"I have absorbed your point of view."

She didn't write him back. Thus, the mist began to gradually lift. Summer began.

On Memorial Day weekend, we took Elijah to my friend Ben's annual Memorial Day barbecue. This was during a brief period when Ben had a lot of rock musicians living at his house, so the party had a vague rock 'n' roll feel to it, meaning that the house smelled bad and there were lots of instruments lying around. Elijah had been very rock-oriented of late. He continually requested to listen to the Hives, the Ramones, and the Aquabats, to the exclusion of all other music. They were his favorite bands. He grabbed me by the hand and said, "Daddy, come rock out in my room." If, in the car, we played any music that he didn't like, he'd say, "No, Mommy Daddy. I want rock 'n' roll!" He was constantly asking us when he was going to "get in a band." I told him it wouldn't be long now.

At Ben's party, Elijah sat inside, on the floor. There was an acoustic guitar next to him.

"I want that," he said.

I put it in his lap. He sat there for a second, and then he started banging on the guitar and plucking the strings wildly.

"One two three rock out!!!!!!!!" he said.

"Oh my God," I said.

He continued to "play" while rocking his head.

"Regina. Come see this!"

My family could be loud, hysterical to the point of melodrama, and we always balanced on the edge of some sort of disaster. I was rude, selfish, profane, and obnoxious. Regina was self-pitying and bossy. Elijah bit people when he was upset. These weren't little things, but they weren't everything, either. We also had a lot of friends, we had a lot of fun, and we loved one another. We would make it through. Regina and I gazed for a while upon Elijah as he thwacked away tunelessly, shouting, "Rock 'n' roll! Rock 'n' roll! Rock 'n' roll!"

My son made me proud.

TWENTY

Endless Summer

May–September 2005

With Elijah's expulsion from preschool, we had the opportunity, in the classic American manner, to remake ourselves. But first, there was a small problem we had to address. We'd run out of money. Also, we were 23,000 dollars in debt. My paychecks stopped arriving with frequency. When they did arrive, they were small. We put 5,000 dollars worth of taxes on credit cards. Our health-insurance premiums kept rising. We were fucked.

We seemed to be falling further and further behind, and it wasn't because we lived outside our means. We'd paid almost exactly the median national price for our house. Our car, when we'd bought it, had been at the median price as well. Plus, it was our only car. Food had been our weakness, admittedly, but when we saw our personal crash coming, we cut the Central Market crap and started shopping at a regular grocery store. We'd bought our TV at a pawnshop and we didn't fix our ten-year-old stereo when it broke. Also, the Silver Surfer had saved me hundreds of dollars a year on weed.

A medical bill here, a plane ticket to visit Nana for Christmas there, a couple of small home improvements—it added up, but we weren't, technically, poor. So how could it be possible that I was having trouble supporting my family? Even taking real dollars into account, I still earned about what my father had at my age. Yet he'd somehow managed to put three kids through college while also raising them in one of the wealthiest neighborhoods in the country. I, on the other hand, was struggling to raise one kid in a neighborhood two blocks from the Interstate on a street that served mainly as a cut-through for beer trucks that were making deliveries to the several liquor stores within walking distance of my house.

Then again, I didn't want to work for anyone else, and neither did Regina. Either one of us probably could have, with a little effort, taken a job that offered good health coverage, possibly life insurance, and maybe even discounted day care. We could have kept our kid at home when he was eighteen months old instead of sending him to Montessori school. We might have double-checked before buying a house down the street from a day-labor center.

But even taking our mildly artsy-fartsy lifestyle choices and assorted mistakes into account, we still should have had enough money to live without the panic of having imminent bankruptcy looming over us. Talking with our friends, and even with people we met randomly, we realized we weren't alone. They all had problems similar to ours: Crime-plagued neighborhoods, crummy schools, battles with a nightmarish health-care bureaucracy, and endless debt. These were austere times. We needed a good national health-care system and guaranteed decent day care as much as any American family, but we knew that with our current government, which had cut health benefits for disabled war veterans and referred to the National Education Association as a "terrorist organization," we probably didn't have much of a shot. Our bootstraps were all we had. So we pinned our hopes on the last frontier of a wheezing American economy. Real estate would save us. It was time to sell the house.

We realized this might be tricky, given the general quality of the Harmon Triangle. After the murder, the cops had opened a permanent substation in an empty apartment in one of the buildings. This calmed things down substantially, and everyone was glad. But once we stopped complaining, the cops stopped paying attention. Soon dudes were once again walking the neighborhood at all hours, drinking malt liquor out of paper bags. If anything, it was worse than before. Every time we stepped onto our front lawn, someone asked us for money. I had to tell people to "get off my property." I had to put up a sign. I hated being that guy, but I lived in constant, and justified, fear that a stray bullet would crash through Elijah's bedroom window or that a drunk driver would smash into the side of our house.

Still, we dithered. Did we really want the hassle of moving? Hadn't we always prided ourselves on being the types of people who liked to live in modestly difficult situations? Then one Saturday night, I went over the edge.

I was peacefully sitting in my lounge chair, watching Montgomery Clift and Elizabeth Taylor in *A Place in the Sun.* From outside, I heard a booming bass from a car stereo. This was common in the neighborhood, as it had been in every neighborhood where I'd lived since 1992. But this time, the bass didn't go away. It just kept booming. I looked through the curtains and watched as a guy got out of the passenger seat of the car, stepped onto my neighbors' lawn, threw something on the grass, and stood there yelling at it.

"What the hell?" I said.

I ran outside, shoeless, in my T-shirt and boxer briefs, and down my front walk, getting close enough so that I could see the license plate.

"Write this down!" I said, and then I relayed the plate number to Regina.

"I don't have a pen!"

"Hurry, or I won't remember it! Where's our flashlight?"

I put on a pair of sweatpants, but no shoes, and walked out into the dark, onto my neighbors' lawn, while Regina looked for the flashlight. I'd taken three steps in his grass when I felt something soft under foot. I heard a little "eep" sound and felt something nip my big toe. Regina was waiting at our porch, in her bathrobe.

"What happened?"

"I got bit."

"You got bit?"

"Yeah. Something bit me."

This time, she had the flashlight. We went back across the street, more carefully this time. A terrified-looking rat was on my neighbor's lawn. Regina poked it with a stick to make sure it was alive. It *eeped* again, and ran away.

"That rat could have rabies," she said.

"Well, that's just great."

"Who would throw a rat out of their car?"

"I hate this neighborhood."

I called 311 while Regina swabbed my big toe with hydrogen peroxide. It had just been a nip. The rat hadn't broken skin. After a few minutes, I was on with police dispatch.

"Someone just threw a rat on my neighbor's lawn."

"Threw a *what*?" said the dispatch woman.

"A rat. He stopped his car at my curb and threw a rat. I don't know if you want to call animal control or what."

She assured me that the police would keep a lookout for the offending car.

"You probably get weird calls like this all the time."

"Not really."

When I got off the phone, I stomped around the room a little.

"Why can't I go outside in my own neighborhood without something weird happening to me?"

"Why did you go outside without shoes on?"

"It was an emergency!"

"Yes, dear."

"We have to get out of here."

And so we posted a FOR SALE sign in the yard. Our neighbors

came over, expressing their grief and disbelief. We played it political, with half-truths. There was nothing wrong with the neighborhood, we said. We love it here. It's just that we're having financial problems and the only way to pull ourselves out of the pit is to sell our house. We didn't tell them about the rat. But don't worry, we said. We're still going to be in Austin.

In reality, we had no idea where we were going to end up. It would probably be in Austin, because local moves are easier, but there was nothing keeping us. Would we buy a less-expensive house, or one at the same price? Values had gone up, so we'd probably end up in an even smaller house in an even worse neighborhood. What about a more expensive house? That wouldn't be smart, because as soon as we'd paid off our debt, we'd get right back into debt. Maybe, we thought, we should go back to renting. Then again, why, if we were just renting, would we do it far away from our families, in a state where 75 percent of people who vote on election day choose to ban gay marriage? All our options felt lousy to me.

We looked around anyway, but especially at one house south and west of downtown. It was 2,600 square feet, two stories, with a remodeled basement that was as large as our current house. I'd have my own office with its own entrance and own bathroom. Regina would have a legitimate studio with a sink and a storage closet. Plus, there was a view from an upper deck of miles of Hill Country. The house was on a quiet street, where the only sounds were from the wind chimes that the current owner had strung all around the vast front yard, and from the wind rustling the surrounding trees and brush. Also, there was a pool, and even a pen where the current owner kept a pot-bellied pig named Olive. It was a bucolic retreat, a compound.

"If we buy this house," I said. "We totally have to keep the pig."

"You just want to *tell* people that you have a pig," Regina said. "You don't actually want it."

"You don't know that."

This house came to be known, in our private mythology, as the

Wildflower House, because it was on Wildflower Lane. It was located in one of the best school districts in the country. Elijah would be going to the high school where we'd seen Beck play when Regina was pregnant. The Wildflower House was a ten-minute drive from the place where Willie Nelson held his annual Fourth of July picnic. We never had a prayer of living there.

In Philadelphia, the first person who'd come through the door had bought our house. Our current place was in much better shape. It would be gone, we figured, within a week. Regina and I looked out the front window for signs of interest, but the only person who picked up a flier was a fat blond prostitute who often tried to bum cigarettes off us. The house went on the market in May. The Wildflower House was gone by mid-June. More than 100 people, probably close to 200, passed through our house that summer. We didn't receive one offer. Not even a nibble. One woman from Seattle summed up the attitude of the prospective buyers.

"You have a really cute house," she said. "Too bad it's so close to the highway."

I felt confused, rootless, and unwanted, which would have been fine if I'd been eighteen. But I was thirty-five, and I had a kid. A miserable legacy of failed adulthood loomed before me. I walked the streets of my neighborhood, listening to Beck's *Mutations* on my iPod. Beck was right. Life was a hopeless journey into a bottomless abyss, only occasionally punctured by ironic Brazilian vacations. This truly was the end of the end. In a sure sign that I, along with the rest of my generation, was now officially old, I thought, "Only Beck understands how I feel."

Then a strange thing happened. Our child started acting like the most charming host at the cutest party in the world. The summer turned delightful.

In our hustle to get the house into "showing shape," we'd moved half of Elijah's toys into the garage. We couldn't keep our house clean under normal conditions. Now it had to be spotless, and we had a toddler at home, all the time. We had to find distractions.

One Tuesday morning soon after Elijah's expulsion, Regina and I took him to one of those malls that hadn't been renovated since the early 1980s, when Chick-fil-A was still a novelty. The provocatively named Inflatable Wonderland drew us there. On its website, Inflatable Wonderland describes itself as "Austin's only indoor inflatable playground for children 12 and under." It also has two slogans, which say so much. One is "Keep it fun!" and the other is "You can't miss us!" The Inflatable Wonderland website also has a strange Bible quote, from Jeremiah 29:11—"For I know the plans I have for you, declares the LORD, plans to prosper you and not to harm you, plans to give you hope and a future." I wasn't entirely sure what that had to do with Inflatable Wonderland, but this was Texas, and it was hard to avoid the Bible.

Inflatable Wonderland comprised two storefronts that took up less square footage than a Disney Store at a higher-end mall. The most amusing attraction by far was "Gorilligan's Island," a mazelike structure with a seven-foot-high inflatable monkey hovering above it. Two puffy halves of a pink circle, with a slit between them, were the entrance. Every time a kid went into Gorrilligan's Island, it looked like they were returning to the womb.

"It's an enormous vagina!" Regina said.

"Do they have an entrance like that at the Disney Princess Clubhouse?"

"Don't be gross."

Elijah snaked his way through the monkey tunnel, went up the inflatable ladder, and came down the slide. He ran off, his arms flapping.

"Daddy-doo! I'm going to the dinosaur! The dragon! It's purple! Purple color! RAWWWWWWR!"

"I guess he's enjoying himself," I said.

Elijah was referring to far and away the best attraction at Inflatable Wonderland, the Hide-n-Seek Dragon, an enormous purple cartoon monstrosity with big bulging eyes and a mouth tall and wide enough to swallow five kids at once. The dragon's insides contain an air blower and the bottom half of an inflatable knight turned upside down. I know this because I flouted the height-and-weight requirement and went inside with Elijah. It looked like fun and I couldn't help myself. I also thought it was hilarious that kids had to exit the dragon through a slit in the back. So did Regina, who said, "I love that they have to come out of the butt."

After a few trips down the Super Slide, I went upstairs to the bathroom. When I returned, our time at Inflatable Wonderland was at an end. A child had snatched one of Elijah's Cheddar Bunnies, and this tragedy had Elijah in hysterics. Still, it had been $5 well spent, because it got us two hours closer to bedtime.

We could only stand Inflatable Wonderland every so often. While I worked, Regina took the boy to a dozen different parks and to the Austin Zoo, a nonprofit entity containing mostly animals that have been rescued from weird traveling Christian circuses. The zoo freaked them both out, because they saw mean kids throwing rocks at the monkeys. Every other child-related activity was crowded, and it was hot besides. Between mid-May and mid-October, the average weather in Austin is about 96 degrees with at least 90 percent humidity. Circumstances had driven us indoors. So we watched a lot of television.

I got to know a lot about children's television in the summer my family tried to find itself. Regina and I said, before Elijah was born, that we wouldn't be parents who depended on TV. But TV, we gradually learned, can sure come in handy sometimes. There were two entire networks, Noggin and the Disney Channel, which devoted all daylight hours, and even some pre-daylight ones, to stupefying toddlers. The shows seemed to hit on three common themes: Be yourself, be creative, and be nice to your friends. *Dora the Explorer* added that you should do all these things bilingually while keeping a sharp eye out for an eye-mask-wearing fox who wants to steal your choco-late boat. This represented a step up from my childhood TV morals of "eat a Scooby Snack" and "run away from Gargamel," but it was still all very retarded. At least the networks didn't air commercials, except promos for their own programming.

Regina and I had two favorites. We liked *Oobi,* a puppet show of sorts, except that the puppets were actual human hands with eyes glued to the knuckles. *Oobi* offered the standard share-and-be-creative message, but it also featured a hilarious character called Grampoo, the apparent legal guardian of the children-hands. Gram-poo made funny faces when he had to eat the awful food the kids cooked for him and he also flirted with Oobi's piano teacher. We also liked *Oswald,* a piano-playing cartoon octopus voiced by Fred Savage from *The Wonder Years.* Oswald shared an apartment in a whimsical big city with his pet dachshund, Weenie. He had many adventures with his friends, who included a finicky penguin named Henry, a roller-skating flower named Daisy, a butterfly who owned a café, and various gingerbread people, robots, and dopey dragons. They, unlike, say, Connie the Cow or the Teletubbies, seemed like children's TV characters with whom we could spend an afternoon if they magically came to life.

Mostly, though, we hated the shows. Unfortunately, Elijah didn't, and we could only watch the John Cleese episode of *The Muppet Show* so many times before he got bored. By the end of the summer, Regina and I were having homicidal fantasies involving the preco-cious little Aryan cartoon girl on *64 Zoo Lane* and the two sickly sweet white fuzzy monsters on *Tiny Planets.* I longed to blow up the *Higglytown Heroes* and I dreamed of shoving "Clay," the Disney Channel's saccharine, giggly asexual mascot, down a garbage dis-posal. Miffy, Maisy, Franklin, Sportacus from *Lazy Town,* Dora the Explorer's prepubescent monkey Boots, Leo the conductor kid from *Little Einsteins,* Tyrone the moose on *The Backyardigans:* They all had to die. I wanted to send Blue to the sausage factory.

Still, television had not pureed Elijah's brain, at least not yet. He'd recently begun talking with great sophistication. We had conversations. One July night, while Regina was mixing up some macaroni and cheese for Elijah, he sat at my feet.

"Let's make up a story," I said.

"OK, Daddy."

"This time *you're* going to tell *me* a story."

"OK!"

"Once upon a time there was . . ."

"A pig."

"And this pig's name was . . ."

"Peenie!"

"OK. And what did Peenie the pig like to do?"

"Pee!"

"Where did he pee?"

"On the potty!"

"So Peenie the pig liked to pee on the potty. And one day Peenie went out walking in the . . ."

"Woods."

"And who did she meet there?"

"Another pig!"

"And what was *that* pig doing?"

"Eating flowers!"

"And what did Peenie do when she met the other pig?"

"She peed on the flowers, Daddy."

While I taught Elijah the finer points of creative storytelling, Regina educated him in her own specialties. He would often run to his easel and ask her to draw him something. Actually, he got a little spoiled, because she could draw anything he asked with remarkable accuracy. After a while, he began to feel that he could do the same. A tall upside-down V, we learned, was his giraffe. When he drew a circle inside another circle, that was a car, and any square represented a supermarket.

"Mama," he said one day. "Draw me thunder."

"Draw you thunder?"

"What color is thunder?"

"I don't know, Elijah. What color *is* thunder?"

"It's white."

"Oh."

"No. Thunder no is white! It's brown!"

"OK."

"Do we eat thunder?"

"Yes."

"No! We no eat thunder! Thunder is brown!"

He also spent much of that summer running around the house shouting: "HIDE! A dinosaur wants to eat me!" or, alternately, "HIDE! A giant rabbit wants to talk to me! Quick, HIDE!" In this case, "hiding" meant one or both of us sitting under a blanket with him, sometimes for long periods of time, and not talking so the monster wouldn't "get" us. While the quiet was a welcome relief, nothing makes an adult brain melt like three hours of mandatory child-imposed hiding per day. After a hiding session, a scene would occur like the following:

Elijah opened the refrigerator.

"Elijah, don't open the refrigerator," Regina said.

"I want to eat somefing."

"What?"

"What I want to eat? I want . . . somefing."

"What?"

"Somefing to eat."

"Do you want fruit?"

"Nooooo."

"Close the refrigerator. Do you want carrots?"

"No! I no want carrots!"

Regina got up and closed the refrigerator. Elijah screamed, ran into the other room, and started thrashing around on the floor. We observed this behavior for a couple of minutes. He popped up. Play could now resume.

"Come in my room, Daddy," he said, grabbing my hand, "and play wif my toys. Come in my room again. And again and again and again."

To pass the time, he and I developed a secret language that had no correlation with reality. I'd begin:

"Hingy dingy bangy bongy."

"Hingy dinky stinky!" Elijah replied.

"Blingo blango pongo pango!"

"Blah blah winky!"

"Pling plang hingy plong bingy!"

"Schlangy schlip slop sloop!"

This secret language caused Regina to shake her head, because it was obvious that Elijah and I actually understood each other. In fact, I'd always understood everything he said, and I could often predict what he'd do before it happened. While I knew I'd never take my son fishing like, say, the dad in *A River Runs Through It*, I also knew for certain that he'd never be a stranger to me. I'd created a clone of myself, only better looking. Regina reluctantly backed me up on this.

"It's not fair," she said. "I only married one Neal. But now I have two."

"Hingy dingy," I said.

"Blingy blangy blongy," said Elijah.

On Saturday mornings, Elijah and I would take our unshakable father-son bond to the Austin Science and Nature Center, a wonderful little preserve sandwiched between two highway overpasses. By ten a.m., the temperature had usually reached 95 degrees. But we still enjoyed the hiking trails, which descended into a limestone-walled canyon with a floor slick with streams and moss, as well as the reptile exhibit; a coyote, a fox, and a bobcat in cages; several live owls that had been hit by cars and were now flightless; and, best of all, three large sandpits full of plaster dinosaur bones. The center provided shovels, brushes, and dustpans for purposes of "excavation." Elijah called it the Dinosaur Park.

"Where'd the monsters go at the Dinosaur Park?" he said, almost every day, whether we were there or not.

"I don't know."

"Monsters sleeping."

"OK."

"Uh-oh. Where are all the monsters?"

Since this was summer, we also did swimming. We'd joined the Jewish Community Center, an expense we definitely couldn't afford. But by joining, we'd moved up on the preschool waiting list. We figured he'd get into school there more quickly, though we never actually got the call.

It had been a while since I'd belonged to a Jewish organization, so I made the mistake of trying to take Elijah swimming at the J on a Saturday. Unfortunately, I'd already promised him a popsicle. When we got there, the guy behind the desk informed us that they don't sell popsicles on Saturday.

"Sorry," I said to Elijah.

"No, Daddy. I want a popsicle now!"

"You can't have one here. It's Shabbat."

"It's not Shabbat!"

"Do you even know what Shabbat is?"

"No!"

"I thought not."

"I want a popsicle!"

"We're not supposed to buy things here on Shabbat. We're Jews."

"No! We're *not* Jews!"

"Yes we are."

"Jews eat popsicles, too!"

Great. My son's first experience with Judaism was that it denied him the thing he loves most in the world. Well, I thought, that's organized religion for you. So on Saturdays, we sought religiously neutral entertainments. The next Saturday, Elijah got up early.

"Daddy. I want orange juice."

"That can be arranged."

"And I want to dance to Johnny Cash music."

I felt a boulder-sized lump catch in my throat.

O joyous day!

"Did you say 'Johnny Cash music'?"

"Uh-huh. I love Johnny Cash music! I want to hear the train song!"

" 'Orange Blossom Special'? Or 'Folsom Prison Blues'?"

" 'Orange Blossom Special.' "

I picked him up.

"Look a yonder comin'," I sang. *"Comin' down that railroad track . . ."*

Johnny Cash didn't, to my knowledge, ever perform a song about bats, but if he had, it would have been my son's favorite song. Bats formed a substantial part of Elijah's early childhood imagination, partly because Austin is home to the largest urban bat colony in North America, under the Congress Avenue Bridge. Hundreds of people gather every night to witness their takeoff. On a Friday evening in July, we decided to go the bridge with Elijah and Hercules. They both got excited.

"What the bats do-ying?" Elijah said.

"They're sleeping. Under the bridge."

"They eating bugs and sleeping."

"Yes."

"They not eating crocodiles."

"No, Elijah. They aren't eating crocodiles."

"Maybe they eating owls."

"Maybe."

"I'm a bat. EEEEEEEEE!"

As we were walking out the door, Elijah said, "I see many beautiful things when we're in the car, like trees and houses and flowers and oranges!"

At the bat bridge, Elijah ran around and shouted "WAKE UP BATS!!!!!" something like 100 times. Twelve-year-old girls came over and showered Hercules with kisses, which Hercules seemed to really like. After a while, the bats came out in great swooping streams, and Elijah gawked in wonder.

We got home around nine p.m., long past Elijah's bedtime. We turned down Harmon Avenue to find a nightmare of howling sirens, and smoke everywhere, and children running down the street, screaming. As we got closer to our house, the smoke didn't dissipate. I assumed disaster.

"Oh my God!" I said. "Is our house on fire?"

"Our house on fire?" Elijah said.

"Wha? Wha? Wha?" Regina said. "Oh God, no!"

Some wires had shorted in an apartment where some guys were doing some work. Those apartment buildings were too crowded. It had just been a matter of time, I thought, before there was a major disaster. There were dozens if not hundreds of kids living in those apartments. I feared for them, but I also feared for us. The next morning, I got up with Elijah at 7:30. He was sitting in his crib.

"There was a big fire, Daddy."

"It was actually a little fire."

"Where'd the fire go?"

"The firemen put it out with water."

"It not at John's house?"

"No."

"There's not fire at our house?"

"No."

"OK, Daddy. I want to get up now."

Please, I silently pleaded to whatever nondenominational entity was listening, let us sell our house.

Regina, meanwhile, decided to tap into ancient pagan superstitions. She went on the Internet to look for spells. The first one she found was "To Break a Streak of Bad Luck." It went: "Go for a walk and pick up seven twigs from the ground, one to represent each day of the week. Traditionally the twigs should be ash for Monday, beech for Tuesday, elm for Wednesday, oak for Thursday, horsechestnut for Friday, yew for Saturday, and elder for Sunday."

Such biodiversity wasn't available in the Harmon Triangle, so Regina just picked up whatever schwag she found in the gutter. She returned home with the sticks, snapped them into pieces, and burned them along with some incense outside in our *chimineya*. As she did this, she chanted: "Ill luck is broken, as these words are spoken." I stood by and watched; I'm not much for chanting.

The second spell was "To Change Your Household Luck." It went: "If you have terrible luck in your daily household affairs and a purification hasn't helped, try this ancient spell. Take an old spoon (it doesn't have to be clean) and walk through your house slowly, visiting each room. Visualize the spoon absorbing the house's malaise. Then walk to a crossroads and bury the spoon there. Don't look back as you return home. Things should start to perk up."

She buried the spoon, and then we were still broke, with an unsold house. We were eating rice and beans for dinner every night. We tried to think of other ways to cut back expenses, but we couldn't give up our electricity, or our health insurance, or our car insurance, or our life insurance, or the payment-plan medical bills that we had because our health insurance didn't cover them.

Regina attempted to cut costs in her own special way: By growing *kombucha*, a Chinese mushroom that, when brewed into a tea, is supposed to have salutary effects. This was supposed to have saved us money both on health care, and, I guess, tea. The strangest thing about *kombucha* is that it "makes babies," little *kombucha*, while brewing in its sun-tea jar. The brewer is then supposed to pass the babies on to friends. That's how an alien symbiote came to live on the bottom shelf of our pantry. Regina took the cure every day. I tried it once. It smelled like overripe vinegar and tasted like dirty socks lightly dipped in apple juice.

One night just before Labor Day, Regina and her *kombucha* friend, Anne Marie, went to a free lecture on macrobiotic cooking at a local yoga center. I would no sooner attend such an event than I would a festival of collegiate a capella groups, so I stayed home with the kid. Elijah acted very sweet and playful that night, and my heart swelled with love for him. I didn't care how broke we were. I wanted to buy him a present. Plus, I didn't feel like watching *Alice in Wonderland* for the third day in a row. So we got into the car and went to Target.

On our last few trips to Target, Elijah had been begging us for a Little People Castle to go along with his farm, zoo, and Noah's Ark. The castle cost only $19, but we couldn't tell him, "It's the castle or it's diapers this month. You decide." I could earn twenty bucks somewhere, I figured. The kid needed the castle.

We went into Target. Elijah immediately started to run toward the toy section. I followed him and grabbed his hand, and we started skipping together, singing, "La, la, la, we're at Target." Everyone got out of our way.

I wandered the toy aisles slyly, not tipping my hand. Elijah was a very good boy. He didn't beg for anything. When he turned his head, I slipped a castle under my arm.

"Time to check out," I said.

He walked away mopily. I walked alongside him, swinging my arm so that the castle came into his view.

"What's that, Daddy?" he said.

"I don't know, son. What *is* that?"

"Are you buying me a *castle*?"

"Yep."

He attached himself to my leg.

"Thank you Daddy! Thank you thank you thank you!"

He ran ahead, beside himself with surprised glee.

"Daddy!" he said. "I'm . . . I'm . . . happy!"

I felt a new emotion, at least for me. It wasn't happiness, or sadness, exactly. Maybe it was a kind of all-knowingness, an understanding that life presents you with limitations and that you have to learn to deal with those limitations and be happy anyway. While I recognized the irony of having this life-changing epiphany while buying my son a plastic toy at a chain store that allowed its pharmacists to deny people birth-control medicine based on religious principles, I cried anyway. I wished I could give Elijah more, could *be* more for him. I just wanted the best for my family, and I felt ashamed that I couldn't give it to them.

Of course, I still wanted other things as well. My ambition still burned, my dreams still lived. And those dreams pointed me in a specific direction. Maybe our house hadn't sold for a reason. Maybe Austin wouldn't be our home forever. In fact, I decided for certain that it would not. Soon my family's life would be free of crime and danger and sleaze. Money problems would plague us no more. Only one place could provide us the transcendent happiness, not to mention the riches, for which we longed. When got home that night, I said, "I think we should move to Los Angeles."

"Definitely," she said.

EPILOGUE
OCTOBER 2005

Before we could breach the magical dreamland that was Hollywood, we had to sell our house. But our decision to leave Texas hadn't changed the general lack of consumer interest in the property. Fortunately, Regina got offered some classes at Austin Community College, where she'd taught occasionally. One day, she received a letter informing her of a raise in her salary.

"Oh my God, Neal! I'm an adjunct professor now! I had no idea!"

I didn't know how to process this. It had been that long since we'd had good news. Maybe Regina's spells had worked. This surprise employment, combined with one of my mysterious periodical upticks in freelance money, allowed us to see to the matter of our son's education, at least temporarily. I'd received a call from Temple Beth Israel, informing us that Elijah had been released from the waiting list and could now attend school in the fall. A great preschool education could be ours for only $720 a month, plus fees.

Instead, we enrolled him for substantially less money at the Children's Discovery Center, which we'd previously derided as a dirty hippie sinkhole. But we'd made a number of friends who sent their kids there, and they had nothing but praise. Also, it was really close to our house. We visited one day. Most of the children were running around in only their diapers. They were covered in mud and paint. The school had a nice library, and it provided organic vegetarian snacks. Also, they didn't have a television, but there was a little garden. It was a "play-based" curriculum, the director told us. Kids were free to do whatever they wanted, whenever they wanted, except at lunch and naptime.

After a couple of trial afternoons when we hung out with him, Elijah started on the morning of Monday, August 15. In the car on the way over, he kept saying, "I don't wanna go to Eamon's school. I don't wanna!" He called it "Eamon's school" because the neighbor kid went there. We took Elijah through the gate. It was 8:30 a.m., and the kids were already dirty. We showed him his cubbyhole and his sleeping mat. Elijah whimpered and clung to my leg.

"Don't leave," he whispered.

But then we did leave, and he howled. I handed him to a teacher. As we walked away, I could hear him scream:

"WHY ARE YOU DOING THIS TO ME???????"

That unsettled us for the rest of the day. But when we came back at four p.m. to pick him up, Elijah was sitting at a table, his mouth covered in blue cupcake frosting. The day after that, he was sliding down into a mud puddle while his teachers squirted him with a hose, and the third day, he was running around with a colander on his head.

We took a step back on Thursday. I arrived and Elijah was standing at the gate, filthy and sobbing.

"What's the matter, buddy?"

"Someone stole my pretzels!"

I took him in my arms.

"We have pretzels at home. Everything's going to be OK."

"No! It'll never be OK!"

This pretzel theft existed out of Elijah's range of understanding. At his previous school, every infraction, no matter how minor, had been punished with a scolding or worse. Here, teachers let the kids "work it out" themselves, and intervened only if things got seriously violent. By comparison with some of the wild long-haired filth pigs that roamed this playground, Elijah was a goody-goody. He didn't dare bite these classmates.

At the old school, Elijah's teachers had given us a list of his infractions nearly every day. Here, they just said, "He had fun." All the teachers were hipsters in their twenties. They looked like people I'd run into at Emo's. They played Ramones songs for the kids and said "Hey, man," to me when I walked into the room. One day, I picked up Elijah to find his head teacher, Jaime, standing in the middle of the playground, jumping up and down with the kids, exclaiming "Dance party! Dance party!" That said, when I picked up Elijah another day, he was splashing around in the toilet, unsupervised. The old school, for its many faults, had at least been clean.

The major difference between the schools, though, was in the art projects. At the Montessori school, Elijah would bring home a sheet from a coloring book that he'd scribbled on listlessly. Often, he'd bring home the same sheet on different days; the school made copies and reused them. Now he was sculpting with clay and making his own paintings with glitter and stick-on googly eyes. He started having conversations with imaginary animals again. One day, I caught him squealing in his room and asked him what he was doing.

"I'm talking to an invisible pickle, Daddy!"

"I didn't know pickles talked."

"Uh-huh. They do. They say 'cheese' and 'milk' and 'super toast.' "

The talking pickles, apparently, worked at Elijah's imaginary restaurant, called, appropriately enough, Fancy. Fancy served as the flagship operation for Elijah's Mario Batali–like imaginary restaurant empire, which included its offshoot, Fancy Chicken, which served only chicken. Elijah gave the other places evocative names that wouldn't be out of place in *Food and Wine*: Popcorn, Raisin, The Bread Place, and Gas Station. Eating in Elijah's room was the closest I'd come to a fancy restaurant in a while. I made sure to tell him that everything was delicious, even his specialty dish, "eggs stuffed with butter inside of Hercules' butt." He was my beautiful boy.

One afternoon, a nice young man came to look at our house. He stayed for a while. The day after that, he brought his girlfriend, his parents, and a bunch of other people we never identified. Regina parked the car on the street, and we watched surreptitiously as this guy walked around our grounds, looking proud, as though he'd discovered a treasure in plain sight.

"Oh my God, Regina. I think he's going to buy our house!"

"Don't jinx it."

"Nothing can jinx this now."

The day after that, he made an offer, and we accepted. Within a month, we'd be subletting the house from him. And a month after that, the moving van would pull out of our driveway. We briefly found ourselves growing nostalgic for our house, the only one Elijah had ever known. That nostalgia lasted until a gang called the Vatos Locos declared, in a graffiti blitz, that they now ruled the Harmon Triangle and that no one could stop them. The fact that the Vatos Locos were just four bored, stupid teenagers who lived in the apartments down the street didn't make us feel any more confident that the neighborhood would be improving soon. We were off to California, to seek our fortune.

As soon as we got the offer, Regina and I began discussing our plans excitedly. I would write many wonderful screenplays that would be immediately purchased and made into movies, and then I would also write my own television show. Nothing could possibly stop that from happening. She would get a teaching job somewhere and also make paintings that would get picked up by an internationally famous gallery. Elijah would surf, or something fun like that.

He'd also evolve into an incredibly talented genius. The signs had already begun to appear. And no matter what he became, I'd still take him to Dodger Stadium all the time.

Unfortunately, we decided to have this conversation while Regina was in Elijah's room and I was in the hallway. Elijah decided this wasn't acceptable. He began to screech. We ignored him, refusing to dignify such blatantly obnoxious behavior.

"Stop talking, guys!"

We ignored him further. He screamed, gave me a little shove, and slammed the door in my face.

Enough.

"You're going to Penalty Chair," I said.

We sat him in the chair and let him stew. His face grew red with what he considered righteous rage. He shrieked and thrashed and said, "No! No No!" Regina and I stared at him stonily, not acknowledging his tantrum.

"Dammit!" he said.

Where had he picked up *that* word?

"Stupid! Dammit! Dammit! Stupid! Dammit! Dammit! Dammit! Dammit! Dammit! Stupid! Dammit! Stupid! Dammit! Daaaaaaaaaaammmmmmmmiiiiiiiiiiit!"

This went on for several minutes, until Elijah looked like the guy in the opening scene of *Scanners* just before explosion. He must have said "dammit" thirty times in a row. Eventually, Regina and I both began to laugh, but we tried desperately to hold it in. We turned away from the Penalty Chair, our bodies heaving, our eyes tearing. Elijah looked at us and grinned.

"What's so funny, guys?"

"Pffffft," Regina said. "Nothing."

Oh, but he knew.

The room was silent for a second, and then Elijah whispered, "*Dammit.*"

A pause.

"Dammit. Dammit. Dammit. Dammit."

Another pause.

"Stupid. Stupid."

By now, we'd completely cracked up.

"Stop it!" I said. "Why are you in Penalty Chair?"

"DAMMMMMMMMMMMIT!"

"Come on, dude."

"Because I yelled when you were trying to talk."

"Are you going to do it again?"

"Yes."

"Wrong answer. Are you going to do it again?"

"No. I'm sorry."

"Good boy."

Elijah stood up, went to Regina, and gave her a hug. I joined them. We were happy. "Family hug!" we said together, and then we all started jumping up and down.

I knew that both good and bad awaited us in California. My family would convulse many more times, only to repair itself again. Careers would rise and fall. There would probably be a major earthquake at some point. But it had still been a long time since something had excited me this much.

"Hey, buddy," I said to Elijah, after we stopped jumping. "Guess what?"

"What?"

"We're moving to Los Angeles."

"Los Angeles? All of us? Even the kitty-cats?"

"Of course the kitty-cats are coming," Regina said. "And we're going to get a new dog, too."

I hadn't heard about this "new dog" plan before, but I tabled it for later. Perhaps, I thought, I'd offer Regina a deal. We could get a dog if the cats went to live with her mother. Hell, as far as I was concerned, we could get a rabid monkey if the cats went to live with her mother.

"There's a beach in Los Angeles and palm trees," Elijah said. "And a jungle and a forest and big dinosaurs!"

"Sure."

"And there's gonna be Sea World in our house. With sharks that bite cows!"

"It's always possible."

"What we going to do in Los Angeles, Daddy?"

I told him what I hoped would soon be true: "Whatever the hell we want to, son."